Farm Accounting
and Management

Farm Accounting and Management

Ford Sturrock
Ph D, MA, B Sc

Director of the Agricultural Economics Unit
University of Cambridge

SIXTH EDITION

PITMAN

PITMAN PUBLISHING LIMITED
39 Parker Street, London WC2B 5PB

Associated Companies
Copp Clark Ltd, Toronto
Fearon-Pitman Publishers Inc, San Francisco
Pitman Publishing New Zealand Ltd, Wellington
Pitman Publishing Pty Ltd, Melbourne

© Ford Sturock 1967, 1971

Sixth edition 1971
Reprinted 1974
First paperback edition 1976
Reprinted 1977, 1978

Reproduced and printed by photolithography and bound in Great Britain
at The Pitman Press, Bath

ISBN 0 273 00230 9

PREFACE TO SIXTH EDITION

THE opportunity has been taken to revise the text thoroughly and introduce decimal currency. One of the chief problems facing farmers is the high cost of capital necessary to keep farming abreast of technical change. A new chapter (21) on Discounted Cash Flow and other methods of capital appraisal has therefore been added. Chapter 13, on the use of farm records to diagnose faults in management, has also been rewritten to take account of gross margins.

The book is intended primarily for students of agriculture in Colleges and Universities—particularly for those who intend to join advisory services here or abroad or who intend to become management consultants. Most of it could be used with profit by students in Farm Institutes. It should also be helpful to accountants who wish to do more for their clients than provide a statement to satisfy the Inspector of Taxes.

Care has been given to provide realistic examples and there is nothing to prevent a farmer from using the instructions given as a "do it yourself" kit to assess his own performance and plan for better results in the future.

The book is divided into three parts. Part I describes the Cash Analysis System of accounting which, in some form, is used by most farmers. The student is introduced to the subject by following the accounts of a farm over two years. This is the minimum necessary for any student who hopes to move on to the planning techniques described in Part III. Indeed anyone who tries to use farm records to advise farmers (or to replan his own farm) without such an elementary knowledge of accounting could be a menace!

On the other hand, a systematic course in double entry bookkeeping is usually a waste of time for an agricultural student. If the farm business is large enough to need double entry, it will have an office and clerk accountants to make the entries. It would be much more useful, in such an organization, if he could use these records to make an appraisal of capital expenditure—or at least understand one preapred by an adviser.

Part II deals with the business side of farming and covers matters such as partnerships, limited companies, valuations, banking, credit and running the farm office.

Part III gives a detailed account of the newer techniques of farm planning. Gross Margin analysis which was first advocated in Britain by the author's department in Cambridge has now become widely accepted by the advisory services and management consultants. Chapter 13 deals with the analysis of past records and the costing of individual enterprises. Chapters 14 to 19 deal with partial and complete budgeting and pass on to illustrate the problems of livestock farming and specialization. Chapter 16 describes Programme Planning. The technique described, which introduces cross substitution, is more flexible than "the Swedish Method" which can often give results that fall far short of the optimum. This chapter is intended to give an insight into the principles that govern the choice and size of farm enterprises. The Farm Institute student can bypass it if he finds it too difficult—all the remaining chapters can be read and understood without it. Indeed, it is quite possible to choose good farm plans by intuition or trial and error. The university student on the other hand may regard this chapter as an introduction to linear programming.

Other features are a chapter on starting a farm and the preparation of capital profiles and this is followed by the new one on capital appraisal. These are aspects of management that are unfortunately sometimes overlooked. It is not enough to devise a new plan—the farmer must find the means to put it into operation. Without careful preparation, a farmer short of capital may promise more than he can accomplish and find himself in a position of acute difficulty.

The final section on taxation is intended as no more than an introduction to a complex subject. A farmer with a taxation problem would, of course, be well advised to obtain professional advice but some knowledge of the subject may help him to understand the implications of the advice he obtains.

Although none of the examples is that of an existing farm, each has been designed to illustrate problems observed on a number of farms.

The author would welcome comments and suggestions for improvements that can be included in a future edition.

February 1971   Ford Sturrock

CONTENTS

PART II: THE BUSINESS SIDE OF FARMING

PART III: FARM ORGANIZATION AND MANAGEMENT

PART I
CASH ANALYSIS METHOD OF BOOK-KEEPING

CHAPTER I

THE VALUE OF KEEPING ACCOUNTS

FARMING, as carried out under modern conditions, is a form of business undertaking and necessitates a large number of financial transactions, both buying and selling. Many farmers are, on their own admission, not interested in figures and account books, and often state with pride that they are able to carry all their business affairs in their heads. But even the smallest shopkeeper is expected to keep some form of accounts and there are many advantages to the farmer in keeping a systematic record of his financial transactions.

Such a record need not be complicated and no farmer should be deterred from keeping a set of accounts on the grounds that it is too involved. The system recommended and described in this book is one which should be easily understood by any one who takes the trouble to do so and the advantages to be obtained from a well-kept set of accounts amply repay the time spent on them.

The keeping of accounts is simply a method of recording financial transactions in a systematic way. Accounts enable a farmer to find out, at any time, the exact financial position of his farming business, and to calculate the profits or losses he has made over any given period of time. In practice, this information is usually calculated at the end of the year, but it would be available at other times if required for any purpose.

The advantages to be derived from keeping farm accounts can be roughly classified into two categories. One deals with purely financial matters as they affect the farmer, and the other with the value of accounts in the organization and management of the farm.

ADVANTAGES OF A FINANCIAL CHARACTER

From a set of farm accounts, a farmer can ascertain his present financial position. This will tell him whether he is solvent, or in other words, whether the value of the things he possesses on the farm, generally called his assets, exceeds the amount of his debts, or liabilities. Many farmers might have been able to avoid bankruptcy had they been conscious of the extent to which their liabilities were increasing in relation to their assets. In making this calculation, the farmer is also able to discover how much money he owes other people and how much there is owing to him.

The difference in value between his assets and liabilities represents the amount of capital he has invested in the farm, and thus he is able to relate his profits or losses to the capital involved.

Any system of accounts involves a record of transactions, and a farmer's account book provides a list of receipts and payments to which, if need be, he can refer at any future time. An accurate record of this nature also ensures that small items of expenditure, which are difficult to memorize, do not escape attention.

One very important advantage of keeping accounts is that the farmer can make a careful check on his profits or losses, and can, therefore, adjust his personal expenditure to the income arising from the farm. There are many instances of farmers who have drifted into serious financial difficulties during a period of depression because they did not scale down their personal expenditure in accordance with their dwindling profits. Any personal expenditure in excess of the profit from the farm results in a reduction of the capital invested in the farm.

The farmer with a well-kept set of accounts has a number of advantages in his business dealings. If he wishes to negotiate with his bank for a loan for the expansion of his business, he is likely to receive more sympathetic treatment than the man who has only a vague idea of his financial position. When a farmer leaves a farm, he has to make a claim from the incoming tenant for compensation for unexhausted improvements. If he has kept accounts, he will have a systematic record of purchases of feeding-stuffs and fertilizers: this will be of great assistance to the valuer who has to assess the tenant right valuation, and the farmer is more likely to receive adequate compensation. Accounts are also of much value in the settlement of an estate after the death of a farmer.

One of the most obvious advantages of keeping accounts is for purposes of taxation. Recent changes in the assessment of income tax on the occupiers of large and medium sized farms have made it essential for accounts to be produced to the Inspector of Taxes. The farmer who neglects to record the details of his farming transactions may well find that he is paying tax in excess of the amount for which he is liable.

The Value of Accounts in Farm Organization and Management

The farmer can derive from a system of farm accounts considerable assistance in the management of his farm. This advantage of keeping accounts is frequently overlooked. When the receipts and payments are properly classified, the accounts for one year can be compared item by item with those of previous years. By so doing, the farmer can check whether expenditure and receipts under particular headings are increasing or decreasing. For example, a comparative study of the expenditure on labour may show an increase, and the farmer is able to discover whether this is due to the use of more labour or an increase in the rate of wages. Such an examination may also indicate possible ways in which economies in expenditure may be made.

It is also possible to make a calculation from the accounts of a farm of the financial value of the farm's output, and this can be used to check up on the efficiency of the organization of the farm. When records are kept of the quantities of produce, or of the numbers of livestock sold, information can be obtained on which crop yields per acre, milk yields per cow, and other measures of output can be calculated.

It may happen that the farmer is not satisfied with the profits he is getting from his farm, and a detailed analysis of the accounts may indicate the weak points in its management. Efficiency may be improved by economies in expenditure or by increasing the produce from the farm: in this way the amount received in sales is increased.

In some cases it is possible, by keeping a small number of additional records, to calculate the profit from individual crops or types of livestock, and to determine the cost of producing them. For example, in the case of milk production, by calculating the cost per gallon of individual items of cost such as foodstuffs or labour, a farmer can compare the results on his farm with those on other farms of a similar type, and so obtain a comparative measure of his efficiency. The items of cost can also be compared with the results of previous years to see whether his methods of production are showing an improvement.

Finally, a close examination of the accounts for one year should provide a basis for future plans. Few farms are so well managed that their organization cannot be improved. It is the farmer who adapts his system of farming to take advantage of existing conditions and prices who is likely to be most successful. Accounts cannot by themselves teach the farmer how to farm, but they can without doubt assist him to use his knowledge of agriculture to the best advantage.

QUESTION

Explain in your own words the reasons for keeping accounts on a farm.

CHAPTER 2

THE CASH ANALYSIS ACCOUNT BOOK

THE farmer who has decided to keep accounts can select one of a number of different systems. The one to be described here is known as the Cash Analysis System: it has the merit of being simple and will give clear and accurate results with the minimum of labour. A number of other methods are in common use, and their merits are discussed in a later chapter.

The Cash Analysis System of farm accounts depends, as its name implies, on the keeping of an Account Book in which all the cash transactions are recorded and analysed. The way in which accounts are kept under this method is best illustrated by taking an imaginary example.

Mr. John Ford entered Manor Farm as a tenant on 1st April, 1968. The farm comprised 300 acres, mainly arable, with buildings for 50 dairy cows. The agreed rent was £1800. When he took the farm, Mr. Ford had £12000 in cash with which to finance the farm and this is his capital.

On taking over the farm, he had to pay £3000 for growing crops and tenant right (the value of manurial residues, cultivations, and other items left by the previous tenant). He also bought £5000 worth of tractors and implements (partly new and partly second-hand from the dispersal sale) and 40 down-calving heifers (£4000) to start the dairy herd. During the year, he paid the following expenses—

						£
Wages	.	.	.	.	.	3400
Fuel	.	.	.	.	.	900
Feeding-stuffs	.	.	.	.	.	1400
Seeds	.	.	.	.	.	460
Fertilizers	.	.	.	.	.	1340
Rent	.	.	.	.	.	1800
Other costs	.	.	.	.	.	700
						£10000

His receipts during the same period were—

						£
Wheat	.	.	.	.	.	4400
Barley	.	.	.	.	.	600
Potatoes	.	.	.	.	.	1500
Milk	.	.	.	.	.	4560
Other receipts	.	.	.	.	.	440
						£11500

These transactions were all recorded in a Cash Analysis Account Book as shown on pages 6 and 7.

ENTERING THE TRANSACTIONS

When the Cash Analysis Book is opened, Sales and Receipts are entered on the left-hand page, which contains columns for the "Date," the "Name and Details," and a number of cash columns. The first of these cash columns is headed "TOTAL RECEIVED," and is followed by columns for the main products sold, in this case "Cereals," "Potatoes," "Milk," and "Other receipts." The right-hand page, for Purchases and Expenses, is similar. The first cash column is headed "Total Paid" and is followed by columns for "Cattle," "Wages," "Feeding-stuffs" etc. These columns are provided so that transactions can be classified as they are entered. The farmer can thus see at any time of the year not only the total spent or received up to that point but also the separate amounts for the purchase or sale of milk, seeds, feeding-stuffs, and other purposes.

At the beginning of the year, Mr. Ford paid the £11000 he owned into the farm bank account ready to start business. As the farm had received this sum, the £11000 was entered as a receipt in the Total Received column and called "Opening Balance, being Cash in Bank." During the year, he entered the transactions detailed above, each item being entered twice, once in the total column and once in the appropriate analysis column. The completed Cash Book is shown in Fig. 1.

CHECKING THE ENTRIES

At the end of the year the columns were totalled. If correctly carried out, every item (with the exception of the opening balance) should have been entered twice. The totals of the analysis columns, together with the balance at the beginning of the year, should thus agree with the Total Paid or Total Received columns. In this example, the checking was done as follows—

SALES AND RECEIPTS

Analysis Columns						£
Cereals	.	.	.	.	.	5000
Potatoes	.	.	.	.	.	1500
Milk	.	.	.	.	.	4560
Other receipts	.	.	.	.	.	440
Total receipts	.	.	.	.	£11500
Add opening balance		.	.	.	11000
Agrees with Total Received Column			.	£22500

(Left-hand page)

SALES AND RECEIPTS

DATE	NAME AND DETAILS	TOTAL RECEIVED	CEREALS	POTATOES	MILK		OTHER RECEIPTS
		£	£	£	£	£	£
	YEAR 1968–69—						
	Opening Balance, being Cash in Bank .	11000					
	Wheat	4400	4400				
	Barley	600	600				
	Potatoes	1500		1500			
	Milk	4560			4560		
	Other receipts . . .	440					440
		22500	5000	1500	4560		440
	£	22500					
	YEAR 1969–70—						
	Opening Balance, being Cash in Bank .	500					

(Right-hand page)

PURCHASES AND EXPENSES

DATE	NAME AND DETAILS	TOTAL PAID £	CATTLE £	TENANT RIGHT £	WAGES £	FEEDING-STUFFS £	SEEDS AND FERTILIZER £	RENT £	FUEL £	IMPLEMENTS £	OTHER COSTS £
	Tenant right .	3000		3000							
	Implements .	5000								5000	
	Dairy heifers .	4000	4000								
	Wages .	3400			3400						
	Fuel .	900							900		
	Foods .	1400				1400					
	Seeds .	460					460				
	Fertilizers .	1340					1340				
	Rent .	1800						1800			
	Other costs .	700									700
		22000	4000	3000	3400	1400	1800	1800	900	5000	700
	Closing Balance, being Cash in Bank .	500									
	£	22500									

FIG. 1. RECEIPTS AND EXPENSES FOR THE FIRST YEAR

The total of £22500 agreed with the Total Received column, showing that the items have been correctly entered and totalled. The Purchases and Expenses columns were similarly added and were shown to agree with the total, £22000 in the Total Paid column.

A second check can now be carried out. The bank account received at the beginning and during the year a total of £22500. As £22000 had been paid out, there should be a balance of £500 left in the bank. From the bank statement, this was found to be correct, thus proving that no transactions had been omitted from the accounts.* This assumes that all transactions have been made through the bank account—payments being made by cheque and receipts being paid into the banking account. This is a practice to be commended.

RULING OFF THE CASH BOOK

To complete the Account Book for the year, the closing balance of £500 was entered in the Total Paid column. Both sides then had the same totals, which were entered level with each other and ruled with a double line. This shows that the account is completed. Finally, the balance was carried down and entered on the opposite left-hand page in the Total Received column, ready to start the accounts for the next year.

In this case, Mr. Ford finished the year with a cash surplus or *credit balance* of £500. If he had spent another £800, he would have finished up with a *bank overdraft* or debit balance of £300. The final lines of the Cash Book would then have appeared as follows—

1968–69	TOTAL RECEIVED £	TOTAL PAID £
	22500	22800
Closing Balance . .	300	
	£22800	£22800

1969–70	
Opening Balance, being Bank Overdraft . .	300

There should be no difficulty in recognizing whether the balance at the end of the year is a credit or a debit. If the Total Received

* It is assumed for the present that all payments are made by cheque, and all receipts paid into the banking account. From the point of view of accounting, it is a practice to be recommended, and students should be accustomed to think in these terms from the beginning. The use of a petty cash box replenished by cheques drawn on the bank is explained in Chapter 9.

column is the greater, the balance must be a credit. If the Total Paid is the greater, the balance must be a deficit, which in this case means a bank overdraft.

Rules for Writing up the Cash Analysis Book

1. Enter the balance at the beginning of the year—a credit balance in the Total Received column and a debit balance or overdraft in the Total Paid column.

2. Enter receipts and payments throughout the year—once in the Total Received or Total Paid column and once in the appropriate analysis column.

3. Total all columns at the end of the year.

4. Add the analysis columns (together with the balance, if any, at the beginning) and check with the Total Paid and Total Received columns.

5. Enter the closing balance and check it with the bank pass-book.

6. Transfer the balance to the opposite page ready to begin the next year.

QUESTIONS

1. You take over a farm of 250 acres and open a banking account with £10000. You start by buying cattle (£4000), and you pay the outgoing tenant £1500 for implements and £1400 for tenant right and crops. During the year you pay—

	£
Wages	2800
Feeding-stuffs	800
Machinery	500
Seeds and fertilizers	920
Rent	1500
Other expenses	1100
Cattle	680

During the year, you receive for—

	£
Crops	3600
Cattle	1600
Milk	1200

Write up the Cash Analysis Account Book, following the procedure given above. The bank account shows a credit balance of £1200.

2. You have been farming for some time and start the year with a bank overdraft of £500. Payments during the year were as follows—

	£
Feeding-stuffs	1100
Rent	300
Fertilizers	350
Cattle	630
Weaner pigs	500
Seeds	150
Calves	120
Wages	400
Rent	300
Poultry foods	150

Receipts for the sale of farm produce were—

	£
Fat cattle	1200
Pork pigs	200
Store cattle	300
Bacon	800
Eggs	650
Poultry	100
Crops	2000

Write up the Cash Analysis Account Book. Is the balance at the end of the year a credit balance or overdraft?

3. After writing up the Cash Analysis Book, a farmer found that the total of the receipts analysis columns plus the opening balance did not agree with the Total Received column. What mistake would you expect to find?

4. In another case, the Account Book was checked and found to be correct, but the balance at the end of the year did not agree with the balance in the bank statement. What mistake had been made?

CHAPTER 3

SIMPLE FORM OF BALANCE SHEET AND TRADING ACCOUNT

HAVING completed the Cash Analysis Book, Mr. Ford was ready to draw up a final statement to see whether he had made a profit or a loss. During the first year, he had spent considerably more than he had received, and his bank balance had dropped from £11000 to £500. On the other hand, the farm was then in full operation and by 31st March, 1969, when he had been farming for twelve months, he possessed a dairy herd, crops, and implements. Thus before he could ascertain his financial position at the end of the year and find out whether he was better or worse off as a result of the year's farming, a valuation of his farm stock was necessary. On that day, therefore, he went round the farm and made a list, or inventory, of the livestock, crops, and implements on the farm. Their value was as follows—

	£
Tenant right (including cultivations and growing crops)	3000
Implements	4000
Dairy herd	4500
	£11500

Thus, if he had sold up and left the farm on 31st March, he could (if his valuations are correct) have realized £11500.

PREPARATION OF TRADING ACCOUNT

The next step was to prepare the Trading Account (or, as it is sometimes called, the Profit and Loss Account). As we have already seen, Mr. Ford spent £22000, and received £11500 during the first year. At the end of that time, however, he had stock and crops on the farm valued at £11500. The question now arises: had he made a profit during the year? Assume for a moment that he had sold up at the end of the year, realizing £11500. If to this is added his receipts (also £11500) he would have received a total of £23000. Total expenditure, however, was only £22000, leaving a margin or profit of £1000. To show this in detail, a Trading Account was drawn up as shown on the next page.

All the items have been copied from the analysis columns in the Cash Book (except that Tenant right and Implements have been given separately). It is customary to put *Purchases and Expenses* on the left and *Sales and Receipts* on the right. The closing

TRADING ACCOUNT FOR YEAR ENDING 31ST MARCH, 1969

Purchases and Expenses—	£	Sales and Receipts—	£
At the beginning of the year—		During the year—	
Tenant right . .	3000	Cereals . . .	5000
Implements . .	5000	Potatoes . .	1500
Dairy cows . .	4000	Milk . . .	4560
		Other receipts .	440
	12000		11500
During the year—		Closing Valuation	
Wages . . .	3400	(31st March, 1969) .	11500
Feeding-stuffs . .	1400		
Seeds and fertilizers .	1800		
Rent . . .	1800		
Fuel . . .	900		
Other costs . .	700		
	22000		23000
NET PROFIT .	1000		
£	23000	£	23000

valuation is also on the right and the opening valuation (there is none in this case) on the left. Having totalled the columns (£22000 and £23000), the difference (£1000) is the profit. This is written in on the *Purchases and Expenses* side, making the totals the same on both sides.

At the end of the first year, the farmer did not in fact give up farming, but the Trading Account is more easily understood if that assumption is made. The fact that Mr. Ford spent considerably more money than he received was inevitable during the first year, when he had to buy implements, livestock, and tenant right to start the farm as a going concern. But it will be clear that this does not mean he had made a loss.

PREPARING A BALANCE SHEET

He then drew up a Balance Sheet, which is a statement showing his financial position at the end of the year.

On the right-hand side is a list of the farmer's possessions or assets, which in this case consisted of stock and crops valued at £11500 and £500 in cash in the bank. On the left-hand side are placed the liabilities, or debts, owing by the farm. In this case there were none, and the Balance Sheet was completed as shown, the balance—£12000—being the amount of capital invested in the business at 31st March, 1969. It is called the Net Capital. The appearance of the Net Capital as a liability in the Balance Sheet may seem strange, but can be explained if the farm and farmer are regarded as two separate units. It can therefore be said that at the end of the year the farm "owed" the farmer £12000, the amount that was invested in the farm at that date.

BALANCE SHEET AT 31ST MARCH, 1969

Liabilities	£	Assets	£
NET CAPITAL . .	12000	Valuation—	
		Tenant right . .	3000
		Implements . .	4000
		Cattle . . .	4500
			11500
		Bank Balance . .	500
£	12000	£	12000

QUESTIONS

1. Draw up a Balance Sheet from the following information—

Valuation

	£
Cattle	2164
Sheep	865
Pigs	1192
Crops	3247
Implements	4221
Tenant right	1246

There is also a credit balance at the bank of £562.

2. A. White took over Woodgate Farm on 1st October, 1969. The Account Book was written up during the year and at 30th September, 1970, the Purchases and Expenses totals were—

	£		£
Wages	583	Pigs	400
Seeds	46	Poultry . . .	1630
Fertilizers . . .	405	Implements . . .	1510
Rent	650	Tenant right . . .	450
Fuel	641	Other costs . . .	423
Feeding-stuffs . . .	642		

Receipts were: wheat £945, barley £724, pigs £1625, eggs £428. The closing valuation was £3245.

Has he made a profit or a loss?

3. On 1st January, 1969, S. Blake took over Church Farm. At that time he had £6000 in the bank. To start the farm, he purchased—

	£
Dairy cattle	3035
Implements	765
Crops and tenant right . . .	1946

Other expenses during the year were—

	£		£
Wages	1721	Machinery repairs . .	141
Fertilizers . . .	391	Service fees . . .	60
Fuel	264	Rent	466
Seed	179	Other costs . . .	342
Feeding-stuffs . . .	1651		

Receipts were: wheat £742, barley £229, cattle £245, milk £4126.

At the end of the year his valuation was as follows—

	£
Dairy cattle	3348
Implements	694
Crops and tenant right . . .	2012

Prepare a Trading Account and Closing Balance Sheet (bank balance at 31st December, 1969, £381).

CHAPTER 4

CLASSIFICATION OF RECEIPTS AND PAYMENTS

IN the previous chapter, we have seen how the Cash Analysis Book was completed for the first year and how the Balance Sheet and Trading Account were drawn up. Mr. Ford is now well established at Manor Farm. He is anxious, however, to start a pig herd. Existing buildings could be converted to take the sows, and the landlord agreed to erect a fattening house for an additional £300 rent. He started the herd by buying twenty gilts. They cost only £800 but there was soon heavy expenditure on feeding-stuffs to rear the first batches of pigs. In addition to this, the second-hand combine harvester proved unsatisfactory and a new one had to be purchased. For these reasons, expenditure outran receipts by £3000. As the farmer started the year with only £500 in the bank, it was obvious that he would have either to slow down the expansion of the pig herd or borrow money. He decided to go ahead with his plans but first of all he had an interview with his bank manager. He produced a programme and was able to convince the bank manager that a loan was justified.

Sales and Receipts	£	Purchases and Expenses	£
Wheat	5037	Wages	4135
Potatoes	1665	N.H.I. stamps for workers .	321
Milk	5013	Workers' income tax . .	245
Calves	110	Electricity . . .	72
Cows	643	Fuel and oil . . .	1216
Fat pigs	3679	Repairs	1008
Sows	54	Small tools . . .	42
Boar	21	Cattle	188
Grazing let	126	Gilts	1300
Grain storage for neighbour	153	Feeding-stuffs . . .	3433
		Seeds	449
		Fertilizers	1194
		Sprays	104
		Rent	2100
		Combine harvester . .	2300
		Fire insurance . . .	166
		Rates	176
		Accountant and valuer .	67
		Stamps and stationery .	12
		Telephone . . .	69
		Other expenses . . .	570
		Private drawings . .	800

CHOICE OF HEADINGS FOR CASH ANALYSIS COLUMNS

To assist in classifying items under the analysis columns, some further explanation is necessary.

Normally, each column of the Cash Analysis Book furnishes one item for the Trading Account. Therefore, the greater the number of columns, the more detail can be given in the final result. On the other hand, if the number of columns is too great the Account Book becomes rather large and clumsy. The choice of headings naturally depends on the type of farm. The following are a few suggestions on the choice of column headings.

Sales and Receipts

1. A column for Total Received.
2. A column for each of the main types of livestock and livestock products sold, e.g. cattle, milk, pigs, sheep, wool, poultry, eggs.
3. A column for each of the main cash crops, e.g. wheat, barley, potatoes, sugar beet, fruit, vegetables.
4. A column for miscellaneous receipts, e.g. minor enterprises and other sources of revenue such as receipts for seasonal grazing, bags sold or work done on contract for a neighbour.
5. A spare column for capital items (e.g. sale of land or implements) or for private receipts (e.g. dividends on shares) paid into the farm bank account. These items are kept separate because they are either omitted from the Trading Account or require special treatment for tax purposes.

With the tendency towards simplification, there are seldom more than four or five major enterprises. For this reason, eight or nine columns may be quite sufficient on the sales and receipts side of the account.

Purchases and Expenses

1. A column for Total Paid.
2. A column for each of the main types of livestock for which purchases are made, e.g. cattle, sheep, pigs, poultry.
3. Columns for the chief livestock variable costs, e.g. feedingstuffs, A.I. and other livestock costs.
4. Columns for the main crop variable costs, e.g. seeds, fertilizers and sprays.
5. Columns for the main common or fixed costs, e.g. wages (including insurance stamps, workers' income tax paid to the Collector of Taxes, employers' liability insurance, and wages paid to the family for work done on the farm), repairs and small tools, fuel and electricity, rent and rates, other overheads (telephone, stationery etc.).
6. A column for capital items (such as land purchased) that do not appear in the trading account and implements that require special treatment for tax purposes.

7. Private drawings (money spent by the farmer on himself and his family, and his own income tax).

When deciding on whether or not to open a column for some item, the *number* of items rather than their size should be the criterion. Egg sales, for example, may have weekly totals and be worth a column even if only a minor enterprise. By contrast, two large capital items could easily go in the same column. They can easily be separated again if necessary.

CHECKING THE ENTRIES

At the end of the year, the columns were totalled and checked as in the previous year.

TOTALS OF ANALYSIS COLUMNS
Sales and Receipts

Milk	£5013
Cattle	753
Pigs	3754
Wheat	5037
Potatoes	1665
Miscellaneous	279
Total receipts	16501
Add opening balance	500
	£17001

The final total, £17001, agrees with the Total Received column and shows that the items were correctly entered.

Purchases and Expenses

Cattle	£188
Pigs	1300
Feeding-stuffs	3433
Fertilizers	1298
Seeds	449
Wages	4701
Fuel and electricity	1288
Repairs and small tools . . .	1050
Rent	2100
Other overheads	1060
Implements purchased . . .	2300
Private drawings	800
	£19967

This total similarly agrees with the Total Paid column.

The second check on the accuracy of the Cash Analysis Book can now be carried out. The difference between the Total Received

(Left-hand page)

SALES AND RECEIPTS

DATE	NAME AND DETAILS	TOTAL RECEIVED £	MILK £	CATTLE £	PIGS £	WHEAT £	POTATOES £	MISCEL-LANEOUS RECEIPTS £
1970	YEAR 1969–70							
	Opening Balance, being Cash in Bank	500						
	Wheat	5037				5037		
	Potatoes	1665					1665	
	Milk	5013	5013					
	Calves	110		110				
	Cows	643		643				
	Fat pigs	3679			3679			
	Sows	54			54			
	Boar	21			21			
	Grazing let	126						126
	Grain storage	153						153
		17001	5013	753	3754	5037	1665	279
	Add Debts receivable at end		515					
			5528	753	3754	5037	1665	279
	Closing Balance, being Bank Overdraft	2966						
	£	19967						

DATE	NAME AND DETAILS	TOTAL PAID	CATTLE	PIGS	FEEDING-STUFFS	FERTILIZER AND SPRAYS	SEEDS	WAGES	FUEL AND ELECTRICITY	REPAIRS AND SMALL TOOLS	RENT	OTHER OVERHEADS	IMPLEMENTS PURCHASED	PRIVATE DRAWINGS
		£	£	£	£	£	£	£	£	£	£	£	£	£
1970	YEAR 1969–70													
	Wages .	4135						4135						
	N.H.I. stamps .	321						321						
	Workers' income tax .	245						245						
	Electricity .	72							72					
	Fuel and oil .	1216							1216					
	Repairs .	1008								1008				
	Small tools .	42								42				
	Cattle .	188	188											
	Gilts .	1300		1300										
	Feeding-stuffs .	3433			3433									
	Seeds .	449					449							
	Fertilizers .	1194				1194								
	Sprays .	104				104								
	Rent .	2100									2100			
	Combine harvester .	2300											2300	
	Fire insurance .	166										166		
	Rates .	176										176		
	Accountant and valuer .	67										67		
	Stamps and stationery .	12										12		
	Telephone .	69										69		
	Other expenses .	570										570		
	Private drawings .	800												800
		19967	188	1300	3433	1298	449	4701	1288	1050	2100	1060	2300	800
	Add Debts payable at end .				862									
		£ 19967	188	1300	4295	1298	449	4701	1288	1050	2100	1060	2300	800
	YEAR 1970–71	£												
	Opening Balance, being Bank Overdraft .	£2966												

FIG. 2. RECEIPTS AND EXPENSES FOR THE SECOND YEAR

and the Total Paid columns should equal the bank balance, as
follows—

Total Paid column	. . .	£19967
Total Received column	. .	17001
Difference	. . . .	£2966

Mr. Ford had therefore spent more than he possessed and, as
already mentioned, had been compelled to borrow money from
the bank. On consulting his bank statement he found that the
bank overdraft was indeed £2966, thus confirming the result
shown above. After proving the entries in this way, the deficit of
£2966 was entered on the Receipts page as "Balance being Bank
Overdraft" and the two sides totalled and ruled off as shown in
the example.

PRIVATE DRAWINGS AND UNPAID ACCOUNTS

In the records, two new items arise in this second year which
are treated in the following way.

PRIVATE DRAWINGS. During the first year, Mr. Ford drew out
no money for private expenses. But during the second year he
spent £800 on living expenses. As this was drawn from the farm
bank account, it was entered as an expense in the Cash Analysis
Book. But as it is not part of the cost of running the farm it is not
transferred to the Trading Account.

UNPAID ACCOUNTS. The receipts and payments so far entered in
the Cash Analysis Book were those actually settled by cash or by
cheque. At the end of the year, however, the farmer owed £862
to Miller & Co. for feeding-stuffs. In addition, he had not received
a cheque for £515 for milk sold during March. Mr. Ford will
no doubt pay this bill during the next financial year and the
Milk Marketing Board will certainly send him a cheque for his
milk during April, 1970. As the feeding-stuffs had been used
and the milk had been produced during the year ending 31st
March, 1970, these transactions must be included in the accounts
for that year. The amounts of these items were therefore added
to the appropriate columns of the Cash Analysis Book, as shown
in Fig. 2.

It will be noted that purchases and sales on credit are not
entered in the Cash Analysis Book at the time when the goods are
bought or sold but only when the money is actually paid or
received. If, however, items are still owing at the end of the
financial year, they must be added to the appropriate columns
in the account book before these totals are transferred to the
Trading Account. They are not, however, also included in the
Total Received and Total Paid columns.

After the Cash Analysis columns had been completed for the

year and ruled the Total Received and Total Paid columns were balanced. The difference between the two sides—in this case an overdraft of £2966—was carried down on the right-hand side as the first entry for the next financial year.

QUESTION

The following is a list of receipts and expenses on a farm for a year. Write up the Cash Analysis Account Book. At the beginning of the year, the bank balance was £345.

Sales and Receipts

	£			£
Wheat	4820	Early potatoes . . .	694
Calves	140	Milk	1654
Turkeys	2806	Old ewes	45
Lambs	650	Old hens	700
Barley	2948	Mustard seed . . .	47
Cocksfoot seed . . .	62	Main crop potatoes . .	1472
Cockerels	720	Hay	44
Sugar-beet	3806	Wool	78
Eggs	9019	Ploughing grant . . .	74
Contract receipts . .	25	Old implements . . .	73
Cottage let	75		

Purchases and Expenses

	£		£
Fertilizers	2648	Sprays and dusts . . .	254
Electricity	368	Welding plant . . .	67
Tyres and spares . . .	63	Day-old turkeys . . .	651
Potato levy . . .	53	Sacks, boxes . . .	207
Day-old-chicks . . .	658	Dairy stores . . .	56
Transport	115	Vet and medicines . .	117
Manure spreading . .	139	Holiday trip to Jersey . .	145
Milk recording . . .	21	Employer's liability and in-	
Casual labour . . .	421	surance stamps . .	240
Telephone	92	Wages	4080
County rates . . .	158	Bank charges . . .	5
Fencing	21	Postage stamps, stationery .	15
Fire insurance . . .	245	Water rates . . .	49
Accountant and valuer .	40	Vehicle insurance . .	107
Tractor	718	Corn drill	306
Private drawings . . .	998	Irrigation equipment . .	317
Harrows	62	Ram	21
Machinery repairs . .	1248	Motor van	466
Tractor cab . . .	34	Poultry cages . . .	104
Income tax (farmer's) . .	261	Income tax (workers' deducted and sent to Inland Revenue)	245

At the end of the year, the farmer owed £171 for machinery repairs, £185 for ewes bought and £40 for water rates.

Add and check the Analysis columns at the end of the year. What is the closing balance?

CHAPTER 5

COMPLETION OF ACCOUNTS FOR THE YEAR

IN the previous chapter, Mr. Ford's purchases and sales for the second year (1969–70) were classified and the columns adjusted for unpaid accounts. As in the first year, an inventory and valuation of live and dead stock on the farm was drawn up on the last day of the financial year (31st March, 1970) and all the necessary information was then available to complete the Trading Account and Closing Balance Sheet.

PREPARATION OF TRADING ACCOUNT

The next step was to draw up the Trading Account as shown below.

TRADING ACCOUNT FOR YEAR ENDING 31ST MARCH, 1970

Purchases and Expenses—	£	Sales and Receipts—	£
Cattle . . .	188	Milk . . .	5528
Pigs	1300	Cattle . . .	753
Feeding-stuffs . .	4295	Pigs . . .	3754
Fertilizers . . .	1298	Wheat . . .	5037
Seeds	449	Potatoes . . .	1665
Wages . . .	4701	Miscellaneous . .	279
Fuel and electricity .	1288		
Repairs . . .	1050		17016
Rent	2100		
Implements . .	2300		
Other overheads . .	1060		
	20029		
Opening valuation . .	11500	Closing valuation . .	16515
	31529		
NET PROFIT . .	2002		
	£ 33531		£ 33531

One new feature will be noted in this Trading Account. The opening valuation is included on the left-hand side in addition to the closing valuation on the right-hand side. The presence of valuation in the trading account can be explained as follows. Assume that the farmer took over the farm at the beginning of the year at valuation, and sold out again at the end. His payments would be £11500 for stock and crop at the beginning, and £20029 for expenses during the year, giving a total of £31529. Receipts would be £17016, plus £16515 for the sale of stock at the end, giving a total of £33531. The difference—£2002—is the Net Profit.

An alternative way of understanding the Trading Account is as follows. Receipts totalled £17016 and expenses £20029, leaving a deficit of £3013. During the year, however, Mr. Ford had started a new pig herd and had bought a large combine harvester. He also had some unsold crops on hand at the end of the year. The valuation had therefore increased by £5015; in fact the farmer had invested the whole of his profit and a substantial sum borrowed from the bank in building up a larger farm business. There is a risk in incurring debt in this way, but the farmer is prepared to take it. The alternative would have been to wait (perhaps three or four years) until he had accumulated enough savings to finance the new pig herd without borrowing. He has chosen to do so on credit, hoping that the profits from the pigs will help to pay off the debt fairly quickly.

The profit can therefore be shown as—

					£
Increase in valuation .	.	.	.		5015
Purchases and expenses	.	£20029			
Sales and receipts	.	.	17016		
Deduct deficit .	.	.	.	.	3013
NET PROFIT	.	.	.	.	£2002

BALANCE SHEET

On this occasion the Balance Sheet is given in more detail and a further definition of a Balance Sheet is given.

A Balance Sheet is a statement drawn up to show the financial position of a business on a certain date. The business in this case is a farm, and on that day the farmer makes a list of all his possessions. These are called his *assets* and consist not only of cash, crops, and implements, but also of any money owing to him, or *debts receivable*. On the other hand, the farmer may owe money either to the bank or to private persons or firms. These debts, which he is liable to be called upon to pay at some future time, are called his *liabilities*, and are generally listed as *debts payable*, as *loans*, or, if owing to the bank, as an *overdraft*.*

The assets of a farm consist of the following—

(a) A valuation of livestock, crops, stores, implements and machinery, and tenant right.

(b) Cash in hand and at the bank.

* In some account books debts receivable are listed as *sundry debtors* or *accounts due to the farm*. Debts payable may also be called *sundry creditors* or *accounts due by the farm*.

(c) Money owing to the farmer for goods sold or for services rendered, but not yet paid, i.e. debts receivable.

Liabilities include—

(a) Overdraft at the bank.

(b) Loans.

(c) Money owing by the farmer for unpaid accounts, i.e. debts payable.

After making a valuation of all his farm assets, Mr. Ford drew up a Balance Sheet showing his financial position at 31st March, 1970. There are two new features in this Balance Sheet. As assets, he not only had livestock, crops, and implements, but a sum of £515 due for milk. As liabilities, he had two items, £2966 owing to the bank as an overdraft, and £862 owing for feeding-stuffs.

CLOSING BALANCE SHEET AT 31ST MARCH, 1970

Liabilities	£	Assets	£
Debts Payable—		Valuation—	
Miller & Co. (Feeding-stuffs) . . .	862	Tenant right . .	3000
Bank overdraft . .	2966	Implements . .	5100
		Cattle . . .	4300
	3828	Pigs	2415
NET CAPITAL . -.	13202	Crops . . .	1700
			16515
		Debts receivable—	
		Milk Marketing Board (milk) . . .	515
£	17030	£	17030

Thus the assets total £17030 and the liabilities £3828, leaving a balance of £13202 which is the Net Capital. When the assets exceed the liabilities and the balance falls, as in this case, on the left-hand side, the business is said to be *solvent*. It means that if on this date the farm were sold up and all liabilities paid off, the farmer would be left with a surplus of £13202 in cash and this is the amount shown as Net Capital. If liabilities exceeded assets, the balance would fall on the right-hand side, and the business would then be *insolvent*, meaning that if the farm were sold up, the assets would be insufficient to pay off the debts or liabilities, and the business might then be bankrupt.

PROVING THE ACCOUNTS

After completing the Trading Account and Balance Sheet, the accuracy of the results is tested in the following way. In the

Closing Balance Sheet, the Net Capital—£13202—was the sur-plus of assets over liabilities on the last day of the financial year. It is also possible to show this in another way. The Net Capital represents the amount of money invested by the farmer in the farm. If he makes a profit and spends it all on living expenses, it is obvious that the amount of money invested in the farm, or Net Capital, remains unchanged. If he does not spend all his profits, but leaves the remainder in the farm business, the Net Capital is increased. On the other hand, if he makes a loss, or spends more on private expenses than the net profit, the Net Capital decreases, and the farmer is said to be "living on his capital."

Mr. Ford made a profit of £2002, but spent only £800 of this on private purposes, and the closing Net Capital should therefore show an increase of £1202. Looking up the Balance Sheets we find that the Net Capital at the beginning of the year was £12000, and at the end £13202—an increase of £1202. This result can be set out formally as follows—

		£
Opening Net Capital		12000
Add Net Profit		2002
		14002
Deduct Private Drawings . . .		800
Closing NET CAPITAL . . .		£13202

This £13202 agrees with the total in the Closing Balance Sheet, and in this way the Trading Account and Balance Sheet are shown to be correct.

LAY-OUT OF TRADING ACCOUNT AND BALANCE SHEET

The general lay-out of the Trading Account and Balance Sheet should be carefully memorized.

Note that the liabilities are placed on the left. If the business is solvent, the balance falls on the left and is the *Net Capital*. Should the liabilities exceed the assets, the business would be insolvent and the balance would fall on the right as the *Net Capital Deficit*.

TRADING ACCOUNT

	£		£
Purchases and Expenses Opening Valuation Balance (if any) is the NET PROFIT		Sales and Receipts Closing Valuation Balance (if any) is the NET LOSS	

BALANCE SHEET

Liabilities	£	Assets	£
Debts Payable . . .		Valuation of live and dead	
Bank overdraft . . .		stock	
NET CAPITAL . . .		Cash in hand and at the	
		bank	
		Debts Receivable . .	

QUESTIONS

1. At Michaelmas you have in hand £2142 worth of cattle, £1521 worth of pigs, £45 worth of poultry, £3165 worth of crops, and £241 worth of feeding-stuffs and fertilizers. Parkinson and Co. owe you £121 for pigs, you owe Mr. Perkins £26 for ploughing and your bank overdraft amounts to £342. Prepare a Balance Sheet and show the Net Capital.

2. You have a bank overdraft of £2321 and a loan from Webster of £3526. Your cattle are worth £2433, sheep £1276, and implements £2747. You are owing £1156 for feeding-stuffs and £342 for seeds. Arrange these details in the form of a Balance Sheet. Is the financial position of the farm sound?

3. Prepare a Trading Account from the following information: opening valuation £10463, sale of vegetables £2844, potatoes £3689, cereals £1585. Payments: wages £1160, seeds £989, fertilizers £378, rent £534, fuel £272, repairs and depreciation £766, other costs £861. The closing valuation was £8232. Why is it particularly necessary to include the closing valuation in an example such as this?

4. Mr. Wilkins of Woodgreen Farm is making up his accounts for the year ending 31st December, 1970. The farm consists of 600 acres on medium soil —mostly arable—in East Anglia. The main crops are cereals and sugar-beet. Cattle are kept to use pasture, leys and arable by-products. The farmer had a sheep flock until recently but they have been discarded to grow more grain.

OPENING BALANCE SHEET AT 1ST JANUARY, 1970

Liabilities	£	Assets	£
Bank overdraft . .	1342		
NET CAPITAL . .	27536	Valuation—	
		Cattle . . .	4580
		Wheat . . .	9236
		Barley . . .	1326
		Oats . . .	1542
		Stores on hand .	671
		Implements . .	8123
		Tenant right . .	3400
£	28878	£	28878

Receipts during the year were—

	£			£
Wheat	4265	Barley		4429
Fat cattle . . .	1306	Straw		429
Oats	2311	Sugar-beet . . .		6967
Calf subsidy . . .	253	Fat cattle . . .		1050
Grazing let . . .	30	Wheat		4261
Hay	1400			

Payments during the year were—

	£		£
Ordinary workers . .	6256	Salary of bailiff . . .	1262
Employers' liability insurance	17	Rates	164
Accountant and valuer . .	125	Fuel and oil . . .	703
Tenant's share of repairs .	641	Fire insurance . . .	220
Telephone	76	Office expenses . . .	84
Electricity	260	Feeding-stuffs . . .	371
Machine repairs . . .	1349	Fertilizers	2568
Seeds	1769	Rent	3860
Sack hire	25	Veterinary charges . .	120
Sprays	391	Machinery purchased . .	1421
		Transferred to private account	2000

The closing valuation was—

	£		£
Cattle	4361	Stores	834
Wheat	7105	Implements . . .	7636
Barley	642	Tenant right . . .	3500

At the end of the year the farmer was owing £342 for repairs, £201 for seeds, and £121 for feeding-stuffs, and £561 for fertilizers. A sum of £145 was owing to him for barley.

Complete the accounts for the year in this order—

(*a*) Write up the Account Book (include the bank overdraft at the beginning of the year, and add amounts owing at the end).

(*b*) Draw up the Trading Account.

(*c*) Draw up the Closing Balance Sheet.

(*d*) Prove the accuracy of the accounts.

5. After completing his accounts, Mr. Wilkins made the following comment, "In the past year I have drawn £2000 for living expenses and my bank overdraft has been replaced by a substantial balance. In spite of this, my accountant tells me I have made a loss. I find this difficult to understand." Can you explain this?

CHAPTER 6

TRADING ACCOUNTS IN MORE DETAIL

IN this chapter, the accounts of Manor Farm are continued for a third year. While the general procedure is the same as before, more detail is given and certain new features are introduced.

It will be recalled that at the end of the second year, Mr. Ford had an overdraft of nearly £3000, the limit agreed with his bank manager, and he also owed over £800 for feeding-stuffs. During the year, the farmer received a legacy of £512, which he promptly paid into the farm account to help to reduce the overdraft. Receipts from the expanded pig herd soon began to increase and there was a welcome rise in crop yields. After two years of expansion, the farmer was content to consolidate his position during the third year. The farm showed a good profit and, as it was not reinvested, farm receipts exceeded expenses by over £3000. This enabled the farmer to pay off the bank overdraft as promised and he finished the year with a credit balance at the bank.

DETAILS OF RECEIPTS AND PAYMENTS

On 1st April, 1970, the third financial year began, and at the end of April Mr. Ford was ready to write up the account book for the first month. He wisely decided, from the time he began farming, to pay all receipts into the bank, and pay all accounts by cheque. It was thus a simple matter to write up the receipts from the counterfoils of the bank paying-in slips and the payments from the details on the cheque counterfoils.

Receipts during April (given on the paying-in slips) were as follows—

1970		£
April 8.	11 Pork pigs (Barr & Co.)	116
8.	1 Fat cow (Benchester market)	57
15.	20 tons wheat (Gavin & Co.)	321
22.	2862 gal. milk (M.M.B.)	515
22.	Walker (ploughing)	42

Payments were—

1970		£
April 1.	Wages	85
1.	N.H.I. stamps	24
8.	Wages	81
8.	Small tools	5
15.	Wages	84
22.	Wages	83
29.	Wages	80
29.	Accountants	45

28

			£
April 29.	Feeding-stuffs (5 tons pig food, Simpson & Wheeler) .		165
29.	Sprays (for cereals, Ace Chemicals Ltd.) . .		18
29.	Small expenses:	£	
	Petrol	6	
	Market	3	
	Nails etc.	2	
	Miscellaneous	1	
		—	12
29.	Private		50

It will be noticed that Mr. Ford does most of his business on a Friday. He visits the town on that day, pays receipts into the bank and cashes a cheque to pay the week's wages. On the last Friday of the month he pays outstanding bills and cashes a cheque for small expenses (£12). He also drew £50 for private expenses.

Details in the Account Book

When copying receipts and payments into the Account Book it is recommended that the following details should be given—

1. Name of person or business firm concerned, for future reference.

2. Numbers of livestock bought and sold, so that the totals can be checked at the end of the year.

3. Quantities of produce sold and materials such as feeding-stuffs bought. This is helpful in calculating yields per cow or per acre and in estimating feeding efficiency.

Checking Entries for the Month

After entering the transactions for April, the columns were totalled and checked. It is desirable that this should be carried out every month, so that mistakes can be corrected without delay.

	£
Total Paid column	3698
Total Received column . . .	1051
Difference which should equal bank overdraft at end of April . . .	£2647

In other words, £1051 was received during the month and £732 was paid out, leaving a surplus of £319. This reduced the bank overdraft from £2966 to £2647.

For the remainder of the year, receipts and payments were entered month by month, as in April.

(Left-hand page)

SALES AND RECEIPTS

DATE	NAME AND DETAILS	TOTAL RECEIVED £	CATTLE £	PIGS £	MILK £	WHEAT £	POTATOES £	MISCELLANEOUS RECEIPTS £	PRIVATE RECEIPTS £
1970 Apr. 8	11 Pork Pigs (Barr & Co.)	116		116					
	1 Fat cow (Benchester Market)	57	57						
15	20 ton Wheat (Gavin & Co.)	321				321			
22	2862 gal. Milk (M.M.B.)	515			515				
	Ploughing (Walker)	42						42	
		1051	57	116	515	321		42	
	Sales for rest of year in shortened form—								
	Cattle	725	725						
	Pigs	6280		6280					
	Milk	5903			5903				
	Wheat	4785				4785			
	Potatoes	2562					2562		
	Miscellaneous	993						993	
	Private	512							512
		22811	782	6396	6418	5106	2562	1035	512
	Less debts receivable at beginning				515				
			782	6396	5903	5106	2562	1035	
	Add depts receivable at end				620				
		£ 22811	782	6396	6523	5106	2562	1035	
	YEAR 1971–72 Opening Balance, being Cash in Bank	£ 667							

PURCHASES AND EXPENSES

DATE	NAME AND DETAILS	TOTAL PAID	CATTLE	FEEDING-STUFFS	SEEDS	FERTILIZERS AND SPRAYS	WAGES	REPAIRS AND SMALL TOOLS	FUEL	RENT	OTHER OVER-HEADS	IMPLE-MENTS BOUGHT	PRIVATE DRAW-INGS
		£	£	£	£	£	£	£	£	£	£	£	£
1970 Apr. 1	Opening Balance, being Bank Overdraft	2966											
	Wages	85					85						
	N.H.I. stamps	24					24						
	Wages	81					81						
8	Small tools	5						5					
15	Wages	84					84						
22	Wages	83					83						
29	Wages	80					80						
	Accountant	45									45		
	Feeding-stuffs (Simpson & Wheeler, 5 ton pig food)	165		165									
	Sprays (Acme Chem. Co.) for cereals	18				18							
	Miscellaneous	12						2	6		4		
	Private	50											50
		3698		165		18	437	7	6		49		50
	Payments for rest of year in shortened form—												
	Cattle	172	172										
	Feeding-stuffs	4453		4453									
	Seeds	315			315								
	Fertilizers and sprays	710				710							
	Wages	4613					4613						
	Repairs and small tools	755						755					
	Fuel	1404							1404				
	Rent	2100								2100			
	Other overheads	1298									1298		
	Implements bought	1476										1476	
	Private drawings	1150											1150
		22144	172	4618	315	728	5050	762	1410	2100	1347	1476	1200
	Less debts payable at beginning			862									
				3756	315	728		762					
	Add debts payable at end			456	305	843		65					
	Closing Balance, being Cash at Bank	667	172	4212	620	1571	5050	827	1410	2100	1347	1476	1200
		£ 22811											

FIG. 3. RECEIPTS AND EXPENSES FOR THE THIRD YEAR

To save space, the remaining transactions are given in a summarized form, as follows—

Receipts—

		£
Cattle	. . . . . .	725
Pigs	. . . . . .	6280
Milk	. . . . . .	5903
Wheat	. . . . . .	4785
Potatoes	. . . . . .	2562
Miscellaneous	. . . . .	993
Private	. . . . . .	512

Payments—

		£
Cattle	. . . . . .	172
Feeding-stuffs	. . . . .	4453
Seeds	. . . . .	315
Fertilizers and sprays	. . . .	710
Wages	. . . . . .	4613
Repairs and small tools	. . .	755
Fuel	. . . . . .	1404
Rent	. . . . . .	2100
Other overheads	. . . .	1298
Implements bought	. . . .	1476
Private drawings	. . . .	1150

At the end of the year the Total Received and Total Paid columns were totalled and again checked with the bank balance, in this case a credit balance carried forward for the next year.

UNPAID ACCOUNTS

Details of unpaid accounts at the beginning and end of the year are given below—

At 1/4/70	£	At 31/3/71	£
Debts payable—			
Miller & Co. (feeding-stuffs)	862	Miller & Co. (feeding-stuffs)	456
		Wills Garage Co. (tractor repairs)	65
		Barker & Wheeler (seeds) .	305
		Farm Supplies Ltd. (fertilizers)	843
Debts receivable—			
M.M.B. (2862 gal. milk) .	515	M.M.B. (3407 gal. milk) .	620

Unpaid accounts are dealt with in the following way. Taking milk as an example, it will be recalled that the £515 owing to Mr. Ford at 31st March, 1970, was added to the receipts for the year ending 31st March, 1970. As the milk had been produced and dispatched from the farm before the end of the financial year, it was properly included in the accounts for that year. The cheque for this milk was received during April and was entered as a receipt in that month. To avoid including this sum in more than one Trading Account, the £515 must be deducted from the receipts for milk in the accounts for the year ending 31st March, 1971. It may seem unnecessary to include this item in the accounts only to deduct it again at the end of the year. It is, however, essential to do so to ensure that the Total Received column contains a complete list of all receipts that can be checked against the bank statement.

At the end of the year, £620 was owing for milk dispatched in March and this sum was therefore added, giving a total of £6523. As this is the precise value of milk produced during the year, this is the sum carried to the Trading Account. Other unpaid accounts were dealt with similarly.

ANNUAL VALUATION

The next step was to take an inventory and valuation of livestock, crops, and other assets at the end of the year. Before completing the Balance Sheet, it is desirable to check the numbers of livestock to make sure that they have all been accounted for.

CHECK ON LIVESTOCK NUMBERS. Take the total at the beginning of the year, add the numbers purchased or born, deduct those sold, died or used during the year, and the final total should agree with the numbers on hand at the end of the year.

The result for this farm was as follows—

	Cattle	Pigs
No. at beginning . .	74	242
No. purchased . . .	2	1
No. born	36	539
Total	112	782
Less—		
No. sold	35	451
No. died	4	93
No. at end . . .	73	238

ITEMS SHARED BETWEEN FARM AND PRIVATE USE

Before completing the Trading Account, there are a number of new items to be taken into consideration. It has already been pointed out that private expenses must be kept strictly separate from farm expenses. In some cases this may be found rather difficult. The farmer may use the farm car occasionally for private purposes. In addition he may use milk or other produce which would otherwise have been sold. Obviously, some allowance must be made in the Trading Account in such cases.

The following are the most important items to be dealt with in this way—

1. Farm produce (such as milk or eggs) used in the house.
2. The farm car or telephone when used partly for private purposes.
3. Farm stores (e.g. fuel) used in the house.
4. Value of the farm-house if included in the rent of the farm.

The dwelling-house is generally used partly as a private house and partly as a farm office, and the accepted rule is to charge two-thirds of the annual value of the house to private use and one-third to the farm.

On the other hand, the farmer may incur private expenses for the benefit of the farm. If he is boarding farm workers in his dwelling-house, he is entitled to charge the cost to the farm Trading Account.

When car, telephone, or similar expenses are shared in this way, the simplest method is to charge them to the farm in the first place and to make an adjustment to the Trading Account at the end of the year. If the accounts are to be used for the assessment of income tax, agreement should be reached with the Inspector on the allowance to be made. All personal benefits, received from the farm, are added to Sales and Receipts as if "sold" by the farm. Similarly any benefits rendered to the farm are added to Purchases and Expenses.

At the end of the year, Mr. Ford made the following allowances: Farm produce consumed £40, private use of farm car £50, and share of rent of farm-house £40. These were added to the Sales and Receipts in the Trading Account.

Trading Account

All information was then ready to complete the Trading Account which, given in detail, is shown below.

The lay-out should be studied and compared with that shown on page 22. In both cases, the purchases of livestock, and the sale of livestock and livestock products (e.g. milk) are given in a sub-total, and this is of advantage in calculating the livestock output—a term which will be explained later. Crop sales are also given a sub-total for a similar reason. It will be noted that the Trading Account for 1970–71 gives more detail. It is not for that reason any more accurate than the Trading Account for 1969–70, but while the inclusion of this additional detail is not essential, the accounts are of greater value as an aid to farm management.

At the end of each year, the farmer should examine his Trading Account and compare it with that of the previous year. He should note any increases or decreases and attempt to find the reason. If costs are rising, he should examine the items responsible and consider whether the increase is justified. They may be rising because of an increase in the production of livestock or crops, in which case the rise in costs should be balanced by an increase in

TRADING ACCOUNT FOR YEAR ENDING 31ST MARCH, 1971

Purchases and Expenses—	£	Sales and Receipts—	£
Cattle	172	Cattle	782
Feeding-stuffs . . .	4212	Pigs	6396
Seeds	620	Milk	6523
Fertilizers and sprays .	1571		
			13701
	6575	Wheat . . . 5106	
Wages	5050	Potatoes . . . 2562	
Repairs and small tools .	827		7668
Fuel and electricity . .	1410	Miscellaneous . . .	1035
Rent	2100		
Other overheads .	1347		22404
Implements purchased .	1476	Non-cash receipts—	
	18785	Credit for private use of—	
		Farm car . . 50	
		Farm house . 40	
		Farm produce . 40	
			130
Opening Valuation . .	16515	Closing Valuation . .	16204
	35300		38738
NET PROFIT . .	3438		
	£38738		£38738

sales or in the valuation. The rise may be due to an increase in prices over which the farmer has no control. But if no explanation can be found, the accounts may indicate where economies can be introduced.

BALANCE SHEETS

The Closing Balance Sheet was then drawn up, preceded by a shortened form of the Opening Balance Sheet, copied from the accounts for the previous year, as follows:—

OPENING BALANCE SHEET AT 1ST APRIL, 1970

Liabilities	£	Assets	£
Bank overdraft . .	2966	Valuation . . .	16515
Debts payable. . .	862	Debts receivable . .	515
	3828		
NET CAPITAL . .	13202		
£	17030	£	17030

CLOSING BALANCE SHEET AT 31ST MARCH, 1971

Liabilities	£	£	Assets	£
Debts payable—			Valuation—	
Miller & Co. (feeding-stuffs) .	456		Cattle	4100
Wills Garage Co. (repairs) .	65		Pigs	2214
			Crops	1320
Barker & Wheeler (seeds) .	305		Implements . . .	5310
			Stores	260
Farm Supplies Ltd. (fertilizer)	843		Tenant right . .	3000
		1669		16204
Opening Net Capital . .	13202		Cash in hand . . .	667
Add Net Profit .	3438		Debts receivable—	
Private receipts .	512		(M.M.B.) . . .	620
	17152			
Less Drawings .	1200			
Produce used	130			
		15822		
		£17491		£17491

Proving the Accounts

The final step is to prove the accuracy of the accounts. At the beginning of the year the capital invested was £13202. As a result of the year's trading this had been increased by the Net Profit, and there were some private receipts paid into the farm account. On the other hand, the capital had been reduced by private drawings, and by the value of farm produce used. Setting this out in tabular form it appears as follows—

		£
Net Capital at beginning of year (per Opening Balance Sheet)		13202
Add—	£	
Net Profit	3438	
Private receipts	512	
		3950
		17152
	£	
Less Private Drawings . . .	1200	
Produce used	130	
		1330
Balance agrees with Net Capital at end of year (per Closing Balance Sheet) . .		£15822

It will be seen that this statement has been inserted in the Closing Balance Sheet showing that the accounts have been correctly completed.

QUESTIONS

The following is a very simple account to be used as a drill of general procedure—

OPENING BALANCE SHEET

Liabilities	£	*Assets*	£
Debts Payable—		Valuation—	8000
Feeding-stuffs . . .	160	Debts Receivable:	
NET CAPITAL . .	8740	Milk	700
		Cash in bank . . .	200
	£8900		£8900

(a) Enter in the Account Book—
Opening Bank Balance £200

Receipts	£	*Payments*	£
Cereals	600	Wages	1500
Milk	8200	Feeding-stuffs . . .	3000
		Rent	800
		Seeds and fertilizers . .	100
		Other costs . . .	1000

Deduct amounts owing at the beginning (see Balance Sheet above) and add those owing at the end—
Owing to the farmer: milk £650.
Owing by the farmer: feeding-stuffs £200, seeds £40.
(b) The closing valuation is £7800; complete the Trading Account, allowing £50 for produce used in the farmhouse.
(c) Complete the Closing Balance Sheet and prove the accounts.

2. Mr. Morris is the tenant of Dairylea Farm, a 100-acre farm with a herd of just over 40 dairy cows. Some heifer calves are reared—the remainder are purchased. The farm is mostly in grass with some kale, silage and direct reseeding of pastures.

OPENING BALANCE SHEET AT 1st JANUARY, 1969

Liabilities	£	Assets	£
Davidson & Stewart (feeding-stuffs)	156	Valuation—	
Farm Supplies Ltd. (seeds) .	45	42 cows . . .	2100
		8 heifers in calf . .	400
	201	19 young stock . .	450
NET CAPITAL. . .	5089	200 hens . . .	100
		Implements . . .	1450
		Tenant right . .	300
			4800
		Debtor—	
		M.M.B. (milk) . .	364
		Cash in bank . .	126
£	5290	£	5290

Receipts during the year were as follows—

	£		£
Milk	4805	Ploughing grant . . .	42
Eggs	465	Contract for neighbour .	21
32 calves . . .	216	Hens sold	30
8 fat and cull cows . .	261		

Payments during the year were as follows—

	£		£
Cowman	609	N.H.I. stamps and insurance	66
Wage of son . . .	530	Water rates . . .	75
Fire insurance . . .	25	Tenant's share of building re-	
Accountant and valuer .	36	pairs	25
Telephone	36	Bank charges and cheques .	12
Fuel	180	Stamps and stationery . .	10
Vehicle repairs . . .	420	Pest destruction . . .	4
Feeding-stuffs . . .	1521	Subscriptions . . .	14
Fertilizers	416	Electricity	72
Rent	650	Seeds	42
Day-old chicks . . .	31	Other expenses . . .	194
Veterinary charges . .	26	Private drawings . . .	702

Produce used in the house is valued at £50, and private use of the car at £40. At the end of the year, Mr. Morris owes £245 for feeding-stuffs, £61 for seeds, £42 for tractor repairs and £32 for veterinary fees. The M.M.B. owed him £321 for milk.

The 43 cows on hand were valued at £2150, the 7 heifers in calf at £350 and the 19 young stock at £445. The 240 hens were valued at £120. The tenant right is £300. Implements were valued at £1233.

Assuming that one cow died, 41 calves were born and 10 heifers were moved into the dairy herd, check the numbers of dairy cows and young stock.

Comment on the financial position of this farmer. (Take into account debtors, creditors and valuations at the beginning and end of the year, the profit and private spending.)

CHAPTER 7

SUMMARY OF PROCEDURE

THE accounts for Manor Farm have now been dealt with for three years, further details being added at each successive stage. In practice, very few accounts would be run in the simple form shown for the first year, but the method shown for the third year would be used throughout. The simpler method of presentation has been given to show how accounts are continued from year to year—the closing balance, valuation, and Balance Sheet for one year becoming the opening cash balance, valuation, and Balance Sheet for the next year.

To summarize the method of keeping accounts by means of a Cash Analysis Account Book, a brief outline of the procedure is given below—

1. Take a valuation of live and dead stock and prepare an Opening Balance Sheet (if not already carried out at the end of the previous year).

2. Copy the opening bank balance into the Account Book.

3. Enter receipts and payments throughout the year, checking the totals once a month with the analysis columns and the bank balance.

4. Total the Account Book at the end of the year, carrying the balance forward.

5. Make a list of unpaid accounts and adjust the analysis columns.

6. Make an inventory of live and dead stock and draw up the closing valuation, checking the livestock numbers.

7. Complete the Trading Account, adding the value of produce used, etc., to the receipts.

8. Complete the Closing Balance Sheet.

9. Prove the accounts. Taking the Net Capital in the Opening Balance Sheet, add—

Net profit (*if any*).
Private receipts paid into the farm account.

deduct—

Net loss (*if any*).
Private drawings.
Value of produce, etc., used.

The result should equal the Net Capital in the Closing Balance Sheet.

In the next section we shall deal with some of the practical details in keeping accounts—the use of a Petty Cash Book and other records, valuations, banking, and income tax—but before doing so, it is important that the general principles of accounting laid down in the preceding chapters are thoroughly understood.

QUESTION

Mr. Starling farms Orchard Farm. His main sales are apples, with a few pears and blackcurrants. Although he owns the land (as is usual with top fruit) the land and buildings are omitted from the balance sheet to prevent any change in their value from affecting the Net Profit.

BALANCE SHEET AT 1ST APRIL, 1967

Liabilities	£	Assets	£
Bank loan . . .	5000·00	Fruit trees . .	4935·00
Debts payable—		Equipment . .	5439·00
NPK Fertilizer Co. .	45·50	Apples in store . .	500·00
Cardboard Cartons		Materials in store .	91·40
Ltd. . . .	281·00	Debts receivable—	
Farm Chemical Co. .	56·12	Williams & Co.	
NET CAPITAL .	6212·00	(apples) . .	378·55
		Balance at bank . .	250·67
£	11594·62	£	11594·62

Receipts during April were—

			£
April 7.	Apples	. . . . .	255·00
21.	Apples	. . . . .	123·65
26.	Apples	. . . . .	56·00
30.	Apples	. . . . .	135·00

Purchase during April were—

		£
April 3.	Regular wages	30·30
8.	NPK Fertilizer Co. (fertilizer) .	45·50
10.	Wages	32·50
14.	Farm Chemical Co. (sprays) .	56·12
17.	Wages	31·50
17.	Road Haulage Co. Ltd. .	25·00
23.	Cardboard Containers Ltd. .	281·00
24.	Wages	33·30
24.	Farm Supplies Ltd. (sprayer) .	10·00
27.	J. Smith Ltd. (tractor repairs) .	42·00
30.	Dillingham R.D.C. (rates) . .	62·50
30.	Private drawings . . .	175·00

Write up the Account Book for April choosing column headings that appear appropriate.
Receipts for the rest of the year were—

	£
Apples	11300·00
Pears	377·00
Blackcurrents	194·00
Other sales	10·00

Payments for the rest of the year were—

		£
Regular wages	. . . .	1254·00
Casual wages .	. . .	2981·00
Trees . .	. . .	518·00
Manures	. . . .	364·45
Sprays and dusts	. . .	743·00
Haulage and transport	. . .	223·00
Packing materials .	. . .	1000·00
Implements purchased	. . .	403·00
Machinery repairs .	. . .	290·00
Fuel . .	. . .	212·00
Contracts	. . . .	130·00
Electricity	. . . .	42·00
Storage Charge	. . .	200·00
Hort. sundries .	. . .	90·00
Insurances	. . . .	66·00
Levies . .	. . .	109·00
Telephone and postage	. . .	40·00
Other payments	. . .	11·00

At 31st March, 1968, the farmer owed A.B. Nurseries £106 for trees, N.P.K. Fertilizer Co. £70, Farm Chemical Co. £45 for sprays, Cardboard Cartons Ltd. £125, J. Smith Ltd. £50 for machinery repairs; and £394·54 was owing to him for apples sold.

(a) Complete the Account Book for the year.

The valuation at 31st March, 1968, was—

		£
Fruit trees	. . . .	5019·00
Equipment	. . . .	4799·00
Unsold apples .	. . .	400·00
Packing materials and sundries .	. .	25·50

(b) Complete the Trading Account. Allow £10 for farm produce used, £52 for the farm-house and £50 for private use of the farm car.

(c) Complete the Closing Balance Sheet.

(d) Prove the accounts.

PART II

THE BUSINESS SIDE OF FARMING

CHAPTER 8

BANKING AND CREDIT

AS has already been stated, every farmer should have a banking account, and payments and receipts should, so far as possible, be made through it. There are many advantages in transacting business in this way, of which the following are the most important—

1. Money is safer in a bank than in the farm office, and the use of cheques avoids the need for carrying large sums of money.

2. A bank cheque can be used as evidence of payment if a dispute should arise.

3. It is easier and quicker to write a cheque than to count out a large sum of money.

4. Money may be borrowed from a bank in the form of an overdraft.

5. A banker's reference may at times be useful as evidence of financial standing, as, for example, in leasing a farm when the applicant is not known to the landlord, or in obtaining credit.

OPENING A BANKING ACCOUNT

When opening a banking account for the first time, a person who is unknown to the bank manager may be asked to produce references. Generally, however, an introduction by some responsible person—preferably one who deals with the same bank— is sufficient. The prospective customer makes his first deposit of money, gives a specimen of his signature, and receives a cheque book and a book of paying-in slips. The bank will record the cheques he draws and the money he pays in on statements that he can examine any time he wishes. Alternatively, the statements will be sent to him as each sheet is filled or at regular intervals according to his instructions. A wallet will be supplied to hold the bank statements.

CHEQUES

A cheque, an example of which is shown overleaf (Fig. 4) is an order to a banker to make a payment of money. The person who writes the cheque is the *drawer* and the person or firm who is to receive the payment is the *payee* (Mr. A. J. Brown). The drawer (F. G. Sturrock in the example given) fills in the date, the name of the payee, the sum of money, and signs his name. It will be noted that the amount of money is given in both words and figures, and to avoid fraud, care should be taken to leave no gaps where additions can be made afterwards. To assist in book-keeping, a brief copy of the details is made in the summary provided in the cheque book or on the counterfoil, or stub.

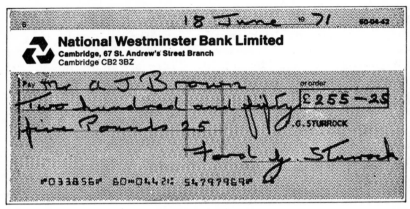

FIG. 4. A CHEQUE

If a customer wishes to draw cash for his own use, he writes *self* or *cash* in the line reserved for the name of the payee and signs the cheque in the ordinary way.

CROSSED CHEQUES. It will be noted that two parallel lines have been printed across the cheque illustrated. Such a cheque is said to be "crossed" and must be paid into a banking account. An "open" cheque with no crossing can be cashed (at the customer's bank only) by anyone, e.g. a farm worker with no bank account.

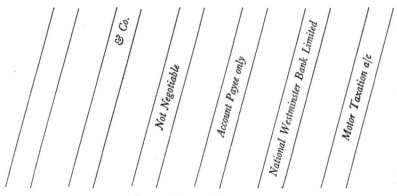

FIG. 5. CHEQUE CROSSINGS

Open cheques, however, are not safe if lost or stolen and are discouraged by the banks. Various types of crossings are illustrated, and while the usual one consists of two plain lines with or without the words "& Co.," other crossings are occasionally used (Fig. 5). As an added precaution against theft, the words "Not Negotiable," "Account payee only," or the name of payee's bank may be added. Sometimes the recipient of the cheque may ask that a special crossing be used, e.g. a borough or county council may request that the cheque for a car licence be marked "Motor Taxation A/c," and the cheque must be paid into that account in the bank. Today, most cheques have a crossing printed on them. If the drawer wishes to make one of these open (e.g. to draw out cash) he can write "Pay Cash" in the crossing and sign his name.

PAYING IN A CHEQUE. On receiving a cheque, the payee, in this case A. J. Brown, completes a paying-in slip. These slips may be obtained in book form or as loose forms. The cheque and the paying-in slip are handed to the bank cashier who initials the entry (and in the case of a book, returns it to the customer).

Instead of paying in a cheque, the payee can endorse it (by signing it on the back) and pass it to someone else to pay into *his* bank account. A shopkeeper, for example, might take such a cheque to oblige a customer who was short of cash or had no bank account of his own.

Formerly the payee had to endorse a cheque by signing it on the back before paying it into his account. As a result of the Cheques Act, 1957, endorsement is no longer necessary except for cheques cashed across the counter, cheques passed to someone else, travellers' cheques and a few other minor exceptions.

ORDER AND BEARER CHEQUES. The cheque illustrated in Fig. 4 (with the phrase "or order" after the payee's name) is known as an "order" cheque. The "bearer" cheque (that could be cashed by someone without a banking account) is now seldom seen and can be ignored.

FORGERY. A bank has to be satisfied that the signature to a cheque drawn on them is genuine before cashing it. If money is paid against a forged signature, the bank may be called upon to make good the loss, unless it can be proved that the customer by carelessness or other circumstances contributed to the forgery.

ERRORS. If when writing a cheque the drawer finds that he has made an error in entering up the details, he may correct it and sign or initial the alteration. It is more satisfactory, however, to destroy the cheque and make out another.

STOPPED CHEQUES. The payment of a cheque can be stopped on the instruction of the drawer in writing. Notice of his death or bankruptcy acts similarly. It is advisable, therefore, to present cheques at the bank without delay. Moreover, if kept too long, the cheque becomes "stale," and will not be paid without reference to the drawer. The usual limit is six months, but some public bodies specify that their cheques must be cashed within a much shorter interval.

DISHONOURED CHEQUES. If a cheque is not properly completed, or if the drawer has insufficient money in his account to meet it, it may be dishonoured by the bank and returned to the payee.

POST-DATED CHEQUES. If, for some reason, the drawer does not wish a cheque to be cashed immediately, he may post-date it. For example, if a cheque is written on 7th January and dated "21st January," the payee cannot obtain payment until 21st January. This practice is not favoured by the banks.

BANK GIRO

The normal way to pay a bill is to send it with a cheque to the creditor. He then sends it to his bank which collects the money from the farmer's bank. This procedure can be shortened, however, if the farmer instructs his bank to pay money straight into the creditor's bank account. Some large firms and public bodies encourage their customers to pay bills in this way. If the farmer wishes to do so, he can fill up a form (or use the one on the back of the bill) and send it with a cheque to his own bank. If he pays several bills at a time in this way, he can make a list of the sums and send one cheque to cover them all. Unless the firm states the name of their bank, however, the method cannot be used. The Post Office also has a Giro system.

To avoid writing and sending cheques for fixed payments which the farmer makes at regular intervals, he can instruct the bank by means of a *standing order* to make payments (e.g. monthly, yearly) for items such as subscriptions and hire-purchase instalments. This is often worthwhile. The bank will continue payments until instructed to stop.

In place of a standing order made by the payer, the payee can take the initiative. A firm that wishes to collect payments in this way, asks its customers to authorize a *direct debit*. This allows the firm to collect payment from the customer's account. This is obviously very convenient for the firm concerned. It is a recent innovation and can be used, for example, to collect life insurance premiums.

PAYING WAGES AND SALARIES

A farmer can legally pay his employees by cheque if they agree. He can go a step further and ask his bank to pay wages directly into the men's bank accounts. This system is more likely for salaried foremen or managers who have their own bank accounts. The system is, however, spreading and allows the employer to avoid carrying large sums in cash.

The Use of More Than One Bank Account

To avoid filling the farm account books with a record of all private receipts and payments made by cheque, some farmers keep two accounts at the bank. Private receipts are paid into a personal account, and to cover living expenses the farmer transfers to his personal account a definite sum from the farm account at monthly or three-monthly intervals. This practice has much to commend it as it reduces the amount of book-keeping and enables the farmer to keep a check on his private expenses. If this method is adopted, the name of the account—"Private A/c" and "Farm A/c," or "No. 1 A/c" and "No. 2 A/c," is entered below the signature when the cheques are written, and on the credit slips when money is paid in.

Bank Charges

Most banks make a charge for keeping customers' accounts. The method of calculating this varies slightly between different banks, but the amount generally charged depends on the number of cheques drawn, the number of items paid in and the size of balance kept. In some cases, no charge is made, but the customer is then expected to keep an agreed minimum credit balance.

Bank charges are deducted from the customer's account at quarterly or half-yearly intervals and should be copied into the Cash Book as a payment when checking the bank pass-book or statement. The twopenny stamp on cheques was a stamp duty which the bank remitted to the Government authorities, but this was abolished on 15th February, 1971.

Current and Deposit Accounts

The banking account from which cheques are paid is known as a "current" account. If a large balance has accumulated, it may be transferred to a "deposit" account. On this interest is allowed, but cheques are not expected to be drawn on it. To withdraw money from a deposit account, the bank may require a few days' notice, but in practice payment can generally be arranged on request.

General Rules

From the book-keeping point of view, the following rules concerning the use of banking accounts should be remembered—

1. When cheques are received, they should be paid into the bank *promptly* lest they become stale or be stopped for some reason.

2. To assist in writing-up the Account Book, the name, date, and a few details of each transaction ("12 bullocks," "feeding-stuffs," etc.) should *always be entered on the counterfoils* of cheques and paying-in slips.

3. All cheques and cash received should be paid *into the bank account.* Any cash required to meet expenses should be obtained by a separate cheque drawn to "self" or "cash."

In this way, all receipts and payments are recorded in the counterfoils of the cheque book, or on the paying-in slips, as well as in the bank statement. If these rules are strictly adhered to, book-keeping is greatly simplified.

Cheques received should not be cashed over the counter or passed on to some other person in payment of a debt. Otherwise there is no proper record of such transactions, and they may easily be forgotten and omitted from the account book.

Some further advantages of having a banking account may be mentioned here. If a farmer is selling goods to a stranger from another part of the country, he may hesitate to accept a cheque until he is sure that the payment will be met. In such a case he may ask his own bank to make a confidential inquiry as to the standing of the person with whom he intends to do business.

In many cases, arrangements can be made that regular receipts, such as cheques from the Milk Marketing Board, and dividends on shares, can be paid directly into a bank account. This saves time in paying in cheques, and avoids the risk of their being mislaid or overlooked. Large sums of money should not be allowed to accumulate on the farm, but should be banked as soon as possible. It is also prudent to deposit securities and insurance policies in a bank strong-room, which is proof against theft or fire damage.

CREDIT

Unless he has large resources at his disposal, the farmer may at times find that he has insufficient money to meet immediate expenses and he may be compelled to borrow money to meet a temporary shortage. He may need a loan to carry out permanent improvements, such as a scheme of drainage or the building of a new cowshed. The borrowing of money does not imply that the farm is showing a loss, and even an efficient farmer may find himself so placed. Credit, or the borrowing of money for business purposes, may be placed in two categories—long-term and short-term—depending on the purpose for which it is required.

SHORT-TERM CREDIT

The need for temporary loans depends on the type of farm. The dairy farmer whose receipts are spread over the year and who receives regular monthly cheques for milk is perhaps in the most favourable position in respect of ready cash. On an arable farm, however, expenses for seed, manures, and feeding-stuffs have to be met throughout the spring and summer when very little money is coming in from sales. By June or July, cash is running short, and it may be necessary to borrow until after the harvest. The same may also be true of a hill sheep farmer, the bulk of whose receipts come once a year at the autumn lamb sales. A short-term loan may also be required to buy store bullocks, which will be sold fat three to six months later.

Two main sources of short-term credit are open to the farmer: a bank overdraft, and credit from merchants and auctioneers. An overdraft is arranged by interview with the bank manager, the farmer giving an estimate of the amount required and his reasons for borrowing. The bank may require the borrower to deposit securities to cover the loan, usually one of the following—

1. Title Deeds of the farm if the farmer is an owner-occupier.
2. Life Insurance policies.
3. Stock Exchange securities.
4. Collateral security. If the farmer has no possessions of his own to offer, a friend or relative may be willing to deposit securities on his behalf or give a guarantee which is acceptable to the bank.

In some cases the bank manager, if he is satisfied as to the integrity of the borrower, may be prepared to advance money without formal security. In this case, the farmer may be asked to fill up a form, similar to a Balance Sheet, giving a list of his possessions and if the net capital (assets less liabilities) is substantial, the bank manager will feel fairly safe in granting an overdraft. But if the bank manager has doubts about repayments the farmer may also be required to sign an "agricultural charge" on his live and dead stock, giving an undertaking that when any part of this stock is sold, he will pay the proceeds into his bank account. The agricultural charge, which is a recent introduction, was made possible by the Agricultural Credits Act of 1928, and takes precedence over ordinary trading debts.

When arrangements satisfactory to the bank manager are concluded, the farmer may borrow up to the specified amount. Interest is charged quarterly or half-yearly at a rate which varies from time to time but is usually 1 or $1\frac{1}{2}$ per cent above the Bank Rate.

Apart from this, the farmer will find that many feeding-stuffs, seeds, and manure merchants and other tradesmen are prepared to allow their bills to remain unpaid for several months. In return, the farmer must expect to pay a somewhat higher price than if the bills were paid promptly. Sometimes the invoice states formally that interest will be charged after a certain interval, or alternatively, an addition for credit may already have been made, discount being given for prompt payment. In some parts of the country, an auctioneer may allow a customer to buy store cattle or sheep on credit, the debt being settled when the livestock are sold. In such cases, however, the livestock may remain the legal property of the auctioneer. In addition, after a poor harvest or during a time of agricultural depression, a landlord may allow a hard-pressed tenant extra time to pay his rent, thus giving him a form of short-term credit.

Another form of credit is hire purchase, which is often used for large implements (such as tractors, combine harvesters) or motor cars. Occasionally it is used for livestock such as cows or store cattle. The operation is as follows. Assume that a farmer buys a tractor for £1000 and pays a deposit of £250, leaving £750 to be paid over two years. The hire purchase company is charging 7 per cent.

		£
Sum borrowed		750
Interest 7% of £750 × 2 years . .		105
		£855

Monthly repayments $\dfrac{855}{24} = £35\cdot62$.

It will be noticed that 7 per cent is charged on the whole amount borrowed for two years, although the amount owing is being reduced month by month. The effective rate is thus nearer 14 per cent. The term "hire purchase" means that the implement (or other asset) bought with the money borrowed remains the property of the finance company and is theoretically on hire to the farmer until the last instalment is paid. If the farmer fails to pay the instalments, the property can usually be taken back and used to repay the balance outstanding. Before this happens, however, a farmer in temporary difficulties should come to some arrangement with the company, e.g. postpone an instalment until after harvest.

On the whole, a bank overdraft is usually the cheapest form of short term credit and will be preferred by the farmer. There are times, however, when the bank refuses a loan, either because the bank manager does not recommend it or because there is a "credit squeeze" and the bank is reducing loans on government advice. The farmer must then turn to other sources of credit. Merchant credit varies but is usually rather more expensive. This is not unreasonable because the farmer is using the merchant's capital and the merchant in turn may have to borrow from the bank or elsewhere. Hire purchase is often used by farmers who have difficulty in obtaining a bank loan. A small proportion of such clients have difficulty in repaying their loans and this raises the costs of the finance company; hence the higher charges.

Much criticism has at times been levelled against credit given by merchants and auctioneers. The disadvantages usually quoted are that, if placed under an obligation to the merchant, the farmer may feel bound to continue to buy his supplies from this source, and a farmer is not in a very strong position to drive a bargain with a man to whom he owes money. Moreover, if he has obtained livestock on credit he is expected to sell again through the same auctioneering firm when he might prefer to dispose of his stock in some other way. On the other hand, men who have started farming with insufficient resources, and without security on which a bank is willing to grant an overdraft, have often been helped over a difficult period by a merchant who had faith in their ability and wished to earn their future goodwill.

Long-Term Credit

Various forms of long-term credit are available to the farmer to carry out permanent improvements to the farm. Such loans may be raised by private arrangement or through one of the officially approved schemes. As the usual form of security is a mortgage on land or buildings, this form of credit is available only to landowners and owner-occupiers.

Advances may be obtained under the provisions of the Agricultural Credits Act of 1928 and 1932 for the erection or reconstruction of farm buildings and workers' cottages, the provision of water supplies, farm roads, and the drainage of land. Agricultural mortgage corporations exist for this purpose and arrangements can be made to pay off loans over periods up to forty years, each instalment consisting partly of interest and partly of repayment of the original loan. Annual repayments depend on the rate of interest when the loan is arranged. The following repayments per £100 borrowed are typical—

	6% £	8% £	10% £
Over 10 years	13·60	14·90	16·30
Over 20 years	8·70	10·20	11·70
Over 40 years	6·70	8·40	10·20

This represents the cost of the improvements to the farmer. Before carrying out a programme of erecting new buildings, for example, he will weigh up the benefits—the saving in labour, the bonus for better quality milk, the increased output by keeping a pig herd—which he expects to gain, and if the increased profit is likely to cover the interest by a comfortable margin, then the farmer is justified in borrowing.

LEASE-BACK

An owner-occupier short of capital to improve his farm or buy more land may sell his farm to an investor (e.g. insurance company) and stay on as a tenant. He may gain by operating on a larger scale; he will lose any rise in value of the land sold.

CONCLUSION

In many countries, the State has taken elaborate measures to provide credit facilities for farmers, by encouraging the formation of special agricultural banks and co-operative credit societies of various kinds. Attempts to introduce similar methods in Great Britain have not met with much success, and the banks and the merchants remain the normal sources of credit. It will be seen that when borrowing from the bank, the owner-occupier or the man who is fortunate enough to possess stocks and shares seldom has difficulty. The established farmer, who has carried on business with success over a number of years, can secure a loan on his personal reputation without formal security. But, the tenant farmer who is not well known and whose need is primarily for short-term credit may have difficulty in borrowing at the beginning of his career when his need for such facilities is greatest. A bank cannot be expected to advance money unless there is reasonable expectation of repayment. An agricultural charge would allow a tenant farmer to pledge his crops and stock but it is unpopular amongst farmers and seldom used. Merchants' associations can inspect the list of charges kept in London and as these take precedence over other debts, merchants, hearing that a farmer has signed one, may press for the payment of their accounts. Thus all other sources of credit may dry up.

In practice, the chief source of short-term credit is the bank and much depends on the local knowledge of the manager and his ability to distinguish between the farmer who needs credit to expand his enterprise on sound lines and the man who wishes to borrow to stave off bankruptcy. The farmer who keeps satisfactory accounts is more likely to receive sympathetic consideration on questions of credit and borrowing than one who has not.

QUESTIONS

1. What advantages are there to the farmer in having a banking account?

2. Explain briefly what you understand by the following—
(a) Crossed cheque; (b) Bank Giro; (c) Lease-back; (d) Stale cheque; (e) Deposit account; (f) Agricultural charge.

3. What sources of credit are available to a farmer who needs ready cash—
(a) To tide the farm over from June until his crops are ready for sale in October?
(b) To build a brick piggery costing £4000?

CHAPTER 9

RUNNING THE FARM OFFICE

IN the examples of farm accounts given in Part I, receipts and expenses were arranged in lists ready for copying into the account book. In practice they do not appear in this form, and the farmer must adopt a system so that all transactions are recorded in a methodical way with the minimum of writing, and in a form convenient for future reference.

To carry out a system of farm accounts on the lines recommended in this book the following books and records are essential—

1. Cash Analysis Account Book.
2. Petty Cash Book.
3. Wages Book.
4. Cheque book counterfoils and receipted accounts.
5. Paying-in slips.

THE CASH ANALYSIS ACCOUNT BOOK

The Cash Book contains a record of receipts and payments with analysis columns for classification of details. Space will probably be required for the annual statements:—opening and closing valuations and Balance Sheets, Trading Account, and lists of unpaid accounts at the beginning and end of the year. Such annual statements may be included in the Account Book or kept separately. Some account books are stoutly bound and are large enough to last for several years. But if the accounts are audited annually, book-keeping may be held up until the Cash Book has been returned by the accountant. For this reason, it is generally more convenient to use a fresh book each year.

PETTY CASH BOOK

As has already been emphasized, payments should, so far as possible, be made by cheque. There are, however, many small items which are paid in cash, and they are frequently a source of trouble in book-keeping. In many cases no proper record is kept, and, as a result, small payments, which may add up to a considerable sum at the end of the year, are omitted from the accounts. It is sometimes recommended that cash payments should be entered in the Account Book as they occur. If this course is adopted, however, the book will be filled with innumerable small items, thus greatly increasing the task of auditing the accounts. In practice it will be found more convenient to enter small cash payments in a Petty Cash Book or note-book from which the totals can be copied into the Account Book once a month.

There are several ways of dealing with petty cash and it is suggested that one of the following should be adopted—

1. A definite sum—say £5—is drawn by cheque (the counterfoil being marked "Petty Cash") and put in a cash box from which small payments are made. When this sum is spent, a further £5 is drawn. At the end of each month, the cash in hand is checked against the payments shown in the Petty Cash Book.

2. The second method is known as the "imprest" system, and is widely adopted by business firms. As before, a lump sum of, say £15, is drawn and put in the cash box. Suppose that at the end of the month, payments amount to £9·84. After checking the balance (which should be £5·16), a cheque is drawn for £9·84, and the money put in the box, bringing the total back to £15.

When payments are made by a foreman or clerk who must account for money placed in his charge, one of these two methods should be used. A Petty Cash Book is kept in the cash box and if the farmer makes payments from his pocket when away from the farm, he should draw the amounts from the cash box. Strict care should be taken that the cash box is kept only for business purposes.

3. If the farmer makes all his own payments and does not wish to keep a cash box, a third method is suggested. This is less accurate, but is frequently adopted in practice. When the farmer needs ready cash he draws a cheque for say £15, marking the counterfoil "Private and Petty Cash." As before, he keeps a note of small farm expenses and totals them at the end of the month. If he finds that he has spent £9·84 for farm purposes, he assumes that the balance (£5·16) has been spent on private expenses. The cheque for £15 is entered in the account book as: £15 in the Total Paid, £5·16 in the Private Expenses, and £9·84 in the Other Expenses or other appropriate columns.

A further point is the method of entering the details in the account book. Assume that the petty cash payments for one month were—

	January					£
Insurance stamps	.	.	.	.	.	5·25
Market expenses .	.	.	.	.	.	1·42
Carriage .	.	.	.	.	.	0·68
Postage stamps .	.	.	.	.	.	0·75
Petrol and oil for car .	.	.	.	.	.	1·44
Nails .	.	.	.	.	.	0·30
						£9·84

In order to classify these, the note-book may have columns corresponding to the headings in the Account Book. This entails using a fairly large book, and is hardly necessary. Apart from insurance stamps, which come under "Wages and insurance stamps," and small repairs, which come under "Repairs and small tools," the balance generally consists of "Other expenses." In this particular case, the farmer was using the imprest system, and he entered the cheque for £9·84 in the Account Book as shown below, the more important items being entered separately—

PAYMENTS

DATE	NAME AND DETAILS	TOTAL PAID	WAGES AND INSURANCE STAMPS	REPAIRS AND SMALL TOOLS	OTHER EXPENSES
January 31	Petty cash— Insurance stamps . Car expenses . Small expenses .	£ 9·84	£ 5·25	£ 0·30	£ 1·44 2·85

WAGES BOOK

In order to calculate deductions for insurance stamps, workers' income tax, etc., a separate Wages Book should be kept, only the weekly total being transferred to the Account Book. Given below is a suggested appropriate ruling for such a book—

Week ending . . . .

NAME OF WORKER	TOTAL EARN-INGS	DEDUCTIONS			PAID TO WORKER
		WORKERS' SHARE OF INSURANCE STAMPS	RENT, MILK, ETC.	INCOME TAX	
J. Brown . .	£ 19·50	£ 1·25	£ —	£ 2·50	£ 15·75
A. Hendry . .	18·70	1·25	0·50	1·25	15·70
T. Armstrong .	20·20	1·25	—	2·70	16·25
	58·40	3·75	0·50	7·45	
Total paid to Workers (transferred to Account Book)		.	.		£47·70

TIME SHEET

Week ending..

Name..

DAY	TIME STARTED	TIME FINISHED	TOTAL HOURS	LESS TIME OFF	HOURS WORKED

Total Hours for Week .   .   .   .   .   .

£

Regular weekly wage .   .   .   .   .

Overtime—weekdays........hours at............   .

Overtime— Sundays........hours at............   .

Piece work   .   .   .   .   .   .

Total earnings   .   .   .   .   .   .

Less payments to be made by worker—
    Income tax   .   .   £

    Rent   .   .   .   .

    Milk, etc.   .   .   .

    Insurance stamps   .

       Paid to worker   .

Received the above sum

Signed..

FIG. 6. TIME SHEET GIVING HOURS WORKED

TIME SHEET For week ending...19 ....
Employee's Name ....
Sheet to be entered up every evening, and the exact time spent on each
separate job to be shown. For team work (e.g. dung carting, seeding, haytime,
harvest, etc.) "horses used" to be entered on ganger's sheet only.

DESCRIP- TION OF WORK DONE	ORDINARY TIME (HOURS)	OVERTIME (HOURS)	PIECE WORK £	TRACTOR USED	CROP AND NAME OF FIELD ON WHICH EMPLOYED
Saturday					
Sunday					
Monday					
Tuesday					
Wednesday					
Thursday					
Friday					
Total				—	— —

Regular weekly wage . . . . £

Weekday overtime.................hours at................. . . .

Sunday overtime.................hours at................. . . .

Piece work and extras . . . .

Total earnings . .

Less payments to be made by worker— £
Income tax . . . . .

Cottage rent or board and lodgings .

Milk.................pints at................. . .

Potatoes at................. . . . .

Insurance (employee's contribution)

Paid to worker . . .

Received the above sum

Signed..

FIG. 7. TIME SHEET SUITABLE FOR COST ACCOUNTING

In the example, J. Brown's regular weekly wage was £17·50 and he received £2 extra for overtime, making a total of £19·50 as Total Earnings. Out of this he was liable for £1·25 for insurance stamps, and £2·50 for income tax, leaving £15·75 which was paid to him in cash. The total wages for the week (£47·70) were transferred to the wages column of the Account Book. Insurance stamps and workers' income tax are also entered in the wages column but only when the stamps are purchased or the income tax forwarded to the Collector of Taxes.

Some employers of large staffs prefer to issue time sheets to the men, who fill in details of the time of starting and finishing and time off. Two forms are illustrated; one gives only the hours worked (Fig. 6), the other gives full details of the work performed, and is suitable for cost accounting (Fig. 7).

As wages are paid in cash, a cheque is usually drawn weekly to cover the cost. The best method is to draw a cheque for the exact amount of the wages—say £47·70. Alternatively, if the Wages Book is not made up at the time, a lump sum of £50 can be drawn and the remaining £2·30 carried over for the next week's wages.

COUNTERFOILS OF CHEQUES AND PAYING-IN SLIPS

The counterfoils in the cheque book and the paying-in slips give a list of receipts and payments transacted through the bank, and they are the chief sources from which the Cash Book is written up.

While the records mentioned are the minimum number required, there are others which may be necessary in certain conditions.

LIVESTOCK MOVEMENT BOOK

To assist in tracing outbreaks of disease, farmers are under a statutory obligation to keep a record of the movement of livestock to and from the farm. Provided that sufficient details are recorded, the Account Book can furnish this information. To avoid producing the Account Book for inspection, a separate record can be kept, ruled as shown below—

LIVESTOCK MOVEMENT BOOK

Date of Movement	Number and Description	Premises or market from which moved; or name and address of person from whom delivery was taken	Premises or market to which taken; or name and address of person receiving them

INVOICE BOOK

When goods are sold on credit, an Invoice Book should be used. Each invoice is completed in duplicate, one copy remaining in the book, thus giving a convenient list of unpaid accounts for use at the end of the year. The other copy is sent as a bill for payment. (See Fig. 8.)

			Ref. No. 5
		Invoice	
			7th July, 1971

Messrs. Smith & Jones
High Street, Bridgetown

Bt. of....J.J.HUNT.......
......CHURCH FARM, ...
....EASTHAM ......

				£
Jan	4	20 dozen Eggs at 20p		4·00
	10	2 Chickens		1·25
				£5·25

FIG. 8. A SPECIMEN INVOICE

RECORDS FOR A RETAIL ROUND

When a product such as milk is sold retail, the roundsman should be provided with a book to record the daily deliveries of milk and cash received either daily or weekly. The example given below has columns for quantities of milk and eggs delivered, and also for cash received during the week (see Fig. 9). Additional columns will be required if butter or other produce is sold, or if more than one delivery is made daily. It is also advisable to supply the roundsman with a receipt book and to insist that he copies details on to the counterfoils before tearing out receipts.

RECORD OF CROPPING

It is useful to keep for future reference a record of the manuring and yields in various fields on a farm. This is often written in a diary, but details are difficult to trace when mixed up with a mass

RETAIL MILK ROUND

Price of Milk _____

Week ending _____

NAME OF CUSTOMER	OWING FROM LAST WEEK	SUN.			MON.			TUES.			WED.			THURS.			FRI.			SAT.			TOTAL DUE	CASH RECEIVED	BALANCE OWING
		MILK	EGGS	CASH	MILK	EGGS	CASH	MILK	EGGS	CASH	MILK	EGGS	CASH	MILK	EGGS	CASH	MILK	EGGS	CASH	MILK	EGGS	CASH			
Thompson, 9 Mill Lane .	£ 0·65	1	–	5	1	–	5	1	–	5	1	12	–	1 1	–	5	1	–	5	1	–	5	£ 0·95	£ 0·95	£ 1 –

FIG. 9. PAGE FROM ROUNDSMAN'S ACCOUNT BOOK

(1 pint milk, 5p, paid each day except Wednesday. Total due at end of week—12 eggs, 25p, 1 pint milk, 5p and 65p owing at beginning—95p. This was received in cash.)

of other notes. A better method is to have a special book with a page for each field, noting crop, yield, manuring, and other details year by year, thus building up a history of each field and of the results obtained.

For this purpose, it is very useful to have a map of the farm. The best maps for the purpose are those published by the Ordnance Survey Department and obtainable from stationers. The 6-inch map (6 inches to the mile) shows field boundaries, and the larger scale 25-inch map gives, in addition, the reference number and acreage of each field.

FILES

All business papers should be stored so that they can be easily traced, and receipts should be kept for seven years in case any dispute of payment should arise. Invoices, receipts, and correspondence should be stored in separate files neatly labelled, and, for convenience of reference, a new set should be started each year. Box-files are satisfactory, or, if accounts are very numerous, concertina files with pockets lettered in alphabetical order are convenient. The old-fashioned method of impaling papers on a spike has little to recommend it; the papers accumulate dust and quickly become torn.

SOME PRACTICAL DETAILS ABOUT RUNNING THE FARM OFFICE

The amount of book-keeping required in a farm varies according to its size and the method of selling the produce. On some specialized farms where fruit and vegetables are dispatched daily to shops or markets, and produce is sold on a retail round, the accounts must be attended to daily, and on larger farms of this kind a full-time office staff is required. In most cases farm produce is sold in bulk and the number of receipts and payments is generally not more than about twenty or thirty per month. Indeed, on some of the more remote hill-farms, the business transactions for a year could be written on one sheet of note-paper.

On an ordinary medium-sized farm, the office routine might be arranged as follows. The majority of payments are made by cheque, the exceptions being wages and petty cash. For small expenses a petty cash box is kept, which is replenished by a cheque, using one of the methods already described. Wages are drawn by cheque weekly, and any surplus is put in the wages box for use the following week. Most of the money received is in the form of cheques, but any received in the form of cash is set aside and paid into the bank.

At least once a week a period is allotted for office work, for filling in the Wages Book and writing cheques for accounts due for payment. A visit can then be paid to the bank to draw cash for wages and if necessary for the petty cash box. Cheques and cash received during the week are paid in at the same time.

At regular intervals—preferably once a month—the Account Book is written up. This is done by copying the details from the counterfoils of the cheque book and paying-in slips which, if the proper routine has been followed, contain a complete list of all payments and receipts. The columns are then totalled and the balance checked with the bank pass-book. It is advisable to check the entries at least once a month, for if a mistake has been made it can be more easily corrected when the details are still fresh in the farmer's mind.

The routine outlined above is simple and foolproof, and ensures that all transactions are recorded in the bank pass-book. On all but a few exceptional farms there should be no difficulty in following the methods suggested. If, however, it is found impracticable to avoid using cash receipts to make farm or private payments, a separate cash account will be found necessary—either in a separate book or in the form of extra cash columns in the Account Book. Further details of an Account Book of this kind are given in Chapter 12, Other Methods of Book-keeping.

CHECKING CASH BOOK WITH BANK BALANCE

If, as suggested, all receipts and payments are passed through the banking account, the Cash Book and bank pass-book will be identical and the balance in both should be the same at all times. If they do not agree, the items in the bank pass-book and Account Book should be compared and it will probably be found that the discrepancy is due to one of the following causes—

1. Bank charges and interest on an overdraft may have been omitted from the Account Book. They are deducted periodically from the banking account, and care should be taken to copy them into the Cash Book as a payment.

2. When a farmer sends a cheque in payment of a bill, the recipient may not present the cheque for payment at once, and when he does so, there may be a slight delay before the farmer's own bank is notified. If the farmer pays in a cheque, his account is usually credited on the same day. Nevertheless, if for any reason the bank pass-book is not up to date, it may be reconciled with the cash book as follows—

On 30th November, a farmer found that the balance in the bank pass-book was £91·23 and in the Account Book £110·25. On checking over the entries, he found that a cheque for £12·13 sent to R. Johnson had not been deducted from his account, and at cheque from C. Barker for £31·15 and paid into the bank had not then been credited—

RECONCILIATION STATEMENT

	£
Balance in bank pass-book	91·23
Add Cheque paid in bank not credited	31·15
	122·38
Less Cheque sent but not presented	12·13
Total agrees with Account Book	£110·25

3. The bank pass-book is a record of the current account, and if money has been paid directly into a deposit account it will obviously not appear in the bank balance. Deposit receipts should therefore not be overlooked when balancing the accounts.

If a farmer accumulates a large bank balance in his farm account, he may decide to invest the money in shares or other securities. In this case, it is best to withdraw this money from the farm accounts altogether: e.g. if a farmer bought 3 per cent Defence Bonds costing £500, this would be shown under payments in the account book as "Private Expenses." Similarly, if a farmer cashed private securities and intended to use the proceeds to buy farm stock, the amount would be entered under "Private Receipts."

CONTRA ACCOUNTS

Occasionally a transaction such as the following occurs. A farmer bought a cow on credit from J. Allan for £50. Later he sold 2 tons of hay to the same man for £14, giving him a cheque for the difference (£36). If the payment of £36 were entered under Cattle, the sale of the hay would be completely unrecorded, and the cattle column would not show the full value of cattle purchased. The two transactions should be regarded as separate items and entered in the Account Book accordingly. As a reminder that they were settled in this way the items may be marked "contra account"—

Under Sales and Receipts:
   Feb. 20.   J. Allan—2 tons Hay (Contra account) . . £14

Under Purchases and Expenses:
   Feb. 20.   J. Allan—1 Cow (Contra account) . . . £50

QUESTIONS

1. A farmer tells you that he has difficulty in dealing with petty cash payments. What advice would you give to him?

2. Assume that you have taken a farm of 100 acres. What account books and records would you consider necessary?

3. Assume that you have just taken an appointment as manager on a 1500-acre arable farm with two foremen. Describe the office organization and record books you would consider necessary.

CHAPTER 10

OWNER-OCCUPIERS AND PARTNERSHIPS

WHILE half the farmers in Great Britain are tenants renting land and buildings from a landlord, the others own the property they farm. As an owner-occupier, a farmer has certain advantages. He has security of tenure, and the knowledge that any improvements that he carries out will be entirely for his own benefit. One might also add that the possession of land gives a certain pride of ownership, which the farmer can never feel for property that belongs to someone else.

On the other hand, the tenant is now protected by law in many ways. If asked to quit, a tenant who has farmed according to the rules of good husbandry and carried out his other obligations can claim compensation for disturbance under the Agricultural Holdings Act, and secure payment for most forms of improvement carried out. A tenant, moreover, is less tied than an owner-occupier and if he prospers can move more easily to a larger farm. It must not be forgotten, however, that an owner-occupier requires a considerable amount of capital, and to buy a farm and stock it may cost five times as much as to stock it as a tenant. The man with a limited amount of money has a choice of purchasing a small farm outright or taking a larger farm as a tenant.

Owner-Occupiers

It is always possible for a farmer with insufficient capital to buy a farm to borrow money by means of a mortgage, pledging the farm as security for the loan. He becomes the legal owner of the farm, and in place of paying rent, he pays interest on the mortgage (in addition to other ownership charges); in course of time he may be able to repay the sum borrowed. If, as has happened in recent years, land values rise, the owner can reap a substantial capital increment. On the other hand, if he buys the farm in a time of prosperity when land values are high, and this is followed by a period of falling prices and agricultural depression (such as happened in 1921) he may be in a less happy position. A landlord might be prepared to forgo part of the rent at such a time, but the mortgage owner generally demands the payment of interest, and in default will have the farm sold to recover the value of his loan.

Owners' Rates and Taxes

Before dealing with the method of keeping accounts as an owner-occupier, a brief explanation is given of the various taxes and levies charged on the ownership of land.

TITHE

Originally, tithe was a gift of a tenth of the produce of land, used for the maintenance of the Church. For many centuries, the produce itself was given, but after 1836 a money payment was substituted. From time to time there has been much discussion on this subject, and the payment of tithe has been represented as a heavy burden on agriculture as an industry. Finally, by a Tithe Act passed by Parliament in 1936, fixed annuities were substituted for tithe rent-charge and payments (with certain minor exceptions) will cease at the end of sixty years.*

DRAINAGE RATES

In certain areas subject to flooding, Drainage Boards have the power to levy rates to recover the cost of the construction and upkeep of drainage schemes. In some cases drainage rates are chargeable to the owner only; in others, both owner and occupier make a contribution.

MORTGAGE PAYMENTS

An owner may have borrowed money on the security of his property, either to buy the farm, to erect buildings or to carry out other improvements. Payments on a mortgage may be for interest only or may include both interest and a gradual repayment of the original sum borrowed.

REPAIRS

The final charge on land ownership is the cost of repairs and upkeep. When a farm is let, the landlord usually agrees to bear a proportion of the cost of structural repairs. In some cases, he supplies the materials and the farmer supplies the labour. In others, the landlord is responsible for the maintenance of roofs and main walls and the tenant for the remainder. At the present time, there is a growing tendency for the landlord to pass the responsibility for repairs to the tenant. Whatever the arrangement, however, both parties will take the cost of repairs into account in negotiating the rent.

If a farmer is an owner-occupier, however, he must expect to pay for such repairs as would otherwise have been carried out by the landlord.

* Strictly speaking, tithe rent-charge came to an end in 1936. The tithe owners received in compensation 3 per cent Government Guaranteed Stock. "Tithe" paid by landowners is now devoted to redemption annuities, one-sixth of the annual payment being set aside to redeem the capital value of the Stock at the end of sixty years. For this reason, only five-sixths of the "tithe" payment can be charged for income tax purposes.

BOOK-KEEPING FOR OWNER-OCCUPIERS

When a farmer owns his farm, he pays no rent, but must meet the costs of ownership mentioned above. In making up his accounts, he can choose one of two methods. He may regard the ownership and tenancy of the farm as a single business, and show the profit on the business as a whole. Alternatively, he may

TRADING ACCOUNT FOR YEAR ENDING 31ST MARCH, 1971

Purchases and Expenses—	£	Sales and Receipts—	£
Cattle	172	Cattle	782
Feeding-stuffs	4212	Pigs	6396
Seeds	620	Milk	6523
Fertilizers and sprays	1571		
	6575		13701
Wages	5050	Wheat £5106	
Repairs and small tools	827	Potatoes 2562	
Fuel	1410		7668
Other overheads	1347	Miscellaneous	1035
Implements purchased	1476		22404
	16685	Non-cash receipts—	
Ownership charges—		Farm car £50	
Tithe £60		Farm house 40	
Building repairs 350		Farm produce 40	
	410	Closing Valuation	130
	17095		16204
Opening Valuation	16515		
	33610		
NET PROFIT	5128		
£	38738	£	38738

FIG. 10. OWNER-OCCUPIER: SIMPLE TRADING ACCOUNT

arrange the accounts to give the profit he makes as an owner and as a tenant separately.

The two methods may be shown by means of an example. Take Mr. Ford's farm for the year ending 31st March, 1971, as described in Chapter 6, assume that he was an owner-occupier and that the farm cost £60,000 originally.

As an owner, he did not have to pay the rent of £2100, but instead he would have paid £60 for tithe and £350 on building repairs which would normally have been paid by the landlord. As an owner-occupier, the Trading Account would be as shown in Fig. 10, above (some details are omitted to save space).

As an owner-occupier, Mr. Ford would therefore have made a Net Profit of £5128, in place of £3438 as a tenant.

The alternative method is to arrange the accounts to show the profit made as a tenant separately from that made as an owner. In this, a column should be set aside in the account book for "Ownership Expenses." A column for "Ownership Receipts" may also be required for sales of timber or gravel, the sale of parcels of land or cottages, and rents received for property not

TRADING ACCOUNT FOR YEAR ENDING 31ST MARCH, 1971

	£		£
Purchases and Expenses .	16685	*Sales and Receipts* . .	22404
Transfer from Ownership		Non-cash receipts . .	130
Account—		Closing Valuation . .	16204
Rental value . .	2100		
Opening Valuation—			
(Tenant's assets) . .	16515		
	35300		
NET PROFIT as occupier	3438		
£	38738	£	38738

OWNERSHIP ACCOUNT

Purchases and Expenses—			£
Tithe	60	*Sales and Receipts*—	
Building repairs . .	350	Rental value . .	2100
	410	(charged to Tenancy Account)	
NET PROFIT as Owner .	1690		
£	2100	£	2100

FIG. 11. OWNER-OCCUPIER: TRADING ACCOUNT AND OWNERSHIP ACCOUNT

included in the annual value of the farm. At the end of the year, an Ownership Account is drawn up similar to the Trading Account. After transferring ownership expenses to the Ownership Account and other expenses and receipts to the Trading Account, the rental value is added as an expense to the Trading Account and as a receipt in the Ownership Account as if paid by the farm to the landlord. The opening and closing valuations of live and dead stock are entered in the Trading Account. A Trading Account and Ownership Account for this alternative method are shown above, using the same figures as in the previous example.

The net result is thus—

				£
Net profit as occupier	.	.	.	3438
Net profit as owner	.	.	.	1690
Net profit as owner-occupier	.	.	.	£5128

By using the second figure, the farmer can see the profit which he would have made as a tenant farmer. This is a useful figure for advisory purposes, as most reports on profits and farming efficiency published in this country assume that the farmer is a tenant. The profit as an owner is also of interest, as it shows the return on the money invested in buying the farm. In this case, he received a return of £1710 on a capital sum of £60,000. The return per £100 invested was therefore—

$$£\frac{1690 \times 100}{60000} = 2 \cdot 8 \text{ per cent.}$$

The corresponding return on the £16204 invested as a tenant is—

$$£\frac{3438 \times 100}{16204} = 21 \text{ per cent.}$$

The return from money invested in the purchase of the farm is thus much poorer than from money invested as a tenant. The exact return varies widely according to circumstances, but a return of under three per cent for ownership and of twelve to twenty per cent as a tenant is quite typical. The return from land ownership also compares poorly with the return from investing in stocks and shares. This might lead one to the conclusion that rents and land values were out of step and that land ownership was a poor form of investment. Land, however, is bought for many other reasons than for the rent it can produce (or save in the case of an owner-occupier). A farmer may buy land to provide greater security and to satisfy pride of ownership. It may also be bought in the hope that land prices will continue to rise in value. There is also the fact that land receives favourable treatment when being assessed for Estate Duty.

PARTNERSHIPS

When two or more persons agree to own and manage a business jointly, they are known as partners. There are a number of situations in which a partnership can operate very successfully.

1. Two friends who wish to start farming may agree to go into

partnership. There are a number of advantages. If the partners have only a limited amount of capital each, they may prefer to operate a large farm jointly rather than two small ones separately. They can divide responsibilities and each can become more specialized in one part of the business. When difficulties occur, one can turn to the other for help and advice. If one partner goes on holiday or is ill, the other can carry on the business until he returns.

2. In some cases a father may take a son into partnership. Psychologically this is often a wise move. A son who must continue to take orders from his father well into middle age may feel frustrated but may be much more contented if recognized at least as a junior partner.

3. A partnership can be used as a means of inducing a man with capital to invest in a farm. He might be unwilling to lend the capital but be willing to take a share in the ownership of the business. If he is content to leave the day-to-day management to his partner, he becomes a "sleeping partner."

4. An experienced manager or foreman may become so useful that a farmer may be anxious to retain his services. One way of doing so is to make him a partner.

A partnership can be quite informal and two friends may carry on a joint enterprise for many years without any formal agreement. Unfortunately, such arrangements can lead to difficulties. The partners may disagree and, in the absence of formal rules, misunderstandings may arise. Worse still, if there is a quarrel and they wish to part company there may be disputes over the division of assets. Even when friends agree and have complete trust in one another, one may die and the other may find his partner's heirs much less sympathetic than was his partner. The heirs might, for example, insist on withdrawing their capital at an awkward time and cause acute difficulties for the remaining partner.

To avoid such difficulties, partners are strongly advised to obtain legal advice in drawing up a formal agreement or *deed of partnership*. This normally states—

1. The name and scope of the business.
2. The amount of capital provided by each partner.
3. The method of sharing profits.
4. The terms under which the partnership can be dissolved.

Legally, all partners are equal and equally able to place orders or incur debts on behalf of the partnership. Indeed (apart from one exception mentioned later) each partner is personally responsible to the limit of his resources for the debts of the partnership.

In the absence of any other agreement, profits are assumed to be divided equally. It is, however, possible to make other arrangements, e.g.—

1. If one partner contributes more capital than another, each might receive interest on capital before the balance is divided.

2. If one of the associates is a sleeping partner, the other might be paid a salary as manager before the balance is divided.

It is also worth noting that it is possible to arrange for a partner to have limited liability for the debts of the business. He must, however, be a sleeping partner who takes no part in the management of the farm.

LIMITED COMPANIES

Instead of forming a partnership, some farmers prefer a limited company. A *joint stock company* is the usual form of business organization. It is owned by the shareholders, who elect a Board of Directors to manage the business. Companies are of two kinds, each with its own set of rules: (1) the public company, often large in size, which raises capital from the public and has its shares quoted on the Stock Exchange, and (2) the private company, which raises its capital privately and is often (although not necessarily) smaller in size. Most farming companies are private. The business structure can be quite simple. A father and son or two friends farming as partners can turn themselves into a company—the partners becoming directors and also shareholders. Other members of the family or a manager or a sleeping partner can also be included as directors or shareholders. The profits of the company can be paid as fees to the directors or as a dividend to the shareholders, or can be retained in the business as a reserve, as the directors decide.

A limited company differs in a number of ways from a partnership, e.g.

1. A limited company is a legal entity quite apart from its members. Directors and shareholders may change but the company, unless dissolved, can continue indefinitely.

2. As its name implies, a limited company has limited liability. This means that if a company becomes bankrupt, the creditors can have the assets of the *company* sold to meet their claims but they have no claim on the personal property of the directors or shareholders. This provision protects the interests of anyone who invests in the company. He may lose his shares but that is all.*
Firms dealing with the company must, however, be warned that

* If the shares are not fully paid up, the shareholder may be required to pay the balance. This is not a common practice in private companies.

liability is limited. It is for this reason that the title of the company, displayed on notepaper and elsewhere, always carries the word "Limited" or "Ltd."

3. A company allows the spreading of ownership without necessarily surrendering control. A farmer can, for example, give shares to his wife or family or to his manager but, if he retains fifty-one per cent or more of the shares in his own hands, he can retain control.

4. Unlike a partner, a director cannot incur debts on behalf of the company unless the rules of the company authorize him to do so. If he goes bankrupt, this need not affect the company.

5. In a private company, the minimum number of directors is one, and of shareholders, two. The maximum number of shareholders is normally fifty. A private company could thus consist at a minimum of the farmer (director and shareholder) and one share assigned to his wife or manager.

The following are the principal rules in forming and managing companies—

1. An agreement is prepared stating that the company will take over the farm business in exchange for shares issued to the farmer and his associates. If he is an owner-occupier, the farmer may prefer to keep the ownership of the holding in his own name and lease the farm to the company. If the farm is tenanted, it will be necessary to obtain the consent of the landlord to the transfer or subletting of the tenancy to the new company.

2. A Memorandum of Association is prepared stating—

The name of the company, e.g. Smith and Son Ltd., Smith and Jones Ltd., Willowbank Farms Ltd.
A declaration that liability of the members is limited.
The object of the company.
The amount of capital and the shares into which it is divided.

3. Articles of Association are also prepared. These are the rules for conducting the company and refer to matters such as the holding of meetings, powers to increase capital or borrow money and the payment of directors.

4. A private company cannot invite the general public to buy shares. Individuals can, of course, be invited privately to do so.

5. A company must have an auditor (usually an accountant).

6. If the directors wish to dissolve a company that is solvent, they can do so. The directors then sell the assets and, after paying debts, can divide the proceeds amongst the shareholders. If the company is insolvent, a creditor who cannot get payment may get an order from the High Court. The company is then wound

up by the Official Receiver and the proceeds are shared out amongst the creditors to pay the debts of the company.

7. A company pays Corporation Tax on its profits; a partnership does not. (*See also* Chapter 22, "Taxation".) Directors' fees qualify for the earned income allowance, dividends do not.

The cost of forming a company is very variable, depending on its size and complexity. A small private company might cost around a hundred pounds or a little more.

At one time, there were substantial advantages from the point of view of taxation in forming a company. Most of these advantages have disappeared but some remain. Take two examples. Individuals pay Surtax but a company does not on profits that have not been distributed (unless they are excessive). When Surtax began at £2000 a year, this was an important consideration. Now that the limit is about £5000, it is less important. On the other hand, a company with a large enough profit has to pay Corporation Tax whereas individuals and partners do not. A further consideration is that when a company is formed this is a new business and the tax rules for new businesses apply. If profits are below average at that point, the timing of the operation may affect tax liability (*see* Chapter 22). The subject is, however, complex, and as the rules are constantly being altered to deal with cases of tax evasion, a farmer would be well advised to obtain up-to-date advice from his accountant and his lawyer to find whether there would be any advantage, in his particular circumstances, in forming a limited company.

CHAPTER II

VALUATIONS

A S already stated, a valuation of assets is made on the date
when book-keeping is first begun, and at the end of every
year afterwards, the closing valuation of one year serving as the
opening valuation of the next.

DATE OF VALUATION

The date on which accounts begin and end is a matter of
secondary importance, provided that the same date is used each
year. In some cases, the calendar year is chosen and accounts
run from 1st January to 31st December. More commonly, book-
keeping begins on the date of entry to the farm. In England,
this is either at Lady-day (25th March) or at Michaelmas
(29th September) and in Scotland at Whitsun (28th May) or
at Martinmas (28th November). Where there is a choice of dates,
a spring valuation is often preferred, particularly in arable
districts. In the autumn, the bulk of the year's crops are still
on hand, and any error in calculating the weight or value of
stacks of grain, clamps of potatoes and other produce will have a
marked effect on the Trading Account and give a misleading
result. In the spring, the bulk of the crops have been sold or used,
and although some of the spring crops are sown, the valuation
generally stands at its lowest point for the year, thus leaving a
smaller margin of error. The valuation on a hill sheep farm is
more easily taken in autumn after the lambs and "cast" ewes
have been sold. In spring, particularly during the lambing
season, the number of lambs and their value is difficult to estimate.

MARKET VALUE OR COST OF PRODUCTION

In making valuations, two methods are possible, one based on
market value and the other on cost of production.

When a farm changes hands, the valuation of live and dead
stock which the incomer takes over is based largely on market
values. But when valuations are made for book-keeping purposes,
cost of production is generally the more satisfactory basis. This
can be shown in the following way. Assume that a farmer bought
five store pigs at £8 apiece, and that the cost of fattening them
was £6 each. When the accounts were closed, their market value
was estimated at £18 each in the closing valuation. In the form
of a miniature Trading Account the result would be as shown on
page 75.

TRADING ACCOUNT FOR YEAR ENDED 31ST DECEMBER, 1970

	£		£
Purchase (5 pigs at £8) .	40	Closing valuation (market	
Expenses	30	value, 5 pigs at £18) .	90
	70		
Net Profit . . .	20		
	£90		£90

The pigs were sold during January, but they realized only £16 each. The result during the second year would be as follows—

TRADING ACCOUNT FOR YEAR ENDED 31ST DECEMBER, 1971

	£		£
Opening valuation . .	90	Sales, 5 pigs at £16 . .	80
		Net Loss . . .	10
	£90		£90

Using the "market value" method, the farmer showed a profit of £20 in the first year, but it was only an "anticipated" profit. In this case, he was too optimistic and the account for the following year showed a loss.

It is a sound maxim in book-keeping not to anticipate a profit before it is realized, and if the pigs had been valued at the cost of production, or £14 apiece (£8 purchase price plus £6 for expenses), the two Trading Accounts would have been as follows—

TRADING ACCOUNT FOR YEAR ENDED 31ST DECEMBER, 1970

	£		£
Purchase (5 pigs at £8) .	40	Closing valuation (cost of	
Expenses . . .	30	production 5 pigs at £14).	70
	70	Net Loss . . .	—
Net Profit	—		
	£70		£70

TRADING ACCOUNT FOR YEAR ENDED 31ST DECEMBER, 1971

	£		£
Opening valuation . .	70	Sales of pigs . . .	80
Net Profit . . .	10		
	£80		£80

By using the latter method, the accounts showed no profit or loss on the pigs until they were sold and the profit realized in the form of cash.

Occasionally, the farmer may find that some of his crops or livestock are not worth the money he has spent on them. Crops may fail through attack by pests, or livestock may be injured, and in these circumstances, there is nothing to be gained by showing crops or stock in the valuation at a price which they would not realize if sold. The valuation should be reduced to the market value, and the expected loss written off during the year in which it occurred.

As a general rule, therefore, *valuations are based on cost of production or market value, whichever is the lower.*

INVENTORY AND VALUATION

To make a valuation for book-keeping purposes, the farmer goes round the farm with a note-book making a list or inventory of the crops, livestock and dead stock.

For convenience, the items may be classified under four headings—

1. Livestock.
2. Harvested crops.
3. Growing crops, and tenant right.
4. Implements and stores.

The first three groups are valued at *cost of production* as explained above.

Implements are dealt with in a slightly different way which will be explained later.

VALUATION OF LIVESTOCK

For valuation purposes, livestock may be divided into two classes: Trading Stock and Productive Stock.

Whereas Trading Stock is valued at "cost of production," Productive Stock is valued at a fixed price termed the Standard Value.

TRADING STOCK. Under this heading are included all livestock intended primarily for sale, e.g.—

Cattle. Bullocks for sale fat or as stores, pedigree cattle reared for sale as breeding stock.

Sheep. Lambs or hoggs for sale fat or as stores, and temporary or "flying" flocks of ewes.

Horses. Horses reared for sale.

Poultry. Fattening cockerels, pullets reared for sale.

As already stated, these should, so far as possible, be valued at "cost of production." The value of purchased livestock, (e.g. store bullocks) is the buying price plus an allowance for their keep up to the date of valuation. If the livestock are home bred, the cost of production is less easily ascertained. When cost accounts are kept, the farmer can calculate the cost of rearing livestock; but if no such records are kept, an estimate must be made. On the whole, it is reasonable to assume that the cost of production is normally a little less than the market value, and at the time of writing the Inland Revenue Department is prepared to accept a valuation of such stock at 25 per cent less than the market value. Thus, a home-reared bullock whose market value was estimated at £80, could be valued at £60.

PRODUCTIVE, OR FIXED, STOCK. Under this heading come all livestock that are not primarily intended for sale, e.g. cows kept to produce milk or calves for rearing, permanent ewe flocks, breeding sows, and laying hens. Working horses, stock bulls, rams, and boars are also placed in this category. Productive livestock, must be sold when old or otherwise unsatisfactory, but this is an incidental receipt and not the chief object for which they are kept. This distinction between trading and productive livestock is of considerable importance in drawing up valuations.

The method of valuing productive livestock is as follows.* A dairy herd that is to be valued for the first time would be valued at the estimated cost of production, which would probably be slightly less than market value. The valuation might be as follows—

	£
20 Dairy cows at £70	1400
5 Heifers in calf at £80	400
5 Heifers (1 to 2 years) at £50	250
6 Calves at £20	120
	£2170

Having once adopted this basis of valuation, the farmer should not change it except under exceptional conditions, and should continue every year to value cows at £70, heifers in calf, £80, and so on, ignoring small fluctuations in market values. A fixed conventional price of this kind is known as a Standard Value.

To show the importance of keeping such values constant, assume that, a year later, the herd still consisted of twenty cows. Market values had increased temporarily and similar dairy cows were selling for £100 each. If the valuation were increased to this figure, the herd would appear in the closing valuation as 20 cows at £100—£2000. The herd therefore appeared in the opening valuation at £1400 and in the closing valuation at £2000—an

* An alternative method of valuing productive livestock for income tax purposes is explained in Chapter 22.

increase of £600. But an increase in valuation means an increase in profit; and by writing up the value of the cows, the profit would have been increased by £600. The herd was the same as before, the cows had not been sold, and the increase in market values had produced no real benefit to the farmer. This £600 profit is therefore fictitious and is known as a "paper profit." If by the end of next year, market values had fallen to £60, the accounts for the next year would have shown a "paper loss" of £800. Juggling with valuations in this way is undesirable and defeats the object of accounting—which is to show the genuine profit or loss on the year's trading.

If prices continue to rise over a long period, allowance must be made for the increased cost of rearing young stock. Old cows retained in the herd should remain at their former value because they were produced at lower costs, whilst newly calved heifers drafted into the herd, having cost more to rear, are shown at an increased value.

Assume that at 29th September, 1964, a farmer had twenty cows valued at £60. During the next year, five old cows were sold and replaced by five home-bred heifers valued at £64. The valuation at 29th September, 1965, would be—

		£
15 Cows at £60		900
5 Cows at £64		320
20		£1220

If, in the following year, four more old cows were replaced by heifers valued at £66, the valuation at 29th September, 1966, would be—

		£
11 Cows at £60		660
5 Cows at £64		320
4 Cows at £66		264
20		£1244

In this way, allowance would be made for the extra cost of rearing replacements but no "paper profit" would be shown on the old cows retained in the herd.

The disadvantage of this system is that, unless the farmer values the cows individually, he may not know the price group of any cow he sells. A slight modification could be made in the following way. The valuation at 29th September, 1965, was: 20 Cows, £1220, and is equivalent to £61 per head. The cows would be carried forward at this value and the valuation at 29th September, 1966, would be—

		£
16 Cows at £61	. . . . . .	976
4 Cows at £66	. . . . . .	264
20		£1240

The average value is now £62 per head and this is used in the succeeding valuation. If falling costs appear likely to last for a considerable period, the value of replacements should be reduced in a similar manner. Other classes of breeding stock, such as ewes or sows, should also be valued at standard prices.

STOCK BULLS, RAMS, AND BOARS. The value of young stock animals is increased until they come into service and written down thereafter until sold. For example, a bull purchased for £140, and expected to be in use for three years, and then sold for approximately £50, would have a depreciation of £30 per year. The value after one year will be £110, and after two years, £80.

VALUATION OF HARVESTED CROPS

Harvested crops, which include grain crops in the stack or in the granary, clamps of potatoes, and other root crops, will be dealt with in two groups.

CROPS FOR SALE. These, such as barley, wheat, or potatoes, should be valued on "cost of production" in much the same way as livestock for sale. If no costing records are available, the valuation is taken as a little less than market price (say 15 per cent less). Quantities of crops are estimated from the cubic capacity of stacks and clamps, with due allowance for tail corn and waste. In assessing the price, a deduction should be made for any costs to be met before the crop is marketed for threshing corn crops, riddling potatoes, and the cost of transport.

FODDER CROPS. These include beans, peas, oats, and other grains grown for feeding, and hay, straw, silage, mangolds, turnips, and other root crops grown for fodder. When a farm changes hands, a professional valuer is usually called in to value such items according to the custom of the district. Fodder crops harvested, or ready to be harvested, may be valued by one of two methods—by market value or by feeding or consuming value.

Market values of hay, oats, beans, and peas are easily ascertained. Mangolds, turnips, kale, and the like are normally grown for use on the farm, and there may be no recognized market value. The valuer therefore uses conventional prices settled by the local valuers' association.

A farmer valuing fodder crops for book-keeping purposes can draw up a list of "standard" values per ton or per hundredweight. These can be based in the first instance on the estimated average cost of production on his own farm or upon published reports of the agricultural economists. As already stated, when dealing with productive livestock these values should be altered only when the general level of costs changes.

GROWING CROPS, CULTIVATIONS, AND MANURES

In addition to harvested crops, crops in preparation must also be valued. This heading, therefore, includes cultivations, growing crops, and manures in the soil which will benefit future crops.

Cultivations are valued at cost, and if the farmer is making his own valuation, he can base it on contractors' prices or, better still, calculate average costs for his own farm. Professional valuers use conventional rates calculated by their associations, modified where necessary to suit local conditions. It is now the rule that cultivations are valued as if done by tractor unless there is good reason (e.g. on a small farm or in an awkward field) for using horses.

Growing crops are valued at the cost of seed, fertilizers and cultivations to date. The cost of carting and spreading manure should also be included.

The last items are farmyard manure and unexhausted manurial residues. When a farm is let to a tenant, the farmyard manure as such usually belongs to the landlord. The tenant, however, is entitled to compensation for the manurial residues of purchased feeding-stuffs and corn fed to the animals producing the manure. The right of a tenant to claim compensation for manurial residues, growing crops, cultivations and the like is known as "tenant right." Formerly the rate of compensation depended on local custom which varied from county to county; but under the Agricultural Holdings Act, 1948, a greater degree of uniformity has been introduced.

The law governing tenant right is too complex and in some respects too rigid to be used in ordinary farm accounting. For accounting purposes, therefore, a tenant farmer would be well advised to accept the figure paid on entry for manurial residues and carry it forward unaltered as one of his assets. If he believes that the value has altered materially and wishes to show the change in his accounts, he should consult a professional valuer.

"Unexhausted manurial residues" is a term used to cover the unexhausted value of manures applied in previous years. For example the beneficial effects of a dressing of lime or slag may be visible for several years after application. Such residues are of two kinds—those derived from artificial fertilizers and those from cake and other feeding-stuffs fed to livestock. Schedules of prices for manurial values have now been prescribed officially in regulations under the Agricultural Holdings Act, 1948. A professional valuer, making a valuation for a farmer who is entering or leaving a farm, goes through the receipts for feeding-stuffs and manures purchased and records of home-grown corn fed during the previous two or three years and calculates the residual values.

When a farm is changing hands, the calculation of the value of tenant right is a matter of great importance. For book-keeping purposes it is not generally necessary to revalue these residues each year. In most cases the amount of farmyard manure and other residues changes little from one year to another, and the same value can be used each year. Valuers frequently give little detail in their statements; and when taking a farm, a farmer would be well advised (after the valuation has been completed) to ask for further particulars. This will not only furnish information for drawing-up future annual valuations, but will be of advantage should the farmer ever leave the farm in ensuring that he obtains the same treatment on quitting as on entering the farm.

If the farming system is radically altered or the numbers of livestock greatly increased or decreased, due allowance must be made in the valuation of farmyard manure and other residues.

It should be noted that when the valuation of farmyard manure and manurial residues is retained at the same figure in the opening and closing valuation, the profit would be unaffected if omitted from the valuations altogether. This fact is generally recognized and for income tax purposes the following arrangement has been made after discussions between the Inland Revenue Department, the Agricultural Department, and the Farmers' Unions—

Where the normal value of tillages, unexhausted manures and growing crops does not exceed £700, and a detailed valuation is not available, a certificate that the value at the beginning of the year did not differ materially from that at the end of the year will usually be accepted.

Even where the normal value exceeds £700 a valuation will not be pressed for in every case, and a similar certificate may be accepted after any inquiry necessary to establish its reasonable accuracy.

The object of the above arrangement is to assist farmers by enabling a detailed valuation to be dispensed with in such cases.

This arrangement, which is limited to cases where detailed valuations are not available, does not prevent a farmer, who so desires, from bringing into his accounts a full detailed valuation of tenant right or waygoing rights and liabilities at the beginning and end of each year. Any farmer who makes a detailed valuation is at liberty to put in that valuation and should in fact do so. The valuation should be made on precisely the same basis as if valuing an outgoing tenant. In other words, the valuation should, in the case of a tenant, be based upon the actual tenancy agreement, and in the case of an owner-occupier, be based on the custom of the country which would, in the absence of a written agreement, be applicable if a tenancy existed.*

In spite of these concessions, it is recommended that tillages, unexhausted manures, and growing crops should be valued. Otherwise, although the effect on the profit may be slight, the list of assets would be incomplete and would not indicate the total sum of money invested in the farm.

VALUATION OF IMPLEMENTS AND FIXTURES

When a farm implement is in use on the farm, it gradually wears out, and in course of time, is replaced by a new one. The value of the implement falls from year to year and to allow for this it is usual to write off a proportion of the cost each year known as a "wear and tear" allowance. For example, assume that an implement is valued at £1600 and that the rate of depreciation is 25 per cent. The method adopted is to calculate the depreciation of wear-and-tear allowance as a percentage of the written-down value at which the implement stands at the beginning of the current year, as follows—

	£
Opening valuation	1600
Less depreciation: 25 per cent of £1600	400
Value at end of 1st year	1200
Less depreciation: 25 per cent of £1200	300
Value at end of 2nd year	900
Less depreciation: 25 per cent of £900	225
Value at end of 3rd year	£675

It will be noted that, in the example given, the depreciation is greatest during the first year (£400), gradually diminishing (£300 and £225 in the second and third years) as the implement becomes older. In practice, new implements do lose value more rapidly than old.

In making these calculations, it is generally sufficient to give the result to the nearest £.

* *Farmers' Income Tax*, published by the Ministry of Agriculture, Fisheries and Food.

To show how the wear and tear allowance is calculated, take a farmer whose implement valuation at 1st January, 1971, was as follows—

						£
Motor car .	.	.	.	.	.	1000
Tractors	.	.	.	.	.	1400
General Implements	.	.	.	.		3300
Small tools .	.	.	.	.	.	200
						£5900

During the year, he purchased a tractor for £1200 and sold the old one for £200. He bought implements worth £500 and sold the old ones for £100. The general implements were valued at £3300 at the beginning of the year and small tools at £200.

DEPRECIATION ALLOWANCES FOR YEAR ENDING 31ST DECEMBER, 1971

IMPLEMENTS	VALUE AT 1ST JAN., 1971	Add PUR-CHASES	Less SALES	SUB TOTAL	Less DEPRECIATION		VALUE AT 31ST DEC., 1971
					RATE	AMOUNT	
	£	£	£	£	PER CENT	£	£
Motor car . .	1000	—	—	1000	25	250	750
Tractors . .	1400	—	200	1200	25	300	900
New tractor .	—	1200	—	1200	60	720	480
General imple-							
ments . .	3300	—	100	3200	25	800	2400
New Implements	—	500	—	500	60	300	200
Small tools .	200	—	—	200	—	—	200
Total . .	5900	1700	300	7300	—	2370	4930

FIG. 12. DEPRECIATION RECORD FOR IMPLEMENTS

Under the present rules for taxation (see Chapter 22), implements can be depreciated by 25 per cent each year. New implements (except motor-cars) can be written down by 60 per cent in the first year and 25 per cent in subsequent years. Motor cars are depreciated by 25 per cent every year. It is best to keep a record of depreciation allowances as shown in Fig. 12. The existing motor car, tractors and implements are each depreciated by 25 per cent after deducting the sales of old implements (which may have been traded-in when replacements were purchased). New tractors and implements are entered separately and depreciated at 60 per cent for the first year. After this calculation has been made, the new valuation (at 31st December, 1971) stands as follows:

		£
Motor car		750
Tractors		1380
General implements		2600
Small tools		200
		£4930

No depreciation allowance is made for small tools (hand hoes, forks, spades, brushes, tools). They wear out rapidly and, as the cost of renewing them is charged under Repairs and Small Tools and not Implements Bought, the cost of buying small tools does not appear in the wear-and-tear calculation. In practice, their numbers vary little and unless there is some substantial change, the same value can be carried forward unaltered from year to year.

Stores including feeding-stuffs, fertilizers, seeds, and fuel stored on the farm are valued at cost.

A VALUATION IN DETAIL

It may seem from the foregoing account that the drawing up of a valuation is a complicated task. In practice, it is less difficult than might be supposed. The description of the methods used by valuers has been given so that, whether the farmer employs professional assistance or carries out his own valuation, he may understand the principles involved and the implications of the method adopted. In the valuation of crops, there are two points that should be borne in mind.

In the first place, the methods of valuation, particularly of fodder and growing crops, vary to some extent from district to district. Indeed two persons using different methods might produce different estimates of the total valuation of the same farm. So far as the Trading Account is concerned, however, it is not the total valuation but the *difference* between the opening and closing valuation that affects the profit. It is of the greatest importance to make the opening and closing valuations by the same methods.

To illustrate this, assume that a farmer had 40 tons of hay at the beginning of a year and 45 tons at the end, both used for feeding. Valuer A considers that the hay was worth £6 per ton.

		£
Opening valuation 40 tons at £6 . . .		240
Closing valuation 45 tons at £6 . . .		270
Increase in value		£30

The £30 represented an increase in production of hay and would increase the profit to that extent. Valuer B took a different view and assessed the hay at £8 per ton.

	£
Opening valuation 40 tons at £8 . . .	320
Closing valuation 45 tons at £8 . . .	360
Increase in value	£40

Although the two estimates were entirely different, the profit in the second case would be only £10 greater than in the first. On the other hand, if the hay were valued at £6 at the beginning by A and at £8 at the end by B, the effect would be as follows—

	£
Opening valuation 40 tons at £6 . . .	240
Closing valuation 45 tons at £8 . . .	360
Increase in value	£120

In this case, the profit would be increased by £120, a result that is entirely misleading. Every care should be taken to adopt a correct basis in drawing up valuations, but it is even more important to use the *same* methods at the beginning as at the end of the year.

In the second place, the farmer should follow the terms of his contract, and show straw and farmyard manure in the valuation only if paid for at entry. Nevertheless, in valuing fodder crops standard values are to be preferred to market prices for the same reason as was recommended for productive livestock. For example, a farmer, who used all his straw for litter, had 10 tons at the beginning and 10 tons at the end of the year. The market price had increased from £2 to £4 per ton. If he valued this at £20 in the opening and £40 in the closing valuation, the accounts would show a "paper profit" of £20, which the farmer was unlikely to realize.

Unless there are reasons to the contrary, it is suggested that a valuation should be drawn up as follows—

Trading livestock: actual cost of production if known, or 75 per cent of the market value.

Productive livestock: standard value.

Crops for sale: actual cost of production if known, or 85 per cent of market value.

Growing crops and tillages: cost of cultivations, seeds and fertilizers up to the date of valuation.

Fodder crops: standard values.

Implements: original cost less depreciation.

Stores: at cost.

Farmyard manure and unexhausted manurial residues: cost at entry, adjusted, if necessary, where the value has increased or decreased since that date. Fig. 13 is an example of a valuation drawn up in accordance with these principles.

INVENTORY AND VALUATION OF LIVE AND DEAD FARMING STOCK, TENANT RIGHT ETC. TAKEN FOR THE PURPOSE OF STOCK-TAKING AS AT 31ST MARCH, 1966

CATTLE

		£	£
93	Cows—in milk	80·00	7440·00
4	Cows—dry	80·00	320·00
34	Heifers—in calf	70·00	2380·00
1	Hereford bull		150·00
40	Buds	24·00	960·00
15	Calves	10·00	150·00
15	Steers	70·00	1050·00
14	Steers and heifers	32·00	448·00
20	Steers	54·00	1080·00
26	Steers	68·00	1768·00
11	Heifers	50·00	550·00
37	Steers and heifers	40·00	1480·00
			17776·00

PIGS

		£	£
60	Sows	30·00	1800·00
124	Pigs	2·00	248·00
3	Boars	20·00	60·00
10	Gilts—in pig	30·00	300·00
165	Pigs—2–4 months	7·00	1155·00
180	Pigs—4–6 months	10·00	1800·00
			5363·00

POULTRY

		£	£
25	Hens	0·20	5·00

CORN AND SEEDS

		£	£
350 ton	Wheat	20·00	7000·00
900 lb	Grass seed	0·10	90·00
			7090·00

HAY

Quantity of clover bales (Bales)

		£	£
25 ton		7·00	175·00

STRAW

Quantity of wheat and barley bales (Bales)

		£	£
30 ton		2·50	75·00

	£	£

FEEDING-STUFFS

90 ton Moist barley	20·00	1800·00
25 ton Feed barley	22·00	550·00
11 ton Feed oats	22·00	242·00
Other feeding-stuffs (given in detail)		916·26
		3507·26

ROOTS

45 ton King Edward ware	18·00	810·00
10 ton King Edward seed		285·00
15 ton Ditto		382·50
15 ton Ditto		315·00
		1792·50

SILAGE

50 ton Silage	3·00	150·00

MANURES

35 ton F.F.C. 51	18·00	630·00
30 ton Nitra shell	13·00	390·00
Manure in heap, 200 tons	0·25	50·00
		1070·00

FUEL AND OIL ETC.

750 gallons Diesel	43·75
50 gallons Petrol	11·25
150 gallons Lubricating oil	67·50
	122·50

CULTIVATIONS AND CROPPING

Artificials used—(given in detail)		3324·70
Seed corn used—(given in detail)		2294·10
2 ton Tic beans		82·00
189 acres Wheat Cultivations thereon	3·30	623·70
50 acres Farmyard manure applied thereon	4·00	200·00
30 acres Oats Cultivations thereon	3·30	99·00
124 acres Barley Cultivations thereon	3·30	409·20
23 acres Tic beans Cultivations thereon	3·30	75·90

		£	£
47 acres Potatoes			
Cultivations thereon		2·30	108·10
48 acres Sugar-beet			
Cultivations thereon		3·00	144·00
96 acres Rye grass			
Cultivations and seed thereon . . .		2·40	230·40
8 acres 4-year Ley			
Cultivations and seed thereon . . .		2·70	21·60
			7612·70

SUMMARY—MARCH, 1970

		£
CATTLE (310)	. . . .	17776·00
PIGS (542)	. . . .	5353·00
POULTRY	. . . . .	5·00
CORN AND SEEDS	. . . .	7090·00
HAY	. . . . . .	175·00
STRAW	. . . . .	75·00
FEEDING-STUFFS	. . . .	3507·26
SILAGE	. . . . .	150·00
ROOTS	. . . . .	1792·50
FUEL AND OILS ETC.	. . .	122·50
MANURES	. . . . .	1070·00
CULTIVATIONS AND CROPPING	. .	7612·70
		44738·96

We value the items contained in the foregoing Valuation at the sum of FORTY-FOUR THOUSAND, SEVEN HUNDRED AND THIRTY-EIGHT POUNDS, NINETY-SIX PENCE (£44738·96).

Signed......................................
Valuers and Surveyors.

NOTE. The values placed on Livestock, Corn and Artificial Manures do not include any subsidies that may become payable.

FIG. 13. FARM VALUATION IN DETAIL

QUESTIONS

1. Explain the following terms—
(a) Standard value.
(b) Tenant right.
(c) Productive livestock.
(d) Wear and tear allowance.

2. You are a farm manager and decide to commence book-keeping from 1st January. Describe briefly how you would proceed to value—
(a) A herd of home-bred Friesian cows.
(b) Store cattle purchased on 15th December.
(c) A clamp of potatoes.
(d) A clamp of mangolds.

(*e*) A field of winter beans sown in October.

(*f*) Ten bacon pigs almost ready for market.

(*g*) A combine purchased twelve months previously for £2000.

3. What is a "paper profit"? Give an example to show how a paper profit may arise through faulty methods of valuation.

4. When taking an annual valuation on 31st March, 1970, a farmer, by mistake, omitted a stack of hay worth £100. What effect is this likely have on the profit of—

(*a*) The year ending 31st March, 1970?

(*b*) The year ending 31st March, 1971?

(*c*) Both years combined?

CHAPTER 12

OTHER METHODS OF BOOK-KEEPING

IN addition to the cash analysis system described, there are many other forms of book-keeping in use, and a brief account of some of the more important is given in this chapter.

MODIFICATION OF THE CASH ANALYSIS SYSTEM

It has been recommended in earlier chapters that all receipts and expenses should be passed through the bank account, and that small cash transactions should be recorded in a separate Petty Cash Book for eventual transfer to the Account Book. If the farmer has a large number of cash transactions and does not wish to pass them through the bank account, he can record them direct in the Account Book. In this case it is desirable to separate cash and bank transactions, to simplify the auditing of the Account Book, and to allow the bank balance to be checked at any time.

To illustrate the method of using these modified cash analysis account books, the following examples are given, using first the Account Book already described (Method 1), and then two modified versions (Methods 2 and 3).

METHOD 1. Assume that at the beginning of a month a farmer has a balance of £15 in the bank and £5 in the cash box. During the month, the following transactions take place—

	£
Paid miscellaneous expenses by cheque	1·00
Drew cash from bank for wages	9·00
Received for milk and paid into bank . . .	12·50
Cashed cheque to cover miscellaneous cash expenses made from the petty cash box (bringing the balance back to £5) .	1·50

The entry of these items is straightforward and is illustrated in Fig. 14.

METHOD 2. Assume that the farmer has the same balance at the beginning of the month. The payments and receipts are as before, but the farmer draws out and pays into the bank odd sums of money which do not necessarily correspond to his receipts and payments.

(a) He pays, as before, miscellaneous expenses by cheque (£1).

(b) He draws a cheque to self for £10. Of this he uses £9 for wages and £1 for miscellaneous cash expenses.

(c) He receives £12·50 for milk sold. Of this, he uses 50p for miscellaneous expenses and pays the £12 into the bank.

Receipts			Payments			
NAME AND DETAILS	TOTAL RECEIVED	DAIRY PRODUCE	NAME AND DETAILS	TOTAL PAID	WAGES	MISCEL-LANEOUS
	£	£		£	£	£
Opening Balance (in Bank)	15·00		Miscellaneous Wages . .	1·00 9·00	9·00	1·00
Milk . .	12·50	12·50	Miscellaneous (per Petty Cash Book)	1·50		1·50
	27·50	12·50		11·50	9·00	2·50
			Closing Balance (in Bank) .	16·00		
£	27·50		£	27·50		

(Other columns omitted) appears vertically between Receipts and Payments sides, and on the far right.

FIG. 14. CASH ANALYSIS ACCOUNT BOOK: METHOD 1

Receipts

NAME AND DETAILS	CASH	BANK	DAIRY PRODUCE	(Other columns omitted)
	£	£	£	
Opening Balance .	5·00	15·00		
Drew cash from bank .	10·00			
Milk . . .	12·50		12·50	
Paid cash into bank .		12·00		
	27·50	27·00	12·50	
£	27·50	27·00		

Payments

NAME AND DETAILS	CASH	BANK	WAGES	MISCEL-LANEOUS	(Other columns omitted)
	£	£	£	£	
Miscellaneous . .		1·00		1·00	
Drew cash from bank		10·00			
Wages . . .	9·00		9·00		
Miscellaneous . .	1·00			1·00	
Miscellaneous . .	0·50			0·50	
Paid cash into bank ·	12·00				
	22·50	11·00	9·00	2·50	
Closing Balance .	5·00	16·00			
£	27·50	27·00			

FIG. 15. CASH ANALYSIS ACCOUNT BOOK: METHOD 2

The list of transactions is therefore—

		£
1. Paid miscellaneous expenses by cheque . . .		1·00
2. Drew cash from bank . :		10·00
3. Paid wages (cash)		9·00
4. Paid miscellaneous expenses (cash) . . .		1·00
5. Received cash for milk		12·50
6. Paid miscellaneous expenses by cash . . .		0·50
7. Paid cash into bank		12·00

In place of using a Petty Cash Book, he opens separate "Bank" and "Cash" columns on the Receipts and Payments pages as shown in Fig. 15. First of all the cash and bank balances are entered on the Receipts pages as shown, and the transactions are then completed as follows—

Item 1. Payment by cheque for £1. This is entered on the Payments page under the Bank and Miscellaneous columns.

Item 2. £10 drawn from the bank. This is a payment by the bank and a receipt of cash, and is entered by means of a "cross-entry": in the Bank column on the Payments page and in the Cash column on the Receipts page. Being a transfer within the farm business, a cross-entry is not entered in any of the analysis columns.

Items 3, 4, 5, and 6 are all cash transactions and are entered in the cash column on the Receipts or Payments page and in the appropriate analysis column.

Item 7. £12 paid into the bank. This is another cross-entry and is entered as a payment by cash and a receipt by the bank.

At the end of the month the bank and cash columns are totalled, showing a bank balance of £16 and a cash balance of £5. Using this method, the farmer need not pay all receipts into the bank but may use them to make cash payments. But unless he records such cash transactions in the Account Book every few days (or keeps a record in a notebook) he may easily forget the details. Cross-entries are a further disadvantage: mistakes are easily made, and as they are not entered in the analysis columns, these columns cannot easily be checked against the totals columns.

METHOD 3. A third method has recently come into use and is shown in Fig. 16. It is a compromise between Methods 1 and 2 described above, and is an attempt to avoid cross-entries. Briefly, the Payments page with Paid in Cash and Paid by Cheque columns is similar to that described in Method 2 and (apart from certain of the cross-entries) is completed in the same way. On the Receipts page, all receipts, whether in the form of cash or cheques, are entered in the Total Received column and in the appropriate analysis column. All cash or cheques subsequently paid into the bank are entered in the Paid into Bank column.

Assuming the same transactions as for Method 2, the entries are made as follows—

Receipts

NAME AND DETAILS	TOTAL RECEIVED	DAIRY PRODUCE	(*Other columns omitted*)	PAID INTO BANK
	£	£		£
Opening Balance .	5·00			15·00
Milk . . .	12·50	12·50		
Paid cash into bank .				12·00
	17·50	12·50		27·00
				—
			£	27·00

Payments

NAME AND DETAILS	PAID IN CASH	PAID BY CHEQUE	WAGES	MISCEL-LANEOUS	(*Other columns omitted*)
	£	£	£	£	
Miscellaneous . .		1·00		1·00	
Drew cash from bank .		*10·00			
Wages . . .	9·00		9·00		
Miscellaneous . .	1·00			1·00	
Miscellaneous . .	0·50			0·50	
	10·50	11·00	9·00	2·50	
Closing Balance . .		16·00			
		£ 27·00			

*Cash drawn from bank.

FIG. 16. CASH ANALYSIS ACCOUNT BOOK: METHOD 3

Item 1. Payment by cheque (£1) is entered in the Paid by Cheque and Miscellaneous columns.

Item 2. £10 drawn from the bank is entered in the Paid by Cheque column only. Such items should be marked to facilitate the checking of the columns at the end of the year.

Items 3 and 4. These two cash payments are entered in the Paid in Cash and appropriate analysis columns.

Item 5. £12·50 received for milk is entered in the Total Received and Dairy Produce columns.

Item 6. Similar to 3 and 4 above.

Item 7. £12 cash paid into the bank is entered in the Paid into Bank column only.

It will be seen that the Paid by Cheque and Paid into Bank

columns correspond to the bank book and the balance should therefore agree with the bank balance. Cash transactions, however, are less easily checked, and for this reason Method 3 is generally used by farmers who employ professional assistance in completing their accounts. An accountant auditing an account book of this kind would check the cash transactions as follows—

						£
Total Received (including cash at beginning)	.	.	.	17·50
Add Cash drawn from Bank	.	.	.	.	.	10·00
Total Receipts to be accounted for	.	.	.	.	27·50
Less Paid into Bank	.	.	.	.	£12·00
Paid in Cash	.	.	.	.	.	10·50
						22·50
Remainder (should agree with cash in hand)	.	.	.	£5·00

SHORT CUT METHOD OF CASH ANALYSIS

The system of cash analysis using a columnar cash book is a clear and efficient system that can be recommended both for teaching and for use. To analyse individual items it is not, however, essential to have a series of columns. Indeed, many farmers merely make a list of receipts and payments and leave it to the accountant to do the analysis afterwards. The quickest way to classify the items for a year is to write a series of account headings on a sheet of paper as shown in Fig. 17 and enter the items under these headings. At the end of the year (or every month or three months) the individual accounts are totalled and checked against the total in the Total Paid or Total Received column. This method has the advantage that any number of accounts can be opened and the farmer is not restricted by the number of columns in the cash book.

After checking the totals at the end of the year, the usual additions and deductions can be made for debtors and creditors before transferring the totals to the Trading Account.

Other modifications of the Cash Analysis Book have been suggested from time to time. Generally they are slight variations of one of the three methods illustrated above, and are designed to assist the farmer to record cash and bank transactions. Fundamentally, there is no essential difference between them, and in all cases the instructions given for completing the Balance Sheet and Trading Account are equally applicable.

DOUBLE ENTRY BOOK-KEEPING

Apart from cash analysis, the most important system in general use is known as "Double Entry" book-keeping. In essentials, the

SHORT CUT METHOD OF CASH ANALYSIS

(Manor Farm, year 1970–71, transactions for April, 1970)

Purchases and Expenses

CATTLE	FEEDING-STUFFS	SEEDS	FERTILIZERS AND SPRAYS	WAGES	REPAIRS AND SMALL TOOLS	FUEL	RENT	OTHER OVERHEADS	IMPLEMENTS BOUGHT	PRIVATE DRAWINGS
—	165	—	18	85	5	6	—	45	—	50
				24	2			3		
				81	—			1		
				84	7			—		
				83				49		
				80						
				437						

Monthly Check April

165	
18	
437	
7	
6	
49	
50	
732	
2966	
3698	(agrees with Total Paid Column)

Opening Balance

Sales and Receipts

CATTLE	PIGS	MILK	WHEAT	POTATOES	MISC. RECEIPTS	PRIVATE RECEIPTS
57	116	515	321	—	42	—

Monthly Check April

57	
116	
515	
321	
42	
1051	(agrees with Total Received Column)

FIG. 17. SHORT CUT METHOD OF CASH ANALYSIS

two methods differ less than might be supposed from a first in-spection.

To take an example, a farmer sells a cow to A. Black for £60. On the cash analysis system this is entered as is shown below.

SALES AND RECEIPTS

NAME AND DETAILS	TOTAL RECEIPTS	CATTLE	(*Other columns omitted*)
A. Black, 1 Cow .	£ 60	£ 60	

In double entry book-keeping, a ledger is used and accounts are opened on separate pages in place of the analysis columns shown above. This transaction would be entered as shown on the next page.

Dr.	CASH ACCOUNT		*Cr.*
To Cattle Account . .	£ 60		£

Dr.	CATTLE ACCOUNT		*Cr.*
	£	By Cash Account (A. Black, 1 cow)	£ 60

Two entries are made for each purchase or sale, one in each of the two accounts affected.

It will be noted that these entries are on opposite sides of the accounts. The theory is that every business transaction involves an exchange—the farmer giving something, and receiving value in return. In this case he gave a cow, and received cash. The rule is that the item is entered on the left-hand side (marked debit or *Dr.*) of the account receiving value, and on the right-hand side (marked credit or *Cr.*) of the account giving value. It follows that the sale of the cow was put on the left-hand side of the Cash Account, as cash was received, and on the right-hand side of the Cattle Account, as the cow was sold. Similarly, if the cow had been purchased, the items would have been entered on the opposite side of the respective accounts.

It will be noted that although this system is known as "double entry," the cash analysis method also involves two entries for each business transaction.

If the £60 were not paid at once, the cow being sold on credit, the method of recording would have been somewhat different. In the cash analysis system, the farmer keeps a note of credit sales in his Invoice Book, and does not record them in the cash book until cash is received.

Using the double entry system, the sale is entered as demonstrated below.

Dr.	A. BLACK'S ACCOUNT		Cr.
To Cattle Account . .	£ 60		£

Dr.	CATTLE ACCOUNT		Cr.
	£	By A. Black Account (1 cow)	£ 60

As before, the £60 is entered on the right-hand side of the Cattle Account.

The second entry cannot, however, at present be shown in the Cash Account as no cash has been received. Instead, an "A. Black Account" (known as a personal account) is opened, and the other entry is made, on the left-hand side, thus giving a record that A. Black owes £60.

When the £60 is paid, a fresh entry is made on the right-hand side of A. Black's Account, and on the left-hand side of the Cash Account

The three accounts now appear as follows—

Dr.	CASH ACCOUNT		Cr
To A. Black Account . .	£ 60		£

Dr.	A. BLACK'S ACCOUNT		Cr.
To Cattle Account . .	£ 60	By Cash Account . .	£ 60

Dr.	CATTLE ACCOUNT		Cr.
	£	By A. Black Account (1 cow)	£ 60

A. Black's Account is now balanced, having an entry of £60 on both sides, thus showing that he no longer owes this sum to the farmer.

There is a further difference. It will be recalled that, in the cash analysis system, the Trading Account consisted of the opening valuation and purchases on one side and the sales and closing valuation on the other. In the double entry system, the valuations are split up and entered in the appropriate accounts. For example, a Cattle Account at the end of a year might appear as shown below.

Dr.		CATTLE ACCOUNT		*Cr.*
	£			£
To Opening valuation .	1500	By Cash (young cattle sold)		300
„ Cash (A. Smith, 1 cow) .	60	„ Closing valuation .		1530
„ Profit and Loss Account	270			
£	1830		£	1830

At the end of the year, *only the balance* (in this case £270) is carried to the final statement which is called a "Profit and Loss Account." By either method, the total profit or loss at the end of the year is the same.

It is not intended to give a full description of double entry book-keeping here, but merely to indicate the general principles so that the student may understand an account kept on this system if he meets one in the course of business.

Double entry book-keeping, with suitable modifications, is universally used by large industrial and trading companies. For such concerns it has several advantages. There is no limit to the number of accounts which can be opened, and where a large number of purchases and sales are made on credit, the accounts give up-to-date statement of the amounts sold, whether for cash or on credit.

On the other hand, a longer period of training is required to master the double entry system, which is more complicated, and if an entry is made on the wrong side of an account, much time may be wasted in tracing it. A farmer usually lacks clerical assistance and the cash analysis system has the advantage of being simple and easily checked. Thus, unless the farm business is very large and complex, the double entry system appears in most cases to have no marked advantage in practice.

COST ACCOUNTS

The two systems so far described—cash analysis and double entry—achieve the same result, which is to show the profit or loss on the farm as a whole. They give no indication, however, of the source of the profit or loss. If, for example, a Trading Account shows a profit of £1500, this is not to say that all branches of the farm have made a profit. Indeed some of the crops or livestock may have made a loss on the year's trading. For all the farmer knows this result might be made up of a profit of £1000 on the dairy herd, a profit of £800 on crops, and a loss of £300 on the poultry flock.

In order to split up the farm accounts to show the profit or loss on separate departments, cost accounts are necessary. Cost accounting has been applied with considerable success in industry and forms a valuable aid to successful management. For example, in a boot and shoe factory, the manager might decide to cost the production of one type of shoe. Records could be kept of the wages of the staff employed in the department making these shoes, and of the leather and other materials supplied. After adding a share of overhead expenses, the total costs of this department, and the cost of manufacture per pair of shoes, could be calculated with considerable accuracy. The manager could then compare this with the selling price, and calculate the profit. If it were unsatisfactory he would be able to decide whether further economies could be made so as to reduce the costs. If economies were impossible, he might decide to close the department down and concentrate on another that was more profitable.

The same technique has been applied to agriculture with the aim of producing a series of Trading Accounts, each relating to one department.

For example the cost account of a potato field might appear thus—

POTATO ACCOUNT 1970—8 ACRES

Purchases and Expenses—		Sales and Receipts—	£
Wages	240	70 tons Potatoes (includ-	
Machinery . . .	25	ing subsidy) . .	1100
Tractor work . . .	48		
Seed	200		
Manures . . .	96		
Rent	56		
Miscellaneous . .	60		
Overheads . . .	107		
	832		
NET PROFIT . . .	268		
£	1100	£	1100

To produce such an account it is necessary to keep records of all labour and materials used on this crop. The cost of manures and seeds purchased are recorded, and notes made of the quantities and value applied to each field. The most difficult task, however, is the allocation of man, machinery and tractor hours. Unlike a factory, where labour is usually employed for long periods on the same work, the farm worker carries out a large variety of operations according to the weather and season of the year. Indeed, it will sometimes be found that in the course of a week he may be employed in several different departments of the farm. In order to charge his labour to the proper account, he must be provided with time sheets. Each day the worker fills in the number of hours, the name of the field, crop, and other particulars of the work on which he has been employed, and whether he has used a tractor. At the end of the week, his wages are noted, and the number of hours of manual and tractor labour is charged to the appropriate department. It may be added that some farmers use time sheets even when cost accounting is not carried out, and find them a convenient check on the amount of overtime worked, and the time spent in carrying out various operations.

In this way, the bulk of the farm purchases and expenses can be charged to the various departments. It will be found that some expenses, car and telephone, work on "odd jobs," and a number of other items, cannot be definitely charged to any account. These are known as "overhead" expenses and are split up between different departments in proportion to the acreage under each crop, or by some other method which seems to give a reasonable result. Receipts are split up in a similar way and the farmer can then calculate the profit from each crop or department on the farm. Cost accounts of this kind have been carried out on a number of farms and much valuable information has been obtained.

This is a very brief outline of the methods employed; and in order to carry out cost accounting in practice, a fairly high degree of skill in accounting is required. The amount of clerical work necessary, particularly in analysing time sheets, is considerable; and unless the farmer has an office staff, the completion of the details may be impossible. It should also be noted that in cost accounting, a number of difficulties arise that are peculiar to agriculture. These may be summarized as follows—

1. Unlike a factory, the various departments of a farm are not independent. To maintain fertility and for other reasons, a rotation of crops is generally necessary, and the farmer can alter the cropping of the farm only within limits. For example, if

40 acres of potatoes were found to give a profit of £800 it could not be assumed that 80 acres would give a profit of £1600. An increase in the area of potatoes might disorganize the work of the farm, and it might not be possible to obtain sufficient casual labour to lift the crop at the proper time.

2. The yields of many crops vary widely from one year to another. For this reason, the profit and cost of production per unit fluctuate from year to year. It might be found that the cost of growing kale could vary from £2 to £4 per ton in different seasons. The profitability of a crop cannot be judged on the results of one year, but only on the average over a number of seasons. Some crops, such as potatoes, are heavily manured, and much of the benefit may be carried over to succeeding crops. The cleaning effects of a root crop may also be seen throughout the rest of the rotation. It is reasonable in such cases to charge a proportion of the cost of manures or cultivations to the following crops. Tables of residual values have been prepared for this purpose, but at best they are only estimates, and no exact value can be given in any particular case.

3. In some cases, "joint products" are obtained in agriculture. For example, grain and straw are obtained from the same crop, and the splitting of costs between these is largely guesswork. Others of the same kind are calves and milk from a dairy herd, or wool and mutton from sheep.

The examples given will serve as an indication of the difficulties that arise in the application of cost accounting methods to agriculture, both in the calculation of costs and in the interpretation of the results obtained. Nevertheless, it is possible to obtain much valuable information from cost accounts. But before embarking on such a system, the farmer should give the matter careful study, and would be well advised to consult the Advisory Economist in his province.

It will be noted that the difficulties discussed above refer mainly to crop costings. In the case of livestock, the results are more easily calculated and highly accurate results may be obtained. In later chapters, details are given of a simpler method of obtaining information about the efficiency of management of a farm.

PART III

FARM ORGANIZATION AND MANAGEMENT

CHAPTER 13

IMPROVING FARM EFFICIENCY

WHEN a farmer has completed his accounts for the year, he is in a position to examine the results. The figure likely to interest him most is the net profit, for unless he has some outside source of income or is prepared to live on his capital, this is the sum on which he must live. The Trading Account shows the profit or loss but little else. The purpose of the remaining chapters is to show how the farmer can use these records and other information to measure his success in the past and to plan improvements for the future.

The first point to note is that the profit is the difference between two large totals—the output and the costs or inputs incurred in obtaining that output. For this reason, a small change in either the output or the inputs can alter the profit quite drastically. In 1967–68 the average farmer in England and Wales obtained £117 output for every £100 spent on inputs—leaving a profit of £17. But this margin is very sensitive to changes in efficiency. A successful farmer who could obtain 10 per cent more output for the same inputs would have had a profit of £28 or 60 per cent above the average. The penalty for failure is equally sharp. A farmer obtaining 10 per cent less output per £100 input would have had a profit of only £5, less than a third of the average profit and less than a fifth of that obtained by the more successful farmer. A 10 per cent increase in costs could produce nearly as much effect. It is thus obvious that quite a small decline in yields or increase in costs that might go unnoticed for months or even years could have a marked effect on the farmer's income. It is for this reason that analysing the past and planning the future can pay large dividends for the time spent on them.

The extent to which profits vary in practice can be illustrated by the results of a survey of farms in 1969 which showed the following range in profits—

PROFIT PER ANNUM		% OF FARMS
Loss: Over £10	. . . .	2
Under £10	. . . .	11
Profit: Under £10	. . . .	31
£10–£20	. . . .	27
£20–£30	. . . .	12
Over £30	. . . .	17
		100

Thus, while the average was £12 per acre, 29 per cent had profits of over £20, and 13 per cent had losses.

Why are some farms so much less successful than others? The types of farm that the adviser is likely to encounter can be classified under the following headings—

1. There is the really badly managed farm. The faults in poor crop and unthrifty stock may be so obvious that no records may be necessary to bring them to light. If this is due to ignorance and incompetence there may be little that one can do. In these days of high costs and narrow margins, such a farmer is unlikely to survive long in business unless he has some other source of income.

2. There is the reasonably well managed farm that, because of some fault that may not be obvious, is less successful than one might expect. This is the type that the farm adviser usually has to deal with. An examination of records may be necessary either to find the faults or to confirm an impression of them gained from observation.

3. There is the farm that looks impressive with high yields and thriving stock but whose costs are excessive. This is a type that can deceive the inexperienced adviser. Records can be most useful in detecting excessive costs.

4. There is the problem farm. It may be too small. If output is below a minimum of say £2000, then no matter how efficiently the farm is managed, a farmer would have great difficulty in obtaining a living. A problem farm may have very infertile soil or some intractable problem of drainage or lack of equipment. Even if a solution can be found, the capital costs of implementing it may be quite beyond the farmer's means. Sometimes there is no solution and the best advice may be to leave the farm.

5. There is the above-average farmer who wishes to be even more successful. This can be disconcerting to an inexperienced adviser because the farmer may be more knowledgeable about his particular field than is the adviser. A comparison with averages —or even premium standards—may be a waste of time, except to demonstrate that the farm is above average. Replanning with the farmer's own high gross margins and capital budgeting for expansion may be more to the point than an analysis of past results.

If we are examining a farm's past records, we require a series of yardsticks or *efficiency factors*. The method of calculating these can be illustrated by taking the Trading Account of Farm B, a dairy farm (Fig. 18).

GROSS OUTPUT. The output of a farm for any particular year is the value of production in that year. To estimate output, take

TRADING ACCOUNT FOR YEAR ENDED 31ST DECEMBER, 1971

Purchases and Expenses—	£	Sales and Receipts—	£
Cattle	1878	Milk	15059
Wages	4525	Cattle	6325
Feeding-stuffs	6272	Eggs	797
Seeds	430	Barley	2182
Fertilizers	986	Miscellaneous	169
Rent	1762		
Repairs and depreciation	1582		
Fuel	724		
Misc. livestock	1101		
Misc. crops	36		
Other costs	1209		
	20505		24532

Opening Valuation—			Closing Valuation—		
Cattle	£11371		Cattle	£9725	
Barley	1200		Barley	200	
Poultry	200		Poultry	200	
Other items	2335		Other items	2335	
		15106			12460
		35611			
NET PROFIT		1381			
		£36992			£36992

FIG. 18. TRADING ACCOUNT FOR FARM B

the sales for the year and adjust for valuation changes. The reason is that sales for 1971 may include crops grown or livestock reared in 1970. The sales may also omit crops or livestock produced in 1971 but still unsold when the accounts are completed. In the present case, sales of barley were £2182. Of this, £1200 was in store at the beginning (opening valuation) and the remaining £982 was grown in 1971. Another £200 worth of the 1971 crop was in store ready for sale at the end of the year. The output was thus £982 plus £200 = £1182. Output can thus be calculated as Sales *less* opening valuation *plus* closing valuation or, more briefly—

$$\text{Crop Output} = \text{Sales} {+ \text{increase} \atop - \text{decrease}} \text{ in valuation}$$

With livestock, there is the complication that some of them may be purchased. If a farmer buys £1000 worth of cattle and sells them six months later for £1400, his output is £400—the gain in value while on his farm. The £1000 paid for the cattle is part of some other farm's output.

In this case, the livestock output is—

						£
Livestock sales .	.	.	.	.		6325
Opening valuation	.	.	.	11571		
Closing valuation	.	.	.	9925		
Less decrease	.	.	.	.		1646
						4679
Less purchases	.	.	.	.		1878
Gross Livestock Output	.	.	.			£2801

Milk, eggs and miscellaneous items need no adjustment (unless the farmer buys milk and eggs for resale).

The general formula is thus—

$$\text{Gross Output} = \text{Sales} \begin{array}{c} + \text{ increase} \\ - \text{ decrease} \end{array} \text{ in valuation, } \textit{less} \begin{array}{c} \text{purchases} \\ \text{of livestock} \end{array}$$

On the Input side, costs are grouped for convenience into variable costs (*see* gross margins below) and fixed or common costs (labour, machinery, rent and other overhead costs). The only other adjustment is an allowance for the farmer's *manual* labour (taken as £500) added to wages. "Machinery and power" comprises implement depreciation, repairs and fuel (including the electricity). *See* Fig. 19.

NET OUTPUT. This measure is sometimes used instead of Gross Output—

$$\text{Net Output} = \text{Gross Output } \textit{less} \text{ purchased feeding stuffs,} \\ \text{and seeds}$$

The justification for these deductions is that farmers who depend heavily on purchased feeding stuffs may appear to have a higher output per acre than other farmers who grow more crops for feeding. By deducting purchased foods, both types of farm are put on an equal footing. The same consideration applies to seeds. Net Output is tending to give way to Gross Margin which has wider uses.

EFFICIENCY RATIOS

The output shows the amount that the farm has produced. But output is economical only if produced at a reasonable cost in resources. The profitability thus depends on the output per unit of input. A good overall measure is *Gross Output per £100 of Inputs.* Another useful measure is *Output (gross or net) per acre.* When comparing output per acre with standards, allowance must of course be made for the quality of the land—an acre of windswept moorland cannot be expected to produce as much as an acre of fen.

Allowance must also be made for the presence on the farm of enterprises such as pigs or poultry that use no land.

LABOUR PRODUCTIVITY. As wages are one of the largest items of cost, the productivity of labour is of vital importance. It is possible to calculate the output per man; but in practice this means translating wages paid to casual workers or women and overtime payments into fractions of "men." It is more convenient to calculate *Output per £100 labour*. "Labour" in this case includes wages and an allowance for the farmer's *manual* labour.

As the farm worker and his implements can be regarded as a unit that does the work of the farm, there is some merit in calculating *Output per £100 labour and machinery*. Another justification for adding these two costs together is that labour and machinery are to an extent substitutes and a farmer who spends more on machines should spend less on labour and vice versa.

So far as the farmer is concerned, the most important measure of success is the profit and it is of interest to compare it with the average of other farms of the same kind. Profits, however, vary for reasons which have nothing to do with the farmers' efficiency as a manager. One farmer is an owner with no debts, a second is a tenant with a very high rent, while a third is paying interest on a large loan. To make a fair comparison, therefore, the profit must be standardized.

NET FARM INCOME. The convention in this country is to express the profit as to a debt-free tenant farmer who pays wages to family workers. When dealing with an owner-occupier, an estimated rent is charged and expenses that would normally be paid by a landlord are omitted. Wages are charged for family workers (except the farmer and his wife) but interest charges are omitted.

The farm income is expected to provide the farmer with—

(a) a return on the capital invested;
(b) a wage for his manual labour (if any); and
(c) a reward for management.

It is, of course, possible to split the profit between these headings either by charging interest on capital* or by making a charge for the farmer's labour.

MANAGEMENT AND INVESTMENT INCOME. This has been shown in the modified Trading Account (*see* Fig. 19) by allowing the farmer £500 for manual labour. On a small farm when the farmer

---

* In the United States, it is usual to charge interest on capital. It is considered that a farmer who has invested heavily should obtain a larger profit. If interest is charged, they are on an equal footing. This profit measure, called *labour income*, is not much used in this country.

MODIFIED TRADING ACCOUNT

Inputs—	£	Outputs—	£
Variable Costs—			
Feeding-stuffs . . .	6272	Milk . . .	15059
Misc. livestock. . .	1101	Cattle . . .	2801
Seeds	430	Eggs	797
Fertilizers . . .	986	Barley . . .	1182
Misc. Crops . . .	36	Miscellaneous . .	169
	8825		
Fixed or Common Costs—			
Wages . . £4525			
Farmer's labour . 500			
	5025		
Machinery and power .	2306		
Rent	1762		
Other Overheads . .	1209		
	19127		
Management and Investment			
Income . . .	881		
	£20008		£20008

Gross Output per acre: $\dfrac{20008}{273} = £73$

Gross Output per £100 inputs: $\dfrac{20008 \times 100}{19127} = £105$

Gross Output per £100 labour: $\dfrac{2008 \times 100}{5025} = £398$

Gross Output per £100 labour and machinery: $\dfrac{20008 \times 100}{7331} = £273$

Net Output:

Gross Output . .		20008
Less feeding-stuffs .	6272	
Less seeds . .	430	
		6702
		£13306

Net Output per acre: $\dfrac{13306}{273} = £49$

Return on Capital = Management and Investment Income per £100 Capital

Capital = average tenant's valuation (£13783) + machinery (£3849)

Return: $\dfrac{881 \times 100}{17632} = 5 \cdot 0\%$

FIG. 19.   MODIFIED TRADING ACCOUNTS FOR FARM B

does all the work, the profit per acre should be greater than on a large farm where all the work is done by paid workers. The effect of charging a wage for the farmer is therefore to put large and small farms on a similar footing.

RETURN ON CAPITAL. This is a useful measure of profitability.

$$\text{Return} = \frac{\text{Management and Investment Income}}{\text{Tenant's Capital}} \times 100$$

Sometimes farm income is used instead of management and investment income. Tenant's Capital in this case is Total Assets not Net Capital. This ratio measures the return to all tenant's capital whether or not it belongs to the farmer.

Having calculated the efficiency factors, standards of comparison are required. The average trading accounts for six typical farm types given in Fig. 20 are based on national averages. The most intensive are the horticultural holdings with an output of £285 per acre. Next are the specialist dairy farms (£72), general cropping farms (£65), cereal farms (£40), cattle and sheep farms (£24), and finally sheep farms (£9). The capital investment and farm income follow the same order.

It will be seen from Fig. 21 that the trading account of Farm B closely resembles the average Specialist Dairy Farm. The output (£73) is almost the same and so also is the output of milk. The inputs on Farm B (£70) are, however, higher—particularly feeding-stuffs and labour. Ideally, the comparison should be with a local group of dairy farms in the same area and of about the same size. In this case, however, the national average is quite suitable. The reader must not, however, expect the trading account of a particular farm always to resemble the pattern so closely as in this case—particularly if the farm being scrutinized has an unorthodox system.

It can be seen that the farm income ("profit") is only £5·00 per acre on Farm B compared to an average of £16·30.* This comparison is not quite fair because the average farm is smaller than this farm. The management and investment income (which largely eliminates the size effect) is, however, also lower (£3·20 compared to £9·30). The farm is thus less profitable than others of its kind—an impression confirmed by the return on capital (5·0 per cent compared to 13·9 per cent) and output per £100 inputs (£105 compared to £115). The output per £100 labour and per £100 labour and machinery is also low. As output is reasonable, and machinery costs per acre seem quite modest, this suggests that labour costs may be too high.

* It is taken for granted in this and subsequent examples that the year chosen is a typical one for the farm concerned.

	TYPE OF FARM					
	SPECIALIST DAIRY	MAINLY SHEEP	CATTLE AND SHEEP	MAINLY CEREALS	GENERAL CROPPING	HORT. HOLDINGS
AVERAGE SIZE (acres) . .	101	459½	258	321½	203	27
NO. OF FARMS	430	84	266	246	313	109
OUTPUT PER ACRE . . .	£	£	£	£	£	£
Wheat	1·00	0·20	1·00	8·50	8·10	—
Barley	1·20	0·40	1·50	14·90	11·30	8·90
Other cereals	0-10	0·10	0·30	0·80	0·50	—
Potatoes	0·30	—	0·20	0·70	13·20	12·30
Sugar Beet	—	—	—	1·10	8·70	—
Fruit	—	—	—	—	—	82·40
Vegetables and Flowers . .	—	—	—	0·30	2·40	55·80
Glasshouse crops . . .	—	—	—	—	—	103·20
Other crops	0·40	0·10	0·40	2·70	2·30	2·30
Total crops . . .	3·00	0·80	3·40	29·00	46·50	264·90
Cattle	9·40	2·30	11·50	4·20	6·10	—
Sheep and Wool . . .	0·90	4·40	6·40	2·00	1·30	—
Pigs	1·50	0·10	0·80	3·70	7·60	10·90
Poultry and Eggs . . .	2·20	0·20	0·40	—	—	—
Milk	54·40	1·40	0·80	0·70	1·60	6·30
Other livestock . . .	—	—	—	—	—	—
Total livestock . . .	68·40	8·40	19·90	10·60	16·60	17·20
Miscellaneous	1·00	0·10	0·40	0·70	1·50	3·20
TOTAL GROSS OUTPUT PER ACRE (i)	72·40	9·30	23·70	40·30	64·60	285·30
INPUTS PER ACRE						
Seed	0·80	0·10	0·50	2·10	4·00	19·80
Fertilizer and Sprays . .	4·10	0·40	1·50	4·80	8·10	20·30
Feeds and Vet. . . .	24·00	2·20	4·10	3·30	6·60	10·00
Wages	8·10	1·10	3·40	6·40	12·50	70·40
Farmer's labour . . .	(7·00)	(1·50)	(2·60)	(1·50)	(2·70)	(24·80)
Machinery	9·20	1·40	3·70	8·00	11·40	50·80‡
Rent	5·00	0·90	2·50	5·40	6·00	12·10
Other	4·90	0·60	1·50	2·20	2·20	30·40
TOTAL INPUTS PER ACRE (ii) .	63·10	8·20	19·80	33·70	53·50	238·60
FARM INCOME PER ACRE . .	16·30	2·60	6·50	8·10	13·80	71·50
MANAGEMENT AND INVESTMENT INCOME PER ACRE ((i)—(ii)) .	9·30	1·10	3·90	6·60	11·10	46·70
EFFICIENCY STANDARDS						
Gross output per acre . .	£72	£9	£24	£40	£65	£285
Gross output/£100 inputs .	115	113	120	119	121	120
Gross output/£100 labour .	479	358	395	510	425	300
Gross output/£100 labour and machinery	298	232	244	253	243	195
Estimated tenant's capital/acre.	£67	£13·50	£35	£46	£58	n.a.
Return on tenant's capital .	13·9%	8·1%	11·1%	14·3%	19·1%	n.a.
Gross margin per acre . .	£43·50	£6·60	£18	£30	£46	£235
Net output per acre . .	£49	£7	£20	£35	£54	£256
Stocking rate (acres/livestock unit)	1·5	1·3†	2·0	3·0	2·2	n.a.
Work units (s.m.d.) per man .	274	270	278	273	256	230

FIG. 20. AVERAGE TRADING ACCOUNT AND EFFICIENCY STANDARDS
(6 Farming Types, England and Wales 1968)*

* Adapted from *Farm Incomes*, 1968, MAFF   † Plus 4·4 acres rough grazing
‡ Includes glasshouse upkeep   n.a. = not available

			FARM		
ACRES:	A	B	C	D
	285	273	57	200
OUTPUT PER ACRE—	£	£	£	£
Wheat	13·60	—	—	—
Barley	10·90	4·30	7·90	6·50
Other cereals	—	—	—	—
Potatoes	—	—	—	—
Sugar Beet	—	—	9·00	—
Other crops	1·00	—	—	—
Total crops	25·50	4·30	16·90	6·50
Cattle	3·10	10·30	—	11·10
Pigs	—	—	69·80	—
Poultry and Eggs	—	2·90	—	—
Milk	—	55·10	—	53·60
Total livestock	3·10	68·30	69·80	64·70
Miscellaneous	1·30	0·60	8·90	1·80
TOTAL GROSS OUTPUT PER ACRE . .	29·90	73·20	95·60	73·00
INPUTS PER ACRE—				
Seed	2·90	1·60	2·60	1·90
Fertilizer and Sprays	4·70	3·70	8·00	6·00
Feeds and Vet.	0·40	27·00	48·50	5·70
Wages	13·80	16·60	0·20	12·50
Farmer's labour	(1·40)	(1·80)	(11·90)	(4·90)
Machinery	6·10	8·40	16·10	10·60
Rent	4·40	6·50	6·90	8·10
Other	1·70	4·40	4·20	5·70
TOTAL INPUTS PER ACRE . . .	35·40	70·00	98·40	55·40
FARM INCOME PER ACRE . . .	—4·10	5·00	9·10	22·50
Management and Investment Income/Acre	—5·50	3·20	—2·80	17·60
Gross Output per acre	£30	£73	£96	£73
Gross Output/£100 Inputs . . .	84	105	97	132
Gross Output/£100 labour . . .	197	398	790	420
Gross Output/£100 labour and mach. .	140	273	339	261
Tenant's Capital/Acre	£54	£65	£93	£63
Return on Tenant's Capital . . .	—10·2%	5·0%	—3·0%	27·9%
Gross Margin per acre	£21·90	£40·90	£36·50	£59·40
Net Output per acre	£26	£49	£45	£64
Stocking density	1·5	1·5	—	1·5
Work Units (s.m.d.) per man . . .	153	358	380	277

FIG. 21. FOUR FARMS ANALYSED

This requires further investigation. The amount of work accomplished per worker can be measured as *Work Units per Worker*. This is 358 (standard about 300), which suggests that labour is used efficiently. *See* notes in Appendix 1. In fact, the farmer has 115 cows and a fair number of young stock looked after by two cow-men. The farmer and the other man employed relieve the cow-men when they have a day off and also do the field work. This seems quite a modest labour staff. As labour is scarce in the area, however, wages are above average.

Another point worth investigation is feeding-stuffs. Scrutiny of the records shows that the yield per cow is 750 gallons and that over 6 lb. concentrates are being fed per gallon. This is excessive and obviously the weakest point in the organization. A 10 per cent increase in milk yields and a 10 per cent decrease in food costs (which would still leave some overfeeding) would raise the profit from less than £1400 a year to over £3500. The density of stocking, 1·5 acres per grazing livestock unit (*see* notes in the Appendix) is quite reasonable, but if the pasture and forage crops are productive less concentrates should be required.

There can be little doubt that efficiency factors, together with a few physical measures such as density of stocking, concentrates per gallon and some specialized ratios such as food costs per £100 output calculated separately for pigs, poultry or cattle can help to highlight weaknesses in organization. The emphasis, however, is on tightening-up the efficiency of existing systems, rather than finding a better one.

One of the drawbacks of using ratios is that they often have more than one interpretation. If, as on Farm B, output per £100 labour is low, this may mean that labour costs are too high. On the other hand, if the output is very low (due to poor yields, for example) this depresses the output per man through no fault of the workers. Farm B is an example.

Another fault of efficiency factors is that they compare the farm with an average. Thus while they are useful in showing how a badly managed farm differs from the average, they are less helpful when dealing with above-average and unorthodox farms. The lessons to be learnt from efficiency factors are also fairly general. A conclusion that "output is low" does not carry any indication of which output is to be raised or how it is to be done. Nonetheless, in the hands of an experienced adviser who is well aware of their limitations, such tests can be useful.

They have the advantage of being easier to prepare than gross margins if the records give little detail. They were popular in the early 1950s when management advice first came into vogue but have since been largely replaced by gross margins.

GROSS MARGINS

Gross margins for farm planning will be described in more detail in the next chapter. They are, however, equally useful for detecting faults in management. Gross margins are calculated by deducting variable costs from the output of each enterprise. For crops, these variable costs are fertilizers, seeds, sprays and dusts.* For livestock they are feeding-stuffs, veterinary expenses, medicines and A.I. They are called variable costs because they vary directly with the acreage of crops or number of livestock. This being so, there are advantages in deducting such costs from output per acre. If for example, the output of barley is £40 and variable costs are £10, then each extra acre of barley will contribute £40 and incur £10 of such costs. It is thus convenient to deduct the one from the other and say that each acre of barley contributes £30 gross margin.

There are, in addition, costs for labour, machinery, rent and overheads. These costs, however, are incurred for the farm as a whole and are therefore named "common costs." Once a machine is bought, its depreciation will continue whether or not it is used. Once a regular worker is employed his cost will continue whether there is work for him to do or not. For this reason, common costs are sometimes called fixed costs. They are not, of course, unchangeable; but unless deliberately altered, they tend to continue. If a plan is changed, therefore, the point is not whether a few man hours are used on a particular crop but whether the labour and machinery can deal with the crops and livestock prescribed.

To take a very simple example, assume that a farmer has 100 acres, cropped as follows—

		£
70 acres Barley @ £30 (gross margin) =	2100
20 acres Potatoes @ £70 (gross margin)	1400
10 acres Cattle @ £20 (gross margin)	200
100 acres @ £37 (gross margin)	3700
Less:	
100 acres Common Costs @ £25	2500
NET PROFIT	£1200

The reason for presenting the results in this form is that it is very much simpler to see the effect on profit of altering or improving the system of farming. Suppose that the farmer by applying

* In this chapter, casual labour is included with "labour", to put farms using casual labour (e.g. for harvesting potatoes) on an equal footing with those that use only regular labour. When preparing budgets for an individual farm, however, casual labour is best treated as a variable cost.

£2 of fertilizer can increase the yields of barley by £3. The effect would be to increase the gross margin per acre by £1. As there are 70 acres, this would increase the total gross margin by £70 and as common costs would be unchanged, the profit would also rise by £70.

Suppose that the farm grew one acre less barley and one more of potatoes. The effect would be a loss of £30 (barley) and a gain of £70 gross margin (potatoes), i.e. a net gain of £40. It may be asked, will this not change the man hours and tractors hours required? The answer is that if the change is not a large one, the regular labour force and machinery will remain virtually unaltered. There will be some changes—more fuel required in one month and less in another, more wear and tear of one machine and a little less of another, some change in overtime. But such changes are unimportant and partly self-cancelling—it is being assumed for this exercise that all work is done by regular staff.

If, on the other hand, the change in the farm programme is so large that an extra man is required, the common costs will rise but in one lump when the man is recruited. It is for this reason that common costs are treated separately from other costs.

Our concern now is to use these gross margins to identify weaknesses in farm organization. If farm income is too low, the faults likely to be found can be classified under three headings—

1. The gross margins per acre or per unit of output may be too low—due to low yields, unthrifty stock, excessive variable costs, such as feeding-stuffs.

2. The intensity may be too low—not enough high-value crops or types of livestock.

3. The common costs may be too high—labour, machinery and power, rent or other overheads.

Each of these faults has different remedies and these are set out in summary form in Fig. 22. Such a system of diagnosis cannot, of course, determine precisely how the remedy is to be applied—that may be a technical matter beyond the scope of this book. But properly applied, the system can give a strong indication of which measures are likely to solve the problem.

There is another matter that can be brought out clearly with the use of gross margins—the level of intensity at which the farmer should aim. Within limits, high output is associated with high income. What, however, are these limits? There are two ways in which output may be increased—

1. The farmer can increase crop yields, for example, by applying more fertilizer. But as more fertilizer is used, diminishing returns apply and the yield begins to fall off. If £1 fertilizer produces £1·50 of crop, it is worth applying. If the next £1

	NORMAL		FAULT 1: LOW GROSS MARGINS		FAULT 2: LOW INTENSITY		FAULT 3: HIGH COSTS	
GROSS MARGIN—								
Barley . . .	70 acres @ £30	£2100	70 acres @ £20	£1400	50 acres @ £30	£1500	70 acres @ £30	£2100
Potatoes . .	20 acres @ £70	1400	20 acres @ £60	1200	10 acres @ £70	700	20 acres @ £70	1400
Cattle . .	10 acres @ £20	200	10 acres @ £20	200	40 acres @ £20	800	10 acres @ £20	200
TOTAL G.M. .	100 acres @ £37	3700	100 acres @ £28	2800	100 acres @ £28	3000	100 acres @ £37	3700
COMMON COSTS	100 acres @ £25	2500	100 acres @ £25	2500	100 acres @ £25	2500	100 acres @ £30	3000
	Profit . £1200		Profit . £300		Profit . £500		Profit . £700	

These examples are, of course, over-simplified but are intended merely to illustrate the principles involved before passing on to deal with detailed examples. The distinction between these three faults is emphasized because the remedies may be quite different. In practice, a farm may have more than one type of fault and need a combination of remedies.

Fault 1. *Low Gross Margins* . (Improve the present system) — Improve crop yields (fertility and drainage problems, diseases etc.). Improve livestock yields, (disease, poor stock, poor housing etc.). Economize on livestock costs (especially feeding-stuffs, utilization of grass and fodder).

Fault 2. *Low Intensity* . (Plan a more intensive system) — Change to more intensive livestock systems. Add pigs or poultry. Grow more high-value crops. Contract for new enterprises.

Fault 3. *High Common Costs* . (Economize on labour, machinery, overheads) — Streamline buildings and layout of fields to economize on labour and machinery. Specialize to ensure full use of expensive equipment. Keep a check on overhead expenses.

FIG. 22. DIAGNOSIS OF FAULTS WITH GROSS MARGINS—OUTLINE SCHEME

produces £1·10, it is just worth applying. If the next £1 produces £0·90, then the application has gone beyond the optimum point. It will be noticed that in this case, the output continues to increase as each extra dose of fertilizer is applied whether the application is justified or not. The gross margin (from which fertilizer cost is deducted) reaches a maximum when the optimum dose is applied and then declines. The size of the gross margin is thus quite a good measure of the extent to which the farmer has attained not the maximum yield but the most profitable one. The same consideration applies to feeding-stuffs. It will thus be apparent that a low gross margin can be due *either* to low yields *or* to excessive variable costs, e.g. overfeeding dairy cows.

2. The second way is to add enterprises with a high gross margin or substitute enterprises with a high gross margin for those with a low one. What is the limit to this process? On well-equipped farms with good soil and ample capital, the limit may be quite high. On poor land or with limited capital resources, the limit may be much lower. But under the right conditions a low-output system can be successful. These conditions are that the land is cheap and that the common costs can be kept to a modest level. The profit will probably be lower per acre than under an intensive system; but if the farmer has enough acres, his *total* profit will be adequate. This can be illustrated by a simple example.

	LARGE-EXTENSIVE ACRES	G.M.	INTERMEDIATE ACRES	G.M.	SMALL-INTENSIVE ACRES	G.M.
Cereals . .	600 @ £25	£15000	210 @ £30	£6300	60 @ £30	£1800
Roots (or vegetables) .	—	—	60 @ £70	4200	40 @ £80	3200
Cattle . .	400 @ £20	8000	30 @ £20	600		
Total G.M.	1000 @ £23	23000	300 @ £37	11100	100 @ £50	5000
Common Costs	1000 @ £18	18000	300 @ £25	7500	100 @ £30	3000
Profit . .	1000 @ £5	£5000	300 @ £12	£3600	100 @ £20	£2000

In this case, the large farm has a gross margin of only £23 an acre. But with 1000 acres, and a simple system, he can keep common costs down to £18, leaving a profit of £5000. The small farm by comparison has an intensive system with a gross margin of £50 an acre, leaving him a profit of £2000. Indeed, if any given farmer is to secure a reasonable living from a small area, he must have a high output per acre. If the farm is too poor to produce such an output, the holding is not viable. The medium or large farm could also have an intensive system, provided the land is productive and the farmer has the capital and ability required to conduct a business on this scale. It is worth noting that the total gross margin is a better measure of size of business than acres. The 1000-acre farm with a total gross margin of £23000 thus has a business four and a half times as large as the 100-acre farm (£5000).

To illustrate this system in practice, Farm B will be analysed again, this time using gross margins.

The crops and livestock were as follows—

Barley .	.	. 32 acres	115 Dairy cows	
Silage .	.	. 100 acres	85 Young Stock	
Rotational grazing .		110 acres	Yield per cow: 750 gallons	
Permanent grazing .		24 acres	Farm Income: £1381	
Woods etc.	.	. 7 acres		

273

Apart from a few acres of barley, this is a specialist dairy farm. Ideally, one should have a group of large specialist dairy farms to compare with this one. There are small specialist dairy farms in the area but the large dairy farms usually carry a fair amount of arable land. It is a group of these that are quoted as an average in Fig. 23. The fact that Farm B is different from the average need not however deter us. In fact, it is interesting to see whether in specializing, Farmer B is doing as well as his neighbours.

The profit on Farm B (£5·00 per acre) is only half the average attained by other farms in the group. This result, while not disastrous, is certainly not adequate for the amount of capital invested. The gross margin from the dairy cows is £50·00 per acre compared to an average of £69·70. The gross margin from land used to rear young stock is usually less than for adult cows, but at £5·10 per acre is very much below the average (£22·90). The livestock density, 1·5 acres of fodder crops per livestock unit (see Appendix 1) is quite reasonable. As already indicated, however, concentrates (at about 6 lb. per gallon) are being used extravagantly for a milk yield of only 750 gallons per cow. Barley, the only arable crop, is average.

Turning now to the common costs, it can be seen that labour costs are about £3 an acre above average. The use of labour can be checked by calculating *Work Units per Worker* (see Appendix 1)—in this case, the answer (358) is above average (300). As already stated, the labour force is quite modest. Other overheads per acre are somewhat above average; this can be investigated but may be due to some item such as repairs that does not occur every year. Machinery and power costs seem to be below

	FARM B			(LOCAL AVERAGE)			FARM D		
	ACRES	G.M. PER ACRE £	TOTAL G.M. £	ACRES	G.M. PER ACRE £	TOTAL G.M. £	ACRES	G.M. PER ACRE £	TOTAL G.M. £
GROSS MARGINS—									
Wheat	—	—	—	16·3	37·50	612	34·0	40·00	1360
Barley	11·7	26·60	312	26·4	27·40	723	—	—	—
Oats	—	—	—	2·8	31·80	91	—	—	—
Potatoes	—	—	—	7·4	59·00	436	52·5	76·40	4013
Dairy Cows	73·3	50·00	3670	33·0	69·70	2299	13·5	42·00	567
Young Stock	15·0	5·10	79	10·3	22·90	236	—	—	—
Other Livestock	—	—	—	0·9	×	75	—	—	—
Poultry	—	—	26	—	—	50	—	×	—
Misc.	—	×	9	—	×	74	—	—	—
Total G.M.	100·0	40·90	4096	100·0	45·90	4596	100·0	59·40	5940
COMMON COSTS—									
Labour	×	16·60	1658	×	13·30	1332	×	12·50	1250
Machinery	×	8·40	844	×	10·40	1044	×	10·60	1060
Rent	×	6·50	645	×	6·00	599	×	8·10	810
Other overheads	×	4·40	443	×	3·40	337	×	5·70	570
Total Common Costs		35·90	3590		33·10	3312		36·90	3690
FARM INCOME	×	5·00	506	×	12·80	1284	×	22·50	2250
FARM SIZE (acres)	273			243			200		

Fig. 23. DAIRY FARMS

average—probably because the farm has fewer arable crops than others in the group. What conclusions should be drawn from this comparison?

1. A farmer specializing in milk production should get better results. He is feeding for about 1000 gallons a cow and obtaining 750 gallons. He must either find some way of raising yields or cutting food costs to match this low yield.

2. One interesting point is the degree of specialization. Although the gross margin per acre for dairy cows (£50·00 per acre) is below average, this is higher than most of the arable crops on the other dairy farms. Thus, unless the farmer were to grow potatoes or some other high-value crops, a change from dairy cows to arable crops would lower his income. Indeed, the other dairy farms could probably increase their income by specializing because the gross margin from cows is higher than most of the arable crops. The limiting factor in their case is no doubt the lack of suitable buildings and the capital to erect them. Farmer B, however, is equipped to carry a large herd and this might give him an advantage. If he could raise the gross margin per acre from dairy cows to the average of £70 per acre, his income would be well above that of the other dairy farmers in the area. The solution is thus to improve the present system.

FARM D

As a contrast Farm D is a successful dairy farm (*see* Fig. 23). The crops and livestock are as follows:

Barley	.	.	.	68 acres
Kale	.	.	.	8 acres
Silage	.	.	.	40 acres
Hay	.	.	.	37 acres
Temporary grazing	.			9 acres
Permanent grazing	.			38 acres
				200 acres

60 Dairy cows
45 Young stock
Yield per cow: 985 gallons
Farm Income: £4500

This farm has the same system as Farm B but shows over four times the profit per acre (£22·50 per acre compared to £5·00). The dairy enterprise with a gross margin of £76 per acre is markedly successful. Indeed, Farm D produces a larger gross margin (£4013) from 53 acres than Farm B does from 73 acres. This is partly due to a reasonably high yield (985 gallons per cow) and partly to the economical use of feeding-stuffs (3 lb. per gallon). The stocking density of 1·5 acres per livestock unit is the same at Farm B but with much less concentrate use. The young stock are also productive and the barley is somewhat above average. The cost of labour per acre is about average and so also are work units per worker (277). Farmer B, by contrast, is very economical in the use of labour (358 work units per man). If this is one of the causes of the low milk yield, the farmer has not gained much advantage.

FARM A

The results, which show a loss of £4·00 per acre, are obviously the worst of the four farms considered. The crops and livestock are as follows:

Wheat	.	.	.	87 acres	Cattle: 23
Barley	.	.	.	127 acres	Loss: £1140
Oats	.	.	.	34 acres	
Beans	.	.	.	10 acres	
Hay	.	.	.	7 acres	
Permanent pasture	.			20 acres	

A glance at Fig. 24 shows that in comparison with other cereal farms all the indices are low—indeed, output is so low that the ratios are not very helpful. Labour, for example, may be excessive; but the low output per £100 labour might simply be due to low

	FARM A			CEREAL FARMS (LOCAL SAMPLE)		
	ACRES	G.M. PER ACRE	TOTAL G.M.	ACRES	G.M. PER ACRE	TOTAL G.M.
		£	£		£	£
Wheat . . .	30·5	20·90	639	23·0	38·00	877
Barley . . .	44·5	26·70	1189	41·8	27·30	1142
Oats . . .	11·9	26·90	320	3·3	29·70	98
Beans . . .	3·5	24·90	87	8·3	23·80	198
Peas, field . .	—	—	—	2·4	35·70	86
Potatoes . . .	—	—	—	0·4	104·00	42
Sugar Beet . .	—	—	—	2·0	66·20	131
Misc. . . .	—	—	—	13·2	—	308
Cattle . . .	9·6	—	—35	5·5	20·40	112
Pigs and Poultry .	—	—	—	0·1	—	55
TOTAL G.M. . .	100·0	21·00	2200	100·0	30·50	3049
Labour . . .	×	13·80	1380	×	7·00	698
Machinery . . .	×	6·10	610	×	8·50	848
Rent . . .	×	4·40	440	×	6·50	655
Overheads . . .	×	1·70	170	×	2·00	203
TOTAL COMMON COSTS	×	25·00	2600	×	24·00	2404
FARM INCOME . .	×	—4·10	—400	×	6·50	645
FARM SIZE (acres) .	285			447		

FIG. 24

output per acre. A comparison of the trading accounts confirms the low output but most of the expenses except for wages seem quite normal. The gross margins in Fig. 24 give a clearer picture. Most of the farm is in cereals with gross margins per acre at or appreciably below average. Barley with 28 cwt. per acre is reasonable, but the wheat (about 20 cwt.) did badly. The gross margin for beans (£24·90) was not very high but was slightly above average for that crop. The cattle enterprise, occupying 10 per cent of the farm is a liability. The farmer buys and fattens stores but the gain does not pay for the food and grazing used, hence the negative gross margin. The common costs are in total only slightly above average. Whereas machinery, rent and overhead costs are quite modest, labour seems to be double what one would expect on such a farm. This fact is confirmed by the fact that work units per worker are only 148 compared to an average of about 275 for an arable farm. This suggests that too many men are being carried.

The faults are not hard to locate. Of more interest is to consider the advice that an adviser should offer. Suppose that he has looked at the farmer's records and is about to visit the farm for the first time. He could prepare a list of queries, somewhat as follows:

1. Can cereal yields be improved, especially wheat? Fertiliser expenditure seems normal. Wrong varieties? Disease problem? (90 per cent of the farm is in cereals.) Drainage? Weeds? Have yields been declining over the last five years?

2. Having dealt with the farmer's immediate problems, it will be necessary to talk over longer term solutions. Suppose that there is a disease or soil fertility problem that can be cured. What would be the effect? If the gross margin for wheat and cattle were each increased by £10 an acre, this would be just enough to wipe out the present loss. If over the next year or two the farmer could increase the gross margin from cereals by another £2 an acre, run the farm with one man less and pay (as seems likely) another £2 an acre rent, he might have an income of about £740 a year— not a very satisfactory living.

3. Technical improvement is thus not enough—a new system is required. If the farmer had 1000 acres of fairly cheap land and a minimum of labour, a low output system of this kind might give an income of £5000 or more a year. But with its present size it is not viable unless cereal yields are quite high. Could the rotation be intensified? Sugar beet? Potatoes? Vining peas? (All would require a quota or contract.) Vegetable crop? (Only feasible if there is a market for them.) Intensive livestock? Barley beef? Pigs? (He could use his own grain.) Intensive livestock would, however, require capital for buildings—unless existing buildings can be converted. There should already be enough

labour to undertake some additional enterprise. These are all matters that can be discussed with the farmer.

FARM C

This is a small farm of 57 acres. Thus, although the farm has a profit of £9·10 an acre, an income of just over £500 is not enough to provide a living. The farmer grows 48 acres of barley and 6

	FARM C			SMALL ARABLE FARMS WITH PIGS AND POULTRY (LOCAL SAMPLE)		
	ACRES	G.M. PER ACRE	TOTAL G.M.	ACRES	G.M. PER ACRE	TOTAL G.M.
		£	£		£	£
Wheat . . .	—	—	—	12·3	32·80	407
Barley . . .	84·2	20·70	1748	51·0	23·10	1178
Oats . . .	—	—	—	2·9	19·10	55
Potatoes . . .	—	—	—	3·1	106·40	333
Sugar Beet . .	10·5	60·00	630	8·7	70·20	608
Fruit etc. . .	—	—	—	1·3	—	358
Misc. . . .	5·3	—	174	16·6	—	634
Cattle . . .	—	—	—	1·7	154·60	264
Pigs . . .	—	(15·70)*	1098	2·1	(31·00)*	2260
Poultry . . .	—	—	—	0·3	(21·40)*	1121
TOTAL G.M. . .	100·0	36·50	3650	100·0	72·20	7218
Labour . . .	×	0·20	20	×	12·00	1202
Machinery . .	×	16·10	1610	×	20·70	2067
Rent . . .	×	6·90	690	×	8·00	799
Overheads . .	×	4·20	420	×	6·20	618
TOTAL COMMON COSTS	×	27·40	2740	×	46·90	4686
FARM INCOME . .	×	9·10	910	×	25·30	2532
FARM SIZE (acres) .	57			57		

* G.M. per £100 Gross Output.

FIG. 25.

of sugar beet. He keeps about 35 sows and sells weaners. The following points are apparent. The gross margins from barley and sugar beet are below average and require investigation. Machinery costs are high, but (as can be seen from Fig. 25) this is perhaps inevitable when arable crops are grown on a small scale. In the case of pigs, gross margin per acre is largely meaningless because they occupy very little land. A more feasible measure is gross margin per £100 gross output. On this farm the figure is £15·70 compared to an average of £31·00. An advisory officer in such a case would raise the following points:

1. Can the yields of barley and sugar beet be increased (26 cwt.

and 13 tons respectively)? Varieties? Drainage? Disease? Weeds? (Expenditure on fertilizers and sprays is quite heavy.)

2. The pig herd should be examined in detail. The farmer sold 618 weaners, which is over 17 per sow. This seems satisfactory. The weaners sell for about £6·65, which seems reasonable if they are under 50 lb. in weight. Food purchased is £2700, to which can be added about £600 for home-grown barley. This is over £90 per sow and litters which seem rather high. Are the sows properly rationed? Judging by other pig herds it should be possible to reduce food costs by at least £900 a year. One possibility is to carry the young pigs on to a larger size. Pork pigs sometimes pay better than weaners when the prices are right, but they need extra housing. Bacon or heavy pigs are a more doubtful proposition because the herd may not be large enough to get a contract.

3. What long-term advice should be given to such a farmer? His farm has a much lower G.M. per acre than the other small farms with which he is being compared. Should he try to intensify his system? Most of these other farms have another worker, often a member of the family. This farmer, however, does all the work single-handed and it is doubtful if he could do much more. (Work units per man 380—a high figure.) To hire a worker would cost £900 or more with overtime. To this might have to be added the upkeep of extra equipment and interest if he borrowed extra capital. The total gross margin would thus have to increase by well over £1000 before the farmer could pay the man's wage and break even, far less increase his net income.

Intensification thus means either a large increase in output or it is not worthwhile. Such a step would thus require very careful planning—particularly if additional capital is required.

On the other hand, improvement of the present system could produce a substantial dividend. An extra £10 an acre from sugar beet and £5 on barley, plus £900 saved on foods, could increase his income to £1700 a year.

ENTERPRISE MANAGEMENT STUDIES

So far, we have been dealing with the farm as a whole and, although gross margins give an insight into the profitability of individual crops and types of livestock, it is often worth going beyond this point to measure the efficiency of one enterprise in some detail. This applies particularly when the enterprise is a large one on which the farmers income largely depends. Some types of livestock indeed lend themselves to such treatment. This is particularly true of some enterprises such as pigs, broilers or laying hens. If such units are large, they have their own specialist labour, equipment and buildings and it is comparatively easy to cost them and show a realistic profit. Such livestock are usually kept under conditions where the farmer can control temperature, heating, lighting and food supplies. It is thus possible to devise very precise efficiency standards.

Some of these enterprises—such as broilers—have largely left the general farm and are managed on factory lines. With strong competition, managers must keep a very careful check on performance. Quite a small variation in efficiency—as little as 0·1 in the food conversion rate—can be of vital importance in the level of profit obtained.

Costing records can also be prepared for dairy herds (e.g. the scheme operated by the Milk Marketing Board) and for beef cattle. With grass-eating livestock however, the standards are not so precise and costs can vary quite legitimately according to system. For this reason, they need care in interpretation.

Crop costings are on the whole rather less useful as an aid to management for the reasons stated in Chapter 12. Nonetheless, a farmer with a large fruit or vegetable enterprise with its own staff, packing sheds etc. on a general farm might well find a departmental account worthwhile.

One example of an enterprise account will be given in this chapter—a pig herd. It is particularly suitable for such analysis and (unlike broilers) it is still a farm enterprise.

FARM E

EFFICIENCY IN PIG PRODUCTION

Farmer E has a herd of 50 sows and sells the progeny as bacon pigs. As a substantial amount of capital is invested in this enterprise it is well worth while to keep a check on results. The trading account for the pig herd is given in Fig. 26. It takes the familiar form—opening valuation and expenses on the left, sales and closing valuation on the right. It is, however, convenient to split this account into two stages in order to obtain the Gross Output of pigs as a separate item to set against the main items of cost.

Having prepared the account in this form, the second stage can be used to calculate costs of labour, foods and other items per £100 of output,* e.g.—

$$\text{Cost of foods per £100 output} = \frac{\text{Cost of foods}}{\text{Gross output}} \times 100$$

---

* Costs per £100 output is a convenient unit. "Costs per pig" would be feasible if the farmer always sold pigs of the same size. In practice, a farmer selling bacon pigs might be tempted to sell a few weaners or porkers if the market were favourable and he will certainly sell cull sows and boars. "Per £100 output" has the advantage that it can be applied to any pig herd.

TRADING ACCOUNT FOR PIG HERD

Stage 1

PURCHASES	£		SALES	£
1 Boar	40		1 Boar	20
15 Sows and gilts . .	495		18 Sows and gilts . .	450
	———		10 Porkers . . .	130
	535		676 Baconers . . .	12844
Opening valuation (pigs) .	5048		16 Casualties . . .	144
	———			———
LIVESTOCK OUTPUT	5583		CLOSING VALUATION	13588
(carried down) . . .	12887		(pigs)	4882
	———			———
	£18470			£18470

Stage 2

COSTS	£		LIVESTOCK OUTPUT	£
Feeding-stuffs . . .	9017		(brought down) . .	12887
Labour	1430			
Share of overheads, medi-				
cines, electricity, repairs,				
water, etc. . . .	1360			
	———			
	11807			
PROFIT	1080			
	———			———
	£12887			£12887

FIG. 26

The results are as follows and are compared with averages—

	FARM E	BACON HERDS	ALL HERDS
Costs per £100 output:	£	£	£
Food . . .	70·00	63·60	65·20
Labour . . .	11·10	9·80	9·40
Other costs . .	10·50	9·50	9·10
	———	———	———
	91·60	82·90	83·70
Profit . .	8·40	17 10	16·30
	———	———	———
	£100·00	£100·00	£100·00

This herd shows a profit of £8·40 per £100 output—only half the average obtained by other herds (£16·30). It does seem, however, that the farmer has chosen one of the more profitable systems because bacon pigs (at this time) are making above average profits.

The costs in this herd are, however, above average. This may mean *either* that the costs are excessive *or* that the output is below average. This can be ascertained by calculating a series of efficiency factors. For this purpose, it is necessary to split the herd into two sections—

> Breeding hard—sows, boars, gilts, unweaned pigs
> Feeding herd —fattening pigs after weaning

BREEDING HERD. The purpose of a breeding herd is to produce weaned pigs at minimum cost. Most of the costs are for feeding sows and a large part of this is the upkeep of the sow itself. Indeed a sow (and litters) producing 18 weaners a year does not use much more food than one producing 14 weaners. For this reason, the more weaners produced per sow, the lower the cost per weaner.

The number of weaners depends on two factors: the number of pigs weaned per litter and the number of litters per year. The number weaned per litter depends in turn on the number born per litter and the number that die before weaning. The number of litters should be at least two per year. Early weaning (e.g. at six instead of eight weeks) can help to increase this.

FATTENING HERD. The success of the fattening herd depends on turning out the maximum value of pigs for the lowest cost of food. This in turn depends on—

(*a*) The food conversion rate, i.e. lb. food per 1 lb. liveweight gain.

(*b*) The cost of food per cwt.

(*c*) The price received for pigs sold.

Results for Farm E are as follows—

BREEDING HERD	FARM E	AVERAGE ALL HERDS
Litters per sow	1·68*	1·95
Pigs born per litter . . .	10·2	10·3
Pigs weaned per litter . . .	8·7	8·6
Pigs weaned per sow per year .	14·6*	16·8
Food cost per weaner . . .	£3·82*	£3·37
Weight at weaning . . .	40 lb	39 lb
Cost of food per cwt. . . .	£1·80	£1·79

FEEDING HERD—		BACON HERDS
Weight of bacon pigs sold (lb.) .	199	202
Mortality	3%	3·4%
Cost of meal per cwt. . . .	£1·80	£1·80
Food conversion rate . . .	3·95*	3·66
Price per score deadweight (bacon) .	£2·53	£2·56

The faults* in this herd are now obvious. In the breeding herd, the food cost per weaner is high—due to too few pigs per sow (14·6 compared with an average of 16·8) and this in turn is due to too few litters per sow (1·68 compared with 1·95). This is probably due to a fault in management in having the sows served at the proper time. The farmer already uses six weeks weaning. Other factors such as litter size, cost of food and size of weaners are satisfactory.

In the feeding herd, the fault lies in the food conversion rate (3·95 compared to an average of 3·66). It will now be necessary to investigate the cause which is likely to be one of the following—

(a) Poor insulation and uncomfortable housing.

(b) A slow-growing strain of pigs (check growth rate of litters from individual sows).

(c) Some sub-acute infection (mortality, however, is not high).

If the litters per sow per year were increased from 1·68 to 1·94 and the conversion rate reduced from 3·95 to 3·66 the profit would be increased from £1080 to nearly £2500. Many "above average" pig herds would show a profit of £3000 to £4000 from a herd of this size.

With such a system of records, a farmer can delegate a fair amount of responsibility to a good pig-man knowing that he can still keep a tight control on levels of efficiency. With a large unit, it would be wise to check the more important factors at least once every six months.

QUESTIONS

1. Calculate efficiency factors for Manor Farm for the first three years of operation. Comment on the performance and make suggestions on how it might be improved in future years.

2. You are a farm adviser and two farmers (F and G) are new clients. Their accountants have given you enough information to prepare these gross margin estimates. You have not yet seen the farms but are now about to visit them to discuss the results. Draw-up a preliminary report on the following lines—

(a) Comment on their past performance and make a list of questions you would ask the farmers to confirm your conclusions.

(b) Would you recommend either of them to change his systems of farming? If so, make a short list of possible improvements explaining in each case how such changes might be expected to benefit the farmer. Assume for this purpose that both farms are in the same region as farms A, B, C and D in this chapter.

	FARM F			FARM G		
	ACRES	G.M. PER ACRE	TOTAL G.M.	ACRES	G.M. PER ACRE	TOTAL G.M.
Wheat . . .	24·4	26·3	641	—	—	—
Barley . . .	—	—	—	60·4	25·9	1564
Oats . . .	—	—	—	—	—	—
Beans (field) . .	—	—	—	39·3	23·1	908
Beans (veg.) . .	5·0	68·3	339	—	—	—
Brassicas . . .	2·9	24·1	70	—	—	—
Other veg. . .	1·6	54·8	90	—	—	—
Dairy cows . .	53·9	65·5	3533	—	—	—
Young stock . .	7·3	−14·5	−106	—	—	—
Beef cattle . .	3·0	9·5	29	—	—	—
Poultry . . .	—	(1·6)*	39	—	(9·8)*	39
Other Income . .	1·9	—	522	0·3	—	25
	100·0	51·6	5157	100·0	25·3	2536
Labour . . .	×	24·0	2404	×	5·1	513
Machinery . .	×	15·8	1576	×	9·6	961
Rent . . .	×	7·9	794	×	4·8	477
Overheads . .	×	8·9	888	×	1·0	102
		56·6	5662		20·5	2053
Farm Income . .		−5·0	−505		4·8	483
Acres . . .			242			700

* Gross Margin per £100 Gross Output.

CHAPTER 14

INTRODUCTION TO BUDGETING

THE aim of this chapter is to plan for the future. As can be seen from the previous chapter, there are two distinct ways in which a farm can be improved. In the first place, it may be possible to farm better without changing the existing farm plan. The farmer may grow heavier crop yields, feed a better dairy ration or breed a pig with a better bacon carcase. Improvements of this kind can have a marked effect on profit and should never be neglected. There are occasions however when the farm plan itself must be altered. The farmer may be producing beef cattle when dairy cows would give a better return. He may be growing oats when it would pay to grow barley and buy any oats required. Quite apart from remedying faults there are many other occasions when a budget may be useful. A farmer might be offered a contract to produce some new crop (e.g. peas for quick freezing) and wonder whether he should accept it. A new machine (e.g. a down-the-row thinner for sugar beet) might come on the market and the farmer wonder whether he should buy one. Eggs might fall in price and the farmer wonder whether he should change to pig production. Quite apart from its effect on profits, a change in the farm plan may entail heavy capital expenditure. Thus before embarking on it, the farmer may need an estimate of the amount so that he can decide whether the results are worth the cost and if so where the funds required are to be found.

Even when the farmer has evolved what he regards as a good system, he should not expect it to maintain him for the rest of his farming career. Changes in methods and prices are continually occurring and the farmer must always be prepared to take advantage of them. It is thus obvious that a farm plan well suited to conditions at one time may be quite out of date ten years later. This does not mean that the farmer should neglect the rules of good husbandry. But within the bounds of good farming there is still a wide choice of methods and the onus is on the farmer to find the one that gives him the best return.

At first sight, it may seem difficult to forecast changes in receipts and expenses that will occur if the farm programme is altered. Fortunately, a method has recently been devised that greatly simplifies this task. This depends on dividing all costs into two groups—*fixed costs* and *variable costs*.

VARIABLE COSTS. In this category we include items such as seed, fertilizers, sprays, feeding stuffs, veterinary expenses, casual labour, transport (e.g. for cattle or sugar beet) and stores (detergents, twine, etc.). These are all costs that vary directly with the area of crops grown and the numbers of livestock. If one acre of wheat needs 3 cwt. fertilizer, 2 acres need 6 cwt. and 10 acres need 30 cwt. If 30 cwt. of meal fattens five pigs then 60 cwt. should fatten ten pigs. Once the farmer has decided on his system of management, these expenses are inevitable and are fairly easy to estimate beforehand.

FIXED OR COMMON COSTS. This category includes regular labour, machinery costs, rent and other overhead expenses such as insurance and telephone. These costs are usually incurred for the farm as a whole and not for any special enterprise. They are thus "fixed" costs in the sense that they do not vary directly according to the crops and livestock kept. They are also "fixed" in the sense that once incurred, they tend to run on whether proper use is made of them or not. Once the farmer has bought a combine harvester, it continues to depreciate at nearly the same rate whether he uses it to cut 100 or 200 acres of corn. Once the farmer has employed a cowman, he must pay his wage every week whether he tends twenty or forty cows. The same consideration applies to the rent and the other overhead expenses.

There is another point. Many fixed items can be bought only in large units. Regular workers can be hired only one at a time. If there is work for one and a half men the farmer may have no alternative but to employ two men. In such a case, the farmer could budget for an increase in crops or livestock (up to a full-time occupation for two men) without any extra wage costs. But if the programme were further expanded, the wage bill would jump (from say £1600 to £2400) when a third worker was recruited. The same consideration applies to tractors and large implements, like a combine harvester or a baler.

This distinction between fixed and variable costs is a very important one and is fundamental to all budgeting. At first sight it may seem rather theoretical but it has a very practical use. A variable cost item such as fertilizer can be measured out and used in the exact quantities required and if there is any left over it can be put back into store. Fixed costs (e.g. regular wages) are a steady stream and tend to run on whether they are used or not.

It will be seen, therefore, that if the farm plan is changed, the variable costs will change in a way that can be budgeted. The fixed or overhead costs on the other hand may hardly change at all—especially if the alteration to the farm programme is not a very extensive one. For example, if the farmer grows an extra 5 acres of barley the extra receipts might be £170 and the variable costs for seed, fertilizer, etc., £40. How about the fixed costs? The barley might need an extra 60 man hours and 30 tractor hours. Should these be charged in the budget? If the farm staff can find the time to cultivate and harvest the extra barley the answer is no, because the farmer has incurred no extra cost.* The net gain from growing five extra acres of barley is thus £170 less £40 = £130 or £26 per acre. This difference is called the *Gross Margin* and is defined as: Output less Variable Costs = Gross Margin.

This gross margin is not of course pure profit. Taking the farm as a whole, about two-thirds of the gross margin is likely to be swallowed up by fixed costs. None the less, the gross margin represents the contribution made by a farm enterprise to these overhead costs. It also shows the gain or loss that can be expected if the enterprise is increased or reduced in size. The gross margin allows only for variable costs and there are occasions (especially if a large change is made to the farm plan) when the fixed costs do alter. But these are best considered for the farm as a whole and will be dealt with at a later stage.

CALCULATIONS OF GROSS MARGINS

1. CASH CROPS. Cash crops are comparatively simple.

Wheat (10 acres)

		£
Output: 280 cwt.		377
Less Variable Costs—		
Seed	£32	
Fertilizer	37	
Sprays, etc.	5	
		74
Gross Margin		£303

Gross Margin per acre £30·30

Potatoes (10 acres)

		£
Output: 80 tons		1040
Less Variable Costs—		
Seed	£258	
Fertilizer	123	
Sprays, etc.	26	
Casual labour (lifting)	100	
		507
Gross Margin		£533

Gross Margin per acre £53·30

* If overtime or an extra bonus were paid to grow this barley, this would of course be a variable cost and would be charged in the budget.

If the farmer had enough regular staff to lift the potatoes without hiring casual labour the gross margin would have been £63·30 per acre.

It is usual to treat grain crops (and indeed any other crop with a recognizable market value) as a cash crop. If barley, for example, is fed to pigs its market value should be inserted as the output when calculating the gross margin for barley and as a food cost when calculating the gross margin for pigs. By giving the barley a gross margin on its own, the farmer can compare barley as a crop with other cash crops on the farm. By charging the pigs with the full market value, he can judge whether it is profitable to market his barley through pigs instead of selling it as grain.

2. LIVESTOCK

Poultry Flock (1000 laying birds)

		£
Eggs sold	. . . .	2950
Culls	. . . .	280
Total sales	. . . .	3230
Less chicks bought .	. . . .	200
Poultry Output	. . . .	3030

Less Variable Costs—

Foods	. . . .	£2190	
Medicines, etc.	. . . . .	40	
			2230
Gross Margin	. . . .		£800

The gross margin is thus £800 for 1000 birds or 80p per bird. The gross margin for pigs is calulated in a similar way. As neither of these enterprises occupies many acres, the return per acre is irrelevant. A better test is the gross margin as a percentage of output. In this case $\frac{800 \times 100}{3030} = 26$ per cent. A reasonable return for both these enterprises is about 25 per cent.

Dairy cows, beef cattle and sheep differ from these enterprises in using substantial areas of pasture and fodder crops, such as kale, silage or hay.* These crops usually have no recognized market value and it is convenient to regard them as part of the livestock enterprise. For this reason, their variable costs for seed, fertilizers, etc., are included in the livestock account.

---

* If hay is grown deliberately for sale, it should be treated as a cash crop. Otherwise, it should be treated as a fodder crop even if an occasional ton of surplus hay is sold.

Dairy Herd (20 cows and followers)

		£
Milk sold		2560
Culls, calves, etc.		210
Valuation increase		50
		2820
Less livestock bought		10
Dairy Herd Output		2810

Less Variable Costs—
    On livestock—

Purchased foods	£980	
Home grown grain (at market value) .	90	
Vet., dairy stores, etc.	186	

On fodder crops—

Seed, fertilizer, etc.	204	
		1460
Gross Margin.		£1350

If this herd requires 50 acres of pasture and fodder crops,* the return per acre is $\frac{1350}{50} = £27$. It is also useful to calculate the gross margin per cow, in this case $\frac{1350}{20} = £67 \cdot 50$. If the return per acre is too low, this is due to a low return per cow or because the fodder crop area is supporting too few stock.

BUDGETING. Having dealt with gross margins, it is now possible to prepare farm budgets. The purpose of a budget is to estimate the effect of some change in the farm programme (such as a change in cropping) or a change in the circumstances of the farm (such as a change in prices). If the change is an extensive one, a complete budget for the farm as a whole will be required. If the change is a simple one, a partial budget will suffice. The latter will be considered first. If a farmer is planning a change, he really has two questions to answer. Firstly, is the change likely to increase the farm profit? Secondly, if the change is worth while, how much capital will be required to carry it out? These two problems should be considered quite separately and care should be taken not to include "once and for all" capital costs in the profit budget. The example that follows will make this distinction clear.

* The acreage of cereal crops used is *not* included. As already mentioned, these are best treated as separate enterprises with their own gross margins per acre.

PARTIAL BUDGETING

There are many problems that can be set out in the form of a partial budget. On the whole, however, two situations are likely to be encountered.

1. INTRODUCTION OR EXPANSION OF A SUPPLEMENTARY ENTERPRISE. Some enterprises such as pigs or poultry can be introduced without displacing any other. In this case, the form of the budget is as follows—

Losses	*Gains*
Increase in fixed costs. Difference (if any) is the estimated increase in profit.	Gross Margin from the new enterprise.

As an example, let us assume that a farmer intends to keep a herd of 10 sows, selling porkers at 150 lb. live weight. The sows should produce 140 fat pigs of which three are retained as gilts; two fattening and one breeding pig die during the year. Housing includes a new fattening house, 4 farrowing pens and huts for in-pig gilts. Beef cattle on the farm have been reduced in numbers and the stockman can care for the pigs. He will be given a bonus of £50 for added responsibility. The gross margin is as follows—

		£
Sales—134 porkers at £13		1742
2 cull sows		40
		1782
Less purchases—boar costs £50, sold for £10 after 2 years, cost per year		20
Pig Output		1762

Less Variable Costs—

Food: 10 sows at 26 cwt. = 260 cwt. at £1·45 .	£ 377	
Boar 20 cwt. at £1·45	29	
Creep food: 140 young pigs at ¼ cwt. = 35 cwt. at £1·90	67	
Fattening pigs: 140 at 4 cwt.* = 560 cwt. at £1·40	784	
	1257	

Other Costs—

10 sows at £5	£50		
140 fatteners at 20p	28		
	—	78	
			1335
Gross Margin			£ 427

* Assume that pigs are weaned at 35 lb. and sold at 150 lb. liveweight; 115 lb. gain at a conversion rate of 3·8 is approximately 4 cwt.

The estimated gross margin is thus £427—approximately £43 per sow or £3·10 per porker produced. For all practical purposes, this is the gain per sow or per fat pig that the farmer can expect whatever the number kept—assuming that he can provide the housing and attention required. Having decided on the number to be kept, a budget can be prepared as follows—

Losses	£	Gains	£
Increase in fixed costs—		Gross margin of new enterprise 10 sows at £43 .	430
Fattening house (40 pigs at £18) . £720			
Farrowing pens (4 at £50) . . 200			
Boar pen . . 50			
Sow huts, trolley, weighing machine, etc. . . . 250	1220		
Charge 10 per cent a year for repairs and replacement	122		
Bonus to stockman	50		
	172		
Increase in profit	258		
	£430		£430

It thus appears that if the estimates are reasonable, an increase in profit of about £250 a year can be expected. Having prepared such a budget, the farmer can use it to estimate the risks that he might face if he introduced the pig herd. If pig prices fell by 5 per cent without a fall in meal prices, the profit would be reduced by $\frac{1762 \times 5}{100} = $ £88. If home grown barley reduced the cost of the ration by 10 per cent profits would be raised by £126 a year.

It should be noted that this budget shows the position say in two year's time *after* the pig herd has been established. The cost of erecting the buildings or of buying the gilts is not included because these are "once and for all" capital items. On the other hand, replacements for breeding-stock and equipment have been provided and for this reason the estimated profit can be maintained indefinitely provided that conditions remain as expected.

CAPITAL BUDGET. A capital budget is intended to show the amount of money that must be spent before the new enterprise is self-supporting. In this case, the farmer would probably buy the gilts two or three at a time spread over the first six months. This will make better use of the farrowing pens and will need less capital than if the gilts were all purchased at the same time. If the gilts farrow a month after purchase, the first sales will occur about six or seven months after the herd has been started and after this point the herd should be self-supporting. The costs for the first six months will thus be as follows—

	£
Housing and equipment	1220
Stock: 10 gilts at £40, 1 boar at £50	450
Working capital; food, etc., for half year . . .	670
Total capital	£2340

In fact, the allowance for food and other costs is slightly generous because the numbers of pigs are being built up during the first six months. On the other hand, a small margin of safety is desirable in case the first litters prove disappointing and the farmer has to wait longer for his first receipts than he expects.

It will be seen in this case that the investment is £2340 or £234 per sow—a much larger sum than many farmers would expect. The return on this capital is: $\dfrac{258 \times 100}{2340} = 11$ per cent. This return is not very high and the farmer in this case might consider whether some better system (e.g. by using home-mixed meals) could be devised before starting this new enterprise.

It will be noticed that the success of this enterprise depends on the fact that a stockman already employed has the time to tend ten sows and no more. If an extra pigman were recruited, it would be necessary to keep thirty or forty sows to pay this addition to fixed costs. In this case, the farmer might conclude that he should choose a part-time unit of ten sows or a full time unit of forty sows—any number between would be less economic.

2. SUBSTITUTION OF ONE ENTERPRISE BY ANOTHER. When dealing with cash crops or with cattle or sheep that require land for fodder crops then the expansion of one enterprise usually means the sacrifice of another. The form of budget is as follows—

Losses	*Gains*
Gross margin from enterprise displaced.	Gross margin from the new enterprise.
Increase in fixed costs. Balance (if any) = Increase in profit.	Decrease in fixed costs.

If the farmer already has the labour and equipment to deal with the change, there will be no change in fixed costs and the budget is a simple one. For example, a farmer intends to grow

10 acres of barley at the expense of oats. He has grown both crops before and can estimate their gross margins—

Losses	£	Gains	£
Gross margin from oats, 10 acres at £21 . . .	210	Gross margin from barley, 10 acres at £25 . .	250
Increase in profit . .	40		
£	250	£	250

In this case, the same equipment will do for either crop. But if the farmer must buy equipment, this is an addition to fixed costs. Assume that a farmer intends to grow 10 acres of potatoes (for the first time) at the expense of barley. He must buy a spinner and hire casual labour to lift the potatoes. The regular staff can deal with the planting and riddling.

Losses	£	Gains	£
Gross margin from barley, 10 acres at £25 . .	250	Gross output from potatoes, 8 tons at £13 . .	4
Increase in fixed costs, Spinner (£96) charge 12½ per cent for repairs and depreciation . . .	12	*Less* variable costs: seed, fertilizer, etc.. £40 casual labour . 10 —	50
	262	Gross margin per acre .	54
Increase in profit . .	278	Total G.M. 10 acres at £54 . . .	540
£	540	£	540

In this case, the gross margin for potatoes has been given in full because it is an estimate based on the yields obtained on neighbouring farms. The margin from barley is based on records from previous years. It appears, therefore, that if the estimates are correct and the farm staff can deal with the cultivation and other work on the potatoes, a change from barley to potatoes would increase profits by £278 or nearly £28 per acre.

A BREAK-EVEN BUDGET. This is a form of budget used when the farmer is uncertain about one item in the budget and wishes to assess the risks involved before he makes a change. Suppose that the farmer in the previous example is rather uncertain about the receipts that he can expect from potatoes, which appear to be more profitable but are also more risky than barley. The risk can be assessed by setting out a break-even budget. This entails a calculation of the return necessary to balance both sides of the budget. At this point there would be neither a profit nor a loss from changing from one crop to the other. In our example, losses on the left-hand side amount to £262. Thus if the potatoes had a gross margin of £262 (or just over £26 per acre) the account would balance and both crops would be equally profitable.

But if the gross margin is £26 per acre and the variable costs are £50, the corresponding output must be £76 per acre. This figure of £76 per acre is the "break-even" point. If the output of potatoes is more than £76, a change to potatoes would be profitable. If the yield is 8 tons, then any price above £10 a ton will show a profit. If the price is £13 a ton, then any yield above 6 tons would pay. With this information, the farmer can decide whether the odds in favour of making a profit are sufficiently attractive to justify the risk.

CAPITAL REQUIREMENTS. When one enterprise replaces another the capital saved from the enterprise given up may partly finance the new one. This is especially true of crop changes. The change from oats to barley shown above is unlikely to entail extra capital because the requirements for both crops are nearly the same. A change from barley to potatoes would require some extra capital as follows—

			£
Seed, fertilizer, etc., for potatoes 10 acres at £50	.	.	500
Less seed, fertilizer, etc., for barley 10 acres at £6	.	.	60
Extra working capital (for variable costs)	.	.	440
Extra fixed capital (spinner) . . .	.	.	96
			£536

The extra capital is thus nearly £54 per acre. This is a large sum but the extra revenue (£28) gives a return of over 50 per cent on the sum invested—a very handsome reward for the trouble and risk entailed. This is a change to a more intensive crop. A change to a less intensive one might entail a withdrawal of capital.

A change from one type of livestock to another can be calculated on similar lines to those shown for the pig herd, the working capital for the enterprise being set against the amount withdrawn from the old one. The cost of buildings and equipment for the new enterprise may be a heavy item, however, whereas equipment for the old enterprise may have very little salvage value to set against it.

CHAPTER 15

INTRODUCTION TO FARM PLANNING

IN this chapter we shall consider methods of planning the whole farm. Gross margins have already been described (Chapter 14) and used to prepare partial budgets for minor changes in the farm programme. Now they will be used to prepare complete budgets for major changes. Before dealing with the details, however, it is necessary to look first at the way in which a farm is organized and financed. It will be seen that gross margins and fixed costs can give a new insight into the way that a farm functions. Not only can they assist the farmer to frame a budget when he has decided on a plan but they can help him to choose for budgeting the plans most likely to be profitable.

Basically, the farm organization can be divided into three parts as shown in Fig. 27. Firstly, there is the farm land occupied either by cash crops or by fodder crops (pasture, kale, silage, etc.) supporting cattle or sheep. As the farmer has only a limited number of acres, these enterprises have to compete for use of the land and the more acres given to one the less there is for the others. So far as land is concerned, therefore, these are *competitive* enterprises.

Secondly there are enterprises, such as pigs and poultry, which usually occupy very little land. If the farmer has the capital and can provide the labour and buildings, pigs or poultry can be added to almost any farm organization without displacing one of the other enterprises. So far as land is concerned, therefore, these are not competitive but *supplementary* enterprises.

Thirdly there is the farmer and his men who supply the labour and equipment to tend the crops and livestock.

Having stated this proposition in concrete terms it can now be stated in financial terms (Fig. 28). Each enterprise—whether cash crop, cattle, sheep, pigs or poultry—has its own output and its own specific (or variable) costs. After paying these costs, each enterprise then contributes its gross margin to the central pool. From this central pool are deducted the fixed costs for regular labour, machinery, rent and other overheads. As already explained, these fixed costs are considered separately because they pay for services provided for the farm as a whole and not for any specific enterprise. On average, the fixed costs absorb about two-thirds of the gross margin, leaving about a third as the net profit.

Having shown the farm organization in this form it is now simpler to see how improvements can be made. We have two

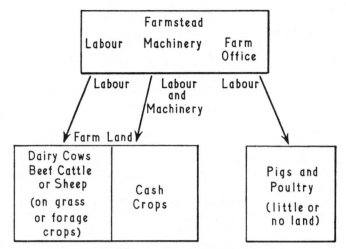

FIG. 27. THE FARM PLAN IN REAL TERMS

Each type of enterprise is provided with labour, machinery and other services.

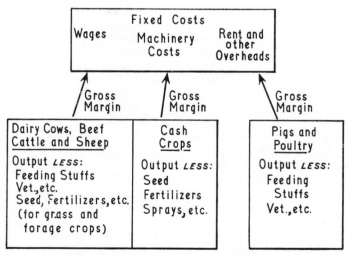

FIG. 28. THE FARM PLAN IN CASH TERMS

Each enterprise should contribute a gross margin to pay for the fixed costs.

propositions. So far as each enterprise (wheat, dairy cows, pigs, etc.) is concerned, its gross margin is—

Output *less* Variable Costs = Gross Margin.

Other things being equal, the higher the gross margin the better. A higher output will increase the gross margin—provided that variable costs are not increased or are not increased to the same extent. If a farmer obtains an extra £2 of grain an acre by applying £1 worth of fertilizer the gross margin is increased. But, if he needs £3 worth, the gross margin will be depressed.

Alternatively a reduction in variable costs will increase the gross margin—provided that output is not reduced to the same extent. If, by better rationing, a farmer can obtain a gallon of milk with 4 lb. of meal in place of 5 lb. the gross margin will be increased. These are all methods of increasing gross margins with improved techniques and better farming.

There is, however, an equally effective way of raising the total gross margin that is sometimes overlooked. A farmer can increase or introduce enterprises that give a high gross margin and reduce or eliminate those that give a low gross margin. In some cases, the choice is a fairly simple one. If barley has a gross margin of £25 per acre and oats has one of £20 then (other things being equal) the more barley and the less oats grown the better.

There are of course often limitations to the size of an enterprise and the farmer cannot always specialize on crops and livestock with the largest gross margins. Potatoes may give twice as high a return per acre as cereals but the area of potatoes is limited by the amount of labour that can be obtained to harvest them, by the risk of eelworm disease and sometimes by quota restrictions. Wheat may pay better than barley but be limited by the area that can be ploughed and sown by December. Dairy cows may pay better than sheep but be limited by the size of the cow-house. A farmer must also choose his crops to fit into a reasonable rotation. The usual restrictions are labour, buildings, capital, and the requirements of good husbandry. In spite of these, however, the farmer usually has a wide choice of alternatives and should use budgets to discover which is the most profitable.

Having dealt with the individual enterprises, we now turn to the second proposition. As already stated—

Total Gross Margin *less* Fixed Costs = Net Profit.

It follows, therefore, that the profit will be increased if fixed costs can be reduced. It must be stated, however, that direct reduction of fixed costs is often difficult to accomplish. The largest single item is labour and while there is often scope for saving man hours through mechanization or work study, the saving of enough labour to spare one man for the whole year may not be easy. Unfortunately, anything less will not reduce the labour bill. So far as machinery costs are concerned, every care should be taken to avoid extravagance because a large part of this item is for depreciation of equipment which has been bought in the past. The purchases may not have been justified at the time but they have been made. Depreciation will, therefore, continue until the equipment is discarded. So far as rent is concerned, once a price is agreed for a farm, it must be paid. Many of the minor overhead expenses, such as insurance, are inevitable and no large savings may be possible.

In practice, a much more fruitful course is to examine fixed costs not by themselves but in conjunction with the total gross margins. When this is done, profitability can often be improved by accomplishing one or other of the following—

1. An increase in the gross margin without an increase (or with a smaller increase) in fixed costs. Labour and machinery make up most of the fixed costs and having paid for them the farmer is entitled to use them fully. It is thus often possible, with careful planning, to intensify production with the existing staff. A farmer buys a sugar beet harvester to save labour and, instead of trying to reduce the labour staff, he uses the man hours saved in October and November to grow more sugar beet or potatoes or drill more winter wheat. Care must of course be taken when intensifying production not to create a seasonal peak that will overtax the labour force. Methods of avoiding this will be shown later.

2. A reduction in fixed costs without a reduction (or with a smaller reduction) in gross margins. This may be more difficult to accomplish but is sometimes possible. A cow-house for 40 cows employing two men might be converted into a yard and parlour requiring only one man. A farmer faced with the loss of an irreplaceable worker might manage to simplify the cropping so that the reduction in gross margin was less than the wage of the man lost.

To summarize, the questions to be asked in replanning a farm are usually as follows—

(a) Are the gross margins from each enterprise high enough? This is a measure of good farming.

(b) Which enterprises produce the highest gross margins and can they be profitably expanded? This is a measure of wise choice of enterprises.

(c) Can fixed costs be reduced? If not, can the programme be rearranged to give a better return from labour and machinery employed? This is a measure of good organization.

In the two examples that follow the first illustrates an increase in gross margins without an increase in fixed costs. (The increase in gross margins is partly due to greater efficiency and partly to a rearrangement of the cropping programme.) The second example includes both a reduction in fixed costs (due to mechanization) and an increase in gross margins (due to changes in the cropping programme).

EXAMPLE I

Farmer D has a dairy and cash crop farm of 120 acres. The dairy herd of 20 cows (housed in an old fashioned cow-house) gives 815 gallons a year and the cash crops include wheat, barley, potatoes and oats. The following is the rotation (9 course)—

Wheat (12)	Barley (12)
Oats (12)	Barley (12)
Potatoes (8) Kale (4)	Ley, 4 years (48)

There are also 12 acres of permanent pasture. The farmer

TRADING ACCOUNT*

Variable Costs		£	Outputs		£
Livestock A.I. . . .		30	Wheat		504
Feeding stuffs . . .		995	Barley		790
Seeds		397	Oats		306
Fertilizers		444	Potatoes		840
Vet. and medicines . .		34			
Casual labour . . .		80			2440
Transport		13	Milk . . £2707		
Contractor		168	Calves and cull cows 217		
Miscellaneous . . .		160			2924
		2321			
Fixed Costs					
Regular labour . £1150					
Repairs . £215					
Fuel . . 120					
Depreciation 380					
	715				
Rent . .	375				
Other overheads	255				
		2495			
		4816			
Net profit . . .		548			
		£5364			£5364

* To simplify the account, sales have been adjusted for valuation changes to give outputs. Grain fed to the dairy herd has been added to crop outputs and also to feeding costs—as if sold at market value by cash crops to the dairy herd.

employs a cowman and a tractor driver. The farm profit is £548, which is somewhat disappointing. The Trading Account is shown in a form suitable for calculating gross margins with outputs on the right and expenses (split into fixed and variable costs) on the left. Now suppose that the variable costs have been deducted from these outputs (the wheat crop, for example, being charged with seeds, fertilizers, etc., and the dairy herd being charged with feeding stuffs, seeds, etc., for fodder crops, etc.). A Budget for the Present Plan now appears with Gross Margins on the right and Fixed Costs on the left. It will be seen that the gross margins total £3043 and of this total £2495 (or 82 per cent) are absorbed by fixed costs. As already mentioned, fixed costs

BUDGET—PRESENT SYSTEM

Fixed	£	%	Gross Margins	£
Wages . . .	1150	38	Dairy herd . . .	1444
Machinery . .	715	24	Barley	566
Rent . . .	375	12	Wheat	392
Other overheads .	255	8	Oats	166
			Potatoes	· 475
	2495	82		
Net profit . .	548	18		
£	3043	100	£	3043

should not amount to more than two-thirds of the gross margins. Does this mean that the fixed costs are too high? Nearly half the total consists of the wages of two men. Could he manage with one? If he specialized either on dairying or on cash cropping, this might be possible but the farmer is reluctant to make so drastic a change. In any case, he is unwilling to part with either of his employees. The second largest fixed cost is for machinery. This amounts to £6 per acre, which seems reasonable for this type of farm. The rent is fixed and the other overheads are fairly small. Thus, although there may be scope for some savings in fixed costs, the amount is unlikely to have much effect on the profit.

Enterprises	Acres	GROSS MARGIN		LOCAL STANDARD
		Total	Per Acre	Per Acre
		£	£	£
Dairy herd . .	64	1444	23	30
Barley . .	24	566	24	26
Wheat . .	12	392	33	30
Oats . . .	12	166	14	21
Potatoes . .	8	475	59	56
	120	£3043		

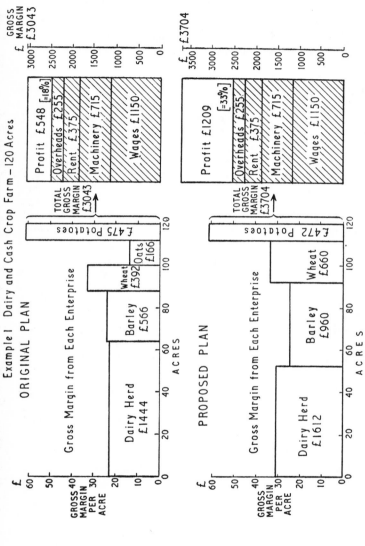

FIG. 29. ORIGINAL AND IMPROVED PLANS FOR 120-ACRE FARM

The weakest points in the present system are the low gross margins per acre for the dairy herd and the oats. In the proposed plan, improved pasture and food rationing increase the gross margin per acre and allow more land for cash crops. The oats are replaced by more profitable cereals. A larger total gross margin with no increase in fixed costs produces a larger profit.

If the fixed costs must be largely accepted, it is essential to increase the gross margins to carry them. At this point, the farmer calls in the District Agricultural Adviser (D.A.A.) and asks for help in replanning the farm. The D.A.A. sets out the margins per acre for the five main enterprises and places the local standards alongside. His comments might be somewhat as follows—

Your wheat, barley and potatoes give results which are fairly close to the average. Thus although some improvement is possible no large increase in revenue per acre can be expected. The oat crop (£14 per acre) however is far below average (£21 per acre). No doubt the yield could be improved but it might be better to change to wheat or barley, which usually give a higher return per acre. Even if oats are needed for feeding, it would still be more profitable to grow wheat or barley for sale and buy any oats required. The crop with the highest gross margin is potatoes (£59 per acre). Unfortunately, it is difficult to obtain casual labour to lift more than 8 acres. It may however be possible to grow more wheat, which is the best of the cereals.

By far the weakest enterprise is the dairy herd, which occupies more than half the farm and gives a margin of only £23 per acre. This is well below the average for dairy cows (£30) and below the level of most of the cash crops. If the gross margin per acre is low, this implies that the margin per cow is low or that too much land is being used per cow. The D.A.A. then calculates the following factors—

1. Acres of fodder crops per cow (including followers): $\dfrac{64 \text{ acres}}{20} = 3 \cdot 2$; Average $2 \cdot 6$

The cows are using too much land and this suggests that either the pasture or fodder crops could be improved.

2. Gross margin per cow: $\dfrac{£1444}{20} = £72$; Average £74, Good £90.

The gross margin per cow could be better. As yields are normal, receipts per cow should be satisfactory. This suggests that the variable costs (of which feeding stuffs are the chief item) may be excessive. On average, the cows are using 36 cwt. of concentrates for 815 gallons. This is equivalent to 5 lb. for every gallon. A ration of 4 lb. concentrates per gallon should be ample. Indeed less should be required because some of the production ration ought to come from the pasture and fodder crops. It should thus be possible to reduce food costs (£995) by at least one-fifth or say £200.

The D.A.A. then examines the pasture and suggests treatment, which includes the use of more fertilizer. If the pasture is improved, the present dairy herd should require fewer acres and the land released could then be used to support more cows or more cash crops. As there are no spare standings in the cowshed, more cash crops will be grown. If a three-year ley is grown in place of a four-year one, this will release 12 acres for cash crops and reduce the fodder crops to 52 acres.

If the pasture improvement can be carried out (and the D.A.A. is confident that this is possible), the new gross margin from dairy cows can be assessed as follows—

$$
\begin{array}{lr}
 & £ \\
\text{Gross Margin at present} \quad . \quad . \quad . \quad . \quad . \quad . \quad . & 1444 \\
\textit{Add} \text{ saving in concentrates} \quad . \quad . \quad . \quad . \quad . \quad . & 200 \\
\hline
 & 1644 \\
\textit{Less} \text{ extra fertilizer (on smaller area)} \quad . \quad . \quad . \quad . & 20 \\
\hline
\text{New Gross Margin} \quad . \quad . \quad . \quad . \quad . \quad . & £1624 \\
\end{array}
$$

G.M.: $\dfrac{1624}{52} = £31$; G.M. per cow: $\dfrac{1624}{20} = £81$

Acres per cow: $\dfrac{52}{20} = 2 \cdot 6$

These results are no better than average and should be attainable. The rotation will now be—

Wheat (12)	Barley (4) Wheat (8)
Barley (12)	Barley (12)
Barley (12)	Ley, 3 years (36)
Kale (4) Potatoes (8)	

Assuming the same gross margins for cash crops as before, the new budget is as follows—

BUDGET—PROPOSED PLAN

Fixed Costs	£	%	Gross Margins	£
As before . . .	2495	67	Dairy herd, 52 acres at £31	1612
Estimated profit . .	1209	33	Barley, 40 acres at £24 .	960
			Wheat, 20 acres at £33 .	660
			Potatoes, 8 acres at £59 .	472
£	3704	100	£	3704

The estimated profit is £1209, compared with £548 at present. Fixed costs now absorb only 67 per cent of the gross margin in comparison with 82 per cent before—not in this case because fixed costs have been reduced but because the gross margins have been increased. It may be of interest to add that of the increased profit of £661, 50 per cent is due to the improved pasture and the release of 12 acres to cash crops, 30 per cent to better rationing of concentrates and 20 per cent to the change from oats to barley.

The exact profit figure calculated in such a budget should not, of course, be taken too seriously. There can be little doubt, however, that the revised programme is very much better than the present one—and this conclusion is unlikely to be upset by quite substantial changes in conditions. Indeed, even if profits were reduced by falling prices or rising costs, the improved programme would offer better prospects of survival than the present one.

QUESTIONS

1. Prepare a further plan for Farmer D on the assumption that he wishes to specialize mainly on milk production. His landlord is prepared to erect a modern yard and parlour (extra rent £250) which will allow one cowman to tend 40 cows.

2. Prepare a further plan for Farmer D on the assumption that he wishes to specialize mainly on cash crops. Dairy cows will be replaced by beef cattle, which give a gross margin of £15 per acre on the pasture and fodder crops used. Prepare a schedule of labour requirements to ensure that the staff employed can deal with the crops grown.

3. Which of these two plans is the more profitable? What change in milk (or crop) prices would be necessary to change the order of preference?

CHAPTER 16

PROGRAMME PLANNING

SO far, we have dealt with farm planning in a fairly simple manner. We have seen that farm income can be increased in a variety of ways. One method is to improve the technical efficiency of enterprises so that they have a higher return in the form of gross margin. A second method, where there is a choice of crops and livestock, is to rearrange the combination of enterprises so as to produce a higher total gross margin for any given input of common costs. It is this second method that will be examined in detail in this chapter.

Once a good plan is formulated, it is a simple matter to test it by preparing a budget. The difficulty is, how is the good plan to be designed in the first place? Even if the new plan is better than the old one, how can one know whether it is the best possible one in the circumstances? It is the aim of this chapter to demonstrate a logical system of rearranging the components of a plan so as to maximize as far as possible the farm income.

The first step is to make a list of the resources the farmer has in the form of land, labour, capital and buildings. The second step is to list the different crops and types of livestock that could be included in the plan, together with their gross margins and requirements of labour and other resources. The third step is to list the restrictions that apply. Sugar-beet may be limited by the acreage that the factory will agree to accept. Potatoes may be limited by quota or the risk of encouraging eelworm damage. The task is thus to choose the combination of crops and livestock that will maximize gross income within the limits of any restrictions that apply.

The best way to demonstrate the process is to take an example, and the one chosen is a cropping programme for an arable farm. To simplify matters, livestock are ignored, but they could be added as a sideline without greatly altering the optimum cash cropping programme.

It will also be observed that in the example given, the rules are strictly and even pedantically applied. For this reason, no plan is allowed to assume more resources than are available. In real life, a little more latitude can be allowed. If labour is short a little extra overtime may solve the problem. For teaching purposes, however, it is best at first to adhere rigidly to the rules. In this way the processes that mould an optimum plan can be much better appreciated. At each stage it is the return to the scarcest factor that counts. If *land* is scarce, the crop with the highest return per *acre* should be chosen. If October *labour* is scarce, the crop with the highest return per *man hour* in that month should be chosen.

Let us take a 300-acre arable farm. The crops that can be grown are wheat, barley, sugar-beet, potatoes, clover cut for hay and then for seed, clover cut for hay only, peas and beans. The labour requirements of these crops are given in man days for the six critical periods of the year when labour "bottlenecks" are most likely to occur. Early spring includes the sowing of grain crops; late spring includes sugar-beet thinning and other weeding. Summer includes hay and silage making. Early autumn includes the grain harvest and late autumn the harvesting of roots and the sowing of winter wheat. These six periods do not cover the whole year but it can be taken for granted that if the plan being tested does not require more labour than is available in these six critical periods, no difficulty is likely at any other time of the year. An estimate is also given of the number of man days of field work that a man could be expected to accomplish during the period concerned. The man days quoted do not account for the whole of the worker's time—an allowance has been made for time lost during bad weather (when crop work is impossible) and for the shorter working day (due to early darkness) in winter.

The periods moreover are not all the same length. Late spring, for example, covers the critical four weeks at the end of May and beginning of June when sugar-beet must be thinned. Late autumn covers about two and a half months from the end of September to the beginning of December. It is assumed in the example that sugar-beet is thinned by hand and harvested by machine. Casual labour is available to help to lift potatoes and this cost has been deducted from the gross margin for potatoes.

The next task is to list the restrictions. These are as follows—

Sugar-beet—maximum contract 50 acres.
Potatoes —limited by quota to 50 acres.
Cereals   —limited to 75 per cent of the arable land (225 acres) as a precautionary measure against disease. (Wheat limited to 150 acres.)
Clover   —limited for the same reason to one year in six (50 acres).

The common (or fixed) costs at present are—

Wages (5 men)   £4000.
Machinery   £3000.
Rent   £1800.
Other costs   £1000.

The aim is to produce a plan that will give the maximum profit within the limits stated without overtaxing the five men employed at any season of the year. As the common costs will not vary appreciably whatever the cropping programme, the greater the total gross margin the greater the profit. The aim is thus to produce the maximum possible gross margin within the limits of the land, labour and other resources available. It might be thought that the problem was thus simply a matter of growing the maximum area of crops with the highest gross margin. Up to a point this is true, but the choice is in fact a more subtle matter than this. Land is not the only resource being used—labour, for example, is also important and indeed costs more. It may thus be just as important to choose crops according to their return per man day as to their return per acre.

LABOUR REQUIREMENTS IN MAN DAYS

CROP	G.M. PER ACRE	EARLY SPRING	LATE SPRING	SUMMER	EARLY AUTUMN	LATE AUTUMN	WINTER
Sugar-beet .	£ 60	1	5	1	—	3	—
Potatoes .	56	2	¼	¼	—	2½	3½
Wheat . .	40	¼	—	—	½	½	—
Barley . .	36	½	—	—	½	¼	—
Clover (hay and seed) .	16	¼	—	1	½	—	—
Clover (hay only) .	10	¼	—	1	—	—	—
Beans . .	20	—	—	—	½	½	—
Peas (threshing)	10	½	—	½	1¼	¼	—
One man supplies .		42	36	31	39	49	41
5 men supply		210	180	155	195	245	205

Fig. 30. Labour Requirements for Critical Periods of the Year (Arable Farm)

The return per man day depends on the season. A farm might have ample labour in midsummer to make all the hay and do all the weeding required. An extra man day at that season would thus be of no value because the farmer already had labour to spare. On the other hand, there might be an acute "bottleneck" in late autumn when sugar-beet is being harvested and winter wheat sown. Indeed, if there is no other limit to growing a few more acres of sugar-beet or wheat, a few extra man days at that season might provide a substantial dividend in extra revenue. The farmer, for example, might have to decide whether to grow more wheat or more sugar-beet. As sugar-beet has a gross margin of £60 and wheat of only £40 an acre, sugar-beet might seem the obvious choice. If land is limited and labour is plentiful this might well be the answer. But if there is land to spare and labour is scarce, then the return per man day should take priority. In this case (*see* Fig. 30) three man days of autumn labour would enable the farmer to grow one acre more of sugar-beet. As this is worth £60, the return is £20 per man day. On the other hand, an extra man day would enable him to grow two acres of wheat worth £80—four times the return from sugar-beet. With labour scarce and land plentiful, wheat would thus be a better choice than sugar-beet.

PLAN 1 (FIVE MEN)

The first step with planning is therefore to set out the return per man day at the various seasons. This is done by dividing the gross margin per acre by the man days per acre at each season of the year.

RETURN PER MAN DAY

CROP	EARLY SPRING	LATE SPRING	SUMMER	EARLY AUTUMN	LATE AUTUMN	WINTER
	£	£	£	£	£	£
Sugar-beet . . .	60	12	60	∞	20	∞
Potatoes . . .	28	224	224	∞	22	16
Wheat . . .	160	∞	∞	80	80	∞
Barley . . .	72	∞	∞	72	144	∞
Clover (seed and hay) .	64	∞	16	32	∞	∞
Clover (hay) . .	40	∞	10	∞	∞	∞
Beans . . .	∞	∞	∞	40	40	∞
Peas	20	∞	20	8	40	∞

FIG. 31. RETURN PER MAN DAY AT VARIOUS SEASONS

The ∞ (infinity) sign simply means that if the crop concerned uses no labour at a particular season, labour is not limiting and the return would be unlimited.

It is now possible to prepare a list of priorities for each labour period and also for return per acre.

To try to settle priorities from seven columns simultaneously could be complicated. The task can be simplified by noting whether any of the periods given are not really limiting and thus not likely to affect the final plan. Looking again at Fig. 30 it can be seen that in winter $3\frac{1}{2}$ man days are needed for riddling and marketing potatoes. As 205 man days are available, this is enough for 58 acres. As only 50 acres can be grown, winter riddling will never restrict the area grown. As no other crop has any vital need at that season, the winter period can be ignored. In the summer period, there are 155 man days. This is enough to do the summer work on 155 acres of sugar-beet, 620 acres of potatoes, 155 acres of clover or 310 acres of peas. As these figures are far above the limits set, summer labour is not limiting and can be ignored. We are thus left with four critical periods—early and late spring, early and late autumn.

The next step is to set out the labour available in these periods and to consider which list of priorities should be used first. Any column can be chosen but for preference the first choice should be

PRIORITY LIST OF ENTERPRISES

CROP	EARLY SPRING	LATE SPRING	SUMMER	EARLY AUTUMN	LATE AUTUMN	WINTER	G.M. PER ACRE
Sugar-beet .	5	8	5	1 =	8	1 =	1
Potatoes .	7	7	4	1 =	7	8	2
Wheat . .	2	1 =	1 =	4	4	1 =	3
Barley . .	3	1 =	1 =	5	3	1 =	4
Clover (S) .	4	1 =	7	7	1 =	1 =	6
Clover (H) .	6	1 =	8	1 =	1 =	1 =	7 =
Beans . .	1	1 =	1 =	6	5 =	1 =	5
Peas . .	8	1 =	6	8	5 =	1 =	7 =

FIG. 32. PRIORITY LIST OF ENTERPRISES

the column that is likely to be most limiting. At this stage, it is difficult to be sure which this is, and when in doubt it is a simple matter to choose returns to land. No. 1 is sugar-beet, and looking along the top row in Fig. 33 it can be seen that there is enough labour in early spring to grow 210 acres, in late spring to grow 36 acres, in early autumn no limit, and in late autumn to grow 81 acres. The maximum possible is thus 36 acres. The labour requirements and gross margin for 36 acres of sugar-beet are thus written in the next line and deducted to show the amount unused and available for other crops (Step 1).

The second crop in priority is potatoes. Unfortunately, they use labour in late spring, and none is available. We therefore turn to the third crop, wheat, which needs no labour at that time. The maximum allowable is 150 acres and as there is enough labour to grow this, it is inserted (Step 2). The fourth crop is barley. The maximum area of cereals is 225 acres, and as 150 have been used for wheat, the maximum for barley is 75 acres. As there is enough labour for this crop, it is added (Step 3). There are now 39 acres still unused and as beans are next in priority they are added (Step 4). All the land is now cropped and the total gross margin is £11640.

It now remains to be seen whether any further improvement is possible. The two scarcest resources appear to be land and late-spring labour. As we have already selected by land priorities, it is worth considering whether it is possible to improve the programme by consulting the priorities in late spring. It may be possible to discard a crop with a low priority at that season in favour of another with a higher one. In late spring, the crop with lowest priority is sugar-beet. An acre less would release five man days. This would permit the growing of 20 acres of potatoes that

CROP (ACRES)	EARLY SPRING	LATE SPRING	EARLY AUTUMN	LATE AUTUMN	ACRES	TOTAL G.M.
						£
Available (5 men) .	210	180	195	245	300	
1. 36 acres Sugar-beet .	36	180	—	108	36	2160
Unused . . .	174	—	195	137	264	2160
2. 150 acres Wheat .	37½	—	75	75	150	6000
Unused . . .	136½	—	120	62	114	8160
3. 75 acres Barley .	37½	—	37½	19	75	2700
Unused . . .	99	—	82½	43	39	10860
4. 39 acres Beans .	—	—	19½	19½	39	780
	99	—	63	23½	0	11640
5. Discard—						
1 acre Sugar-beet .	1	5	1	3	1	60
39 acres Beans	—	—	19½	19½	39	780
	100	5	83½	46	40	10800
6. 18 acres Potatoes .	36	4½	—	45	18	1008
	64	½	83½	1	22	11808
7. 22 acres Clover (for seed) . . .	5½	—	11	—	22	352
	58½	½	72½	1	0	12160

FIG. 33. PROGRAMME FOR PLAN I

need only ¼ man day per acre. One acre less of sugar-beet means the loss of £60 but 20 acres of potatoes would bring in £1120. Unfortunately, there are no acres to spare. It might, however, be worth discarding the crop with the lowest gross margin per acre (i.e. beans) to make way for potatoes. This is done (Step 5).

The next step is to add the maximum acreage of potatoes. There is enough labour for 50 acres in early spring, 20 acres in late spring and only 18 acres in late autumn. In Step 6, therefore, we add 18 acres of potatoes.

There are now 22 acres unused. What crops should be selected? We have selected for return per acre and per man day in late spring. The next bottleneck is late autumn, when labour is now almost exhausted. Wheat, barley, sugar-beet and potatoes are all at maximum. The one man day in late autumn would permit 2 acres of beans or 4 acres of peas. The farmer decides that two acres of beans are not worth the trouble. Peas are less profitable than clover for seed. There is in fact ample labour to put the remaining 22 acres in clover (Step 7).

The total gross margin is thus £12160 and (apart from a switch from two acres of clover to beans, which would add a further £8) this is probably the best programme that can be produced. It will be noted that the first four relatively simple steps produced £11640 in gross margin. The final adjustments (Steps 5, 6 and 7) were more complex and added only £520. It is now possible to set out the plan in the form of a budget.

BUDGET FOR PLAN I

COMMON COSTS	£	GROSS MARGINS	£
Wages (5 men)	4000	150 acres Wheat at £40	6000
Machinery	3000	75 acres Barley at £36	2700
Rent	1800	35 acres Sugar-beet at £60	2100
Other costs	1000	18 acres Potatoes at £56	1008
	9800	22 acres Clover at £16	352
Net Profit	2360	300	
	£12160		£12160

The estimated profit is thus £2360, or £7·90 per acre. This is a reasonable but modest return. It should be remembered, however, that this is from crops alone. Such a farm would probably also carry a livestock enterprise, which would augment the profit.

PLAN 2 (FOUR MEN)

Suppose that this farmer is faced with the loss of one of his workers, who is about to retire. Labour is scarce locally and it will be hard to find a replacement. If he operates the farm with one man less, the cropping will be rather less intensive but, on the other hand, he will save the wages of one man. The farmer, therefore, wishes to know whether on balance he can maintain his profit with only four men. If not, then he must make a special effort to recruit another. The plan is constructed much as before except that less labour is available. Selecting as before first on return per acre, sugar-beet is the first choice. There is only enough labour in late spring for 28 acres of sugar-beet (Step 1). The four man days unused allow the growing of 16 acres of potatoes and then 144 acres of wheat (2nd and 3rd priorities).

As there is no labour to spare in late spring or late autumn, the only remaining crop that can be inserted is clover, and this is limited to 50 acres.

Labour is now exhausted at two periods, and 62 acres are left unused. For this reason, an attempt should be made to select for returns per man day at these periods. Fig. 32 shows that

CROP	EARLY SPRING	LATE SPRING	EARLY AUTUMN	LATE AUTUMN	ACRES	TOTAL G.M.
						£
Available (4 men) .	168	144	156	196	300	
1. 28 acres Sugar-beet .	28	140	—	84	28	1680
	140	4	156	112	272	
2. 16 acres Potatoes .	32	4	—	40	16	896
	108	—	156	72	256	2576
3. 144 acres Wheat .	36	—	72	72	144	5760
	72	—	84	—	112	8336
4. 50 acres Clover .	12½	—	25	—	50	800
	59½	—	59	—	62	9136
5. Discard—						
6 acres Sugar-beet	6	30	—	18	6	360
	65½	30	59	18	68	8776
6. 68 acres Barley .	34	—	34	17	68	2448
	31½	30	25	1	—	11224
7. Discard—						
12 acres Clover .	3	—	6	—	12	192
1 acre Potatoes .	2	¼	—	2½	1	56
	36½	30¼	31	3½	13	10976
8. 13 acres Barley .	6½	—	6½	3¼	13	468
	30	30¼	24½	¼	—	11444
9. Discard—						
1 acre Barley . .	½	—	½	¼	1	36
Add—						
1 acre Wheat .	¼	—	½	½	1	40
	30¼	30¼	24½	—	—	£11448

FIG. 34. PROGRAMME FOR PLAN 2

potatoes and sugar-beet are bottom of the list. A switch to one of the other crops thus seems desirable. None of the other crops uses labour in late spring. This period is thus not a problem. Attention should therefore be given to late autumn labour. The first priority is clover, but this is already at its maximum. The next crops in order of priority are wheat and barley. If one acre of sugar-beet were given up the loss would be £60. The three man days released would, however, allow the growing of 6 acres of wheat (G.M. £240) or 12 acres of barley (G.M. £432). A change to barley would seem to be advantageous. As there are 62 acres of land still idle, which could be put in barley, this would be made possible by releasing 6 acres of sugar-beet, which could also be put in barley, making an extra 68 acres. This has been done (Steps 5 and 6).

As this move obviously pays, it might be worth growing even more barley. There is no land to spare, but to replace clover (G.M. £16 per acre) with barley (G.M. £36 per acre) would be an advantage. The present area of cereals (144 + 68) is 13 acres short of the maximum and this could be put into barley. To grow 13 acres of barley requires three and a quarter man days in late autumn and there is only one day to spare. This is a trifling deficit but, adhering strictly to the rules, we should discard one acre of potatoes to release the extra labour needed.

It is now possible to prepare a budget for Plan 2 with four men.

BUDGET FOR PLAN 2

COMMON COSTS	£		GROSS MARGINS	£
Wages (4 men) . .	3200	145 acres	Wheat at £40 .	5800
Machinery . . .	3000	80 ,,	Barley at £36 .	2880
Rent	1800	22 ,,	Sugar-beet at £60	1320
Other costs . . .	1000	15 ,,	Potatoes at £56 .	840
		38 ,,	Clover at £16 .	608
	9000			
Net Profit . . .	2448	300		
	£11448			£11448

In comparison with the five-man plan, the gross margin has fallen by £712 from £12160 to £11448. With less labour, fewer acres of root crops are grown and there is a slight shift from wheat to barley to ease the labour bottleneck in late autumn. On the other hand, this loss is largely compensated by a saving of £800 in wages. On balance therefore the profit has risen by £88. The verdict is thus that if the farmer adjusts his farming programme, the departure of one man need not cause any loss.

PLAN 3 (FOUR MEN, MORE MECHANIZATION)

A farmer faced with the loss of a man might well attempt to compensate for this by further mechanization. Assume, for example, that he has taken the advice of the local Agricultural

Adviser, who suggests that the purchase of a larger sugar-beet harvester with a hopper would save a man day an acre and would add £40 a year to his costs. He adds that a precision drill and root thinner would save three man days an acre in spring. This equipment would add £60 to annual costs. It is comparatively easy to calculate the effect on the farm programme. We set out first the new labour requirements per acre and then the labour still unused in Plan 2. To this is added the labour that would be saved on the existing 22 acres of sugar-beet. There is now enough labour in late spring (at two days per acre) for an extra 48 acres and in autumn for an extra 11 acres. There is, however, another

	EARLY SPRING	LATE SPRING	EARLY AUTUMN	LATE AUTUMN	ACRES	GROSS MARGIN
New sugar-beet labour requirements (per acre) . . .	1	2	—	2		
Labour unused in Plan 2	30¼	30¼	24½			
Saved by machines (on 22 acres already grown) . . .		66		22		
Labour available .	30¼	96¼	24½	22		
Discard—						£
15 acres Potatoes .	30	3¾	—	37½	15	840
13 acres Clover .	3¼	—	6½	—	13	208
	63¼	100	31	59½	28	1048
28 acres Sugar-beet .	28	56	—	56	28	1680
	35½	44	31	3½	—	£632

FIG. 35. PROGRAMME FOR PLAN 3

way to increase the beet acreage. With the new labour requirements, sugar-beet now uses less labour (two man days) in late autumn than potatoes (two and a half man days) and provides £4 more in gross margin. As there is ample labour in late spring, there is nothing to prevent the farmer changing all the potatoes to sugar-beet. Is it possible to grow even more sugar-beet? The 22 acres already grown, plus 15 taken from potatoes, makes 37. As the maximum is 50 acres, 13 more can be added. The 15 acres of potatoes will release thirty-seven and a half days in late autumn, and adding this to the twenty-two already available makes fifty-nine and a half. This is enough (at two days per acre) for the extra 28 acres of sugar-beet.

Some small further adjustments are possible—the switching of 5 acres of barley to wheat or even the introduction of a few beans —but these will be ignored. A budget for Plan 3 is given. It will be seen that the extra mechanization has had a substantial effect and has enabled the farmer to specialize on sugar-beet. This entails some cost for extra sugar-beet machines, but the farmer can now discard potato machinery. On balance, profit has risen by £532 and is more than for Plan 1 with five men.

BUDGET FOR PLAN 3

COMMON COSTS	£	GROSS MARGINS	£
Wages (4 men) . .	3200	145 acres Wheat at £40 .	5800
Machinery . . .	3100	80 acres Barley at £36 .	2880
Rent	1800	50 acres Sugar-beet at £60	3000
Other costs . . .	1000	25 acres Clover at £16 .	400
	9100	300	
Net Profit . . .	2980		
	£12080		£12080

This example indeed illustrates clearly the economic effect of introducing machines. Much is written about the effect of mechanization on "lowering costs of production." In fact, mechanization increases costs. It is, however, worthwhile if it enables the same staff to increase output or a smaller staff to maintain the same output. The machine must, however, break a "bottleneck" that would otherwise hamper an increase in production.

RULES FOR PROGRAMMING

No very precise rules can be given and some trial and error is necessary to find the best way of solving a problem.

1. Set out a list of the limiting resources (e.g. land, labour at critical periods, space available for livestock, capital etc.).

2. Make a list of the enterprises from which a choice is to be made and the resources (land, labour etc.) that each one requires and the gross margin that it is expected to make.

3. Calculate the return (in gross margin) per unit of input (per acre, man day, etc.) to give a list of priorities.

4. Choose the resource that seems most limiting and insert the maximum number of units of the enterprise giving the highest return to that resource. Deduct all the resources required. Repeat with the next enterprise in order of priority until one resource runs out.

5. Fill up with any other enterprise not requiring the resource concerned.

6. Attempt to substitute one enterprise for another. Pay attention to the priorities for any other resource exhausted or in short supply.

7. Prepare a budget for the plan.

8. If the plan seems unsatisfactory, start again with a different resource. Change to a different resource after Stage 4 instead of Stage 5, or at any other point where there is an interesting alternative.

These are the rules so far as one can give them. It must be admitted that intuition and a flair for what is likely to work may be of more use in the final stages than any of the rules given. The list of priorities really applies only until some of the resources run out. After that point, it is the cross-substitution rate that matters. In other words, if land is available and wheat can be added, the gain is the gross margin (say £40 an acre). But if all the land has been used and wheat is substituted for barley (£36 per acre), the gain is only £4 an acre.

Some of the final substitutions given in this chapter may seem difficult to recognize. The following are a few of the typical solutions. Assuming, for example, that the problem is one of a cropping programme and that the main limitations are land and labour.

1. If labour is exhausted at one point and land is still available, then substitute a crop giving a high return per day at that period for one giving a low return—even if the gross margin per acre is less, e.g. 16 acres are unused and late autumn labour is exhausted. If an acre of potatoes (G.M. £56 per acre) is given up, it releases enough labour to grow 5 acres of wheat (£40 per acre). It would thus pay to discard 4 acres of sugar-beet—

LOSS		£	GAIN		£
4 acres Sugar-beet at £60	.	240	20 acres Wheat at £40	.	800
16 acres idle	. . .				
Net Gain	. .	560			
		£800			£800

2. If land is exhausted and labour is still available, the substitution should be in the opposite direction, i.e. substitute a crop with a high return per acre (the scarcest resource) for one with a low return per acre, even if this means the use of more labour (within the limits of the amount available).

3. If both land and labour are exhausted at one or more points, try substituting a crop with a high return per acre for one giving a low return. It may also be necessary to discard

another crop to release enough labour to make the change. Suppose in (1) above that land was not idle but under clover (G.M. £10 per acre) and that clover is discarded to provide land and sugar-beet is discarded to provide labour.

LOSS	£	GAIN	£
4 acres Sugar-beet at £60 .	240	20 acres Wheat at £40 .	800
16 „ Clover at £10 .	160		
	400		
Net Gain . .	400		
	£800		£800

This change is profitable because the gain from changing 16 acres of clover into wheat is greater than the loss from changing 4 acres of sugar-beet to wheat.

The example given concentrates on two resources—land and labour. It is, however, possible to programme with other resources if they are likely to limit the scope of any plan prepared. An obvious one is capital, and a farmer very short of money may have to make a difficult choice between enterprises and calculate carefully how to make the best use of the amount of capital available. It is even possible to programme for space in livestock buildings if there is very little available and the farmer can choose between different types of cattle or pigs or in-wintered sheep. The student should, however, be wary of including too many restraints. Capital can be borrowed and new buildings can be erected. It is thus best to plan first for the best and most profitable use of the land and labour available, without limiting capital. Then if the plan is promising enough and the farmer lacks only capital to carry it out, he should use the plan to convince his bank manager that he needs more capital and could make good use of it.

It is also possible to introduce livestock alongside crops in programming labour requirements. But while it is realistic enough to include fodder crops with cash crops because the same field staff probably attend to both, one must be cautious about including the tending of livestock in the same programme. To do so implies that labour is fluid between crops and livestock and that stockmen with an hour to spare can spend the time cultivating a field and that tractor men can similarly come in to feed livestock. Many small farmers do, in fact, switch from crops to livestock in this way, but on a large farm where workers tend to be specialists this is not very practical. In this case the livestock and crops should be programmed for labour as separate units.

Another point is worth emphasis. The programming in this

chapter has been conducted as a game with exact quantities of resources and rigidly precise constraints. Even so, the answers given are quite realistic; indeed there are many arable farms whose basic plan closely resembles them. It must be admitted, however, that farming is less predictable than these planning exercises seem to imply. Risk and uncertainty are inevitable but this is no reason for failing to plan to make the best use of the resources available. The standards being produced for work of this kind usually have a margin of safety built in. The labour days available, for example, include an allowance for bad weather, and if conditions are unusually bad more overtime may be worked.

In practice, however, it is not necessary to be so pedantically exact as in the exercises in this chapter. An experienced Agricultural Adviser faced with a labour bottleneck in a plan may avoid the necessity of cutting down on a profitable crop by suggesting some new machine or a better work method. Nevertheless, for teaching purposes, practice with a model such as that used in this instance is an excellent education in the economic forces that determine the profitability of alternative plans. To begin with, the rules should be adhered to precisely. As practice is gained, however, they can be relaxed.

LINEAR PROGRAMMING

In the account of programme planning given in this chapter, only a few variables were handled at one time—mostly five crops and four time periods to which the labour requirements had to be fitted. While a matrix of up to about 5 × 5 can be done by hand and can be used to solve a number of interesting problems, anything more complex would be beyond the hand methods described above. In deciding on the optimum organization of a farm, there might be more crops to choose from and some of the crops might have alternatives, e.g. lift sugar-beet by machine, by hand or by contractor. With livestock there might be several methods of feeding using either hay, silage, fodder roots or sugar-beet tops, and for concentrates there might be the alternatives of buying or using home-grown grain. There might also be numerous restrictions, e.g. that only one third of sugar-beet can be harvested in time for winter wheat, or that potatoes cannot be grown more than one year in three. These complications can easily raise a matrix to 30 or 40 enterprises and a similar number of restrictions. Such a problem can be solved with a computer and a technique known as linear programming.

Linear programming can be used to solve problems on individual farms. It can also be used to answer more general problems such as the optimum system for farms in an area. The purpose of such an investigation is not to produce a blue print to which all farms should conform; each holding has peculiarities that affect its own best programme. A general study of this kind can, however, indicate the general direction in which farm systems might be guided. The same technique can also be used to show the changes in the farming system that should follow from changes in conditions—in prices, supply of labour, technical improvements and the like. The technique can also be used to determine the optimum size of holding for a family farm. These are only a few of the uses now being found for the technique of linear programming in farming. There can be little doubt that its use will extend.

QUESTIONS

1. Try the following variations on the four-man plan—

    (a) A six course rotation—wheat, wheat, barley, barley, barley, break (clover, legumes or roots).

    (b) No limit on cereals. If your plan shows an increased profit (at existing yields), how much would cereal yields have to fall before this plan no longer pays?

2. Try a three-man plan—

    (a) With standards as in Plan 1.

    (b) With labour-saving sugar-beet machinery. As cereals are likely to be important, is it worth starting to select by returns per man day in early autumn?

3. Try the effect of (a) the improved beet-harvester alone in Plan 3, (b) the precision drill and thinner alone. Compare these results with both machines together. Repeat with five men and six men.

4. Try a two-man plan—

    (a) With standards as in Plan 1.

    (b) With improved sugar-beet machinery.

    (c) With a large combine harvester that saves a quarter man day per acre in early autumn.

CHAPTER 17

PLANNING A LIVESTOCK FARM

IT is sometimes said that gross margins are less useful on a livestock than on an arable farm. On an arable farm, there are usually a number of crops from which to choose and gross margins are obviously useful in deciding which to include in the rotation. On a livestock farm, by contrast, the choice may be far more limited. Sometimes, as on a mountain sheep farm, this is because there is no real alternative. Sometimes, as on a dairy farm, it is because a unit large enough to employ labour efficiently may force the farmer into specialization, leaving little room for anything else on the farm. But if the choice is very limited, what part can gross margins play in improving farm management?

The answer is that gross margins are just as useful as a guide to planning as on arable farms. There is, however, a change in emphasis. On an arable farm the problem is *what* to produce and *how much* of each enterprise. On a livestock farm what to produce may be obvious and the problem in planning is *how* to produce it. In other words, the emphasis is not on choosing between gross margins but on the size of the gross margin itself. Farm improvement is thus concerned with the internal organization of the enterprise chosen. On a grassland farm with a high rainfall and good dairy buildings, dairy cows may obviously be the most profitable enterprise. But within a dairying enterprise there is a wide choice of methods of feeding, housing and management, and each of these affects the size of the gross margin. Indeed, one could even regard different dairy systems as alternative enterprises within which to make a choice.

As already stated, the gross margin from livestock is—

Output less

(a) Variable cost of livestock, e.g. purchased feeding-stuffs, veterinary charges, medicines etc.

(b) Variable costs of fodder crops, e.g. seeds, fertilizers, sprays etc.

It will be seen that there are two kinds of variable costs—animal costs that vary with the number of animals, and crop costs that vary with the acreage of fodder crops. In planning, it is usually worth keeping these separate because stock numbers can be altered without changing the fodder crops and vice versa.

For example, the gross margin of a herd of 30 dairy cows and followers might be shown as follows—

		£	£
Output (milk, calves, cull cows, *less* replacements)			4500
Less animal variable costs—			
Concentrates		1400	
Vet, A.I., dairy stores etc. .		300	
			1700
Gross margin (without forage costs)			£2800

$$\text{Gross margin per cow } \frac{2800}{30} = £93$$

The next point to calculate is the return per acre. Suppose that these cows utilize—

Grazing	.	.	.	.	30 acres
Hay and silage	.	.	.	40 acres
Kale .	.	.	.	.	5 acres
Cereals	.	.	.	.	5 acres
					80 acres

The cows thus use the produce of 80 acres and it would be possible to calculate the gross margin per acre from the whole of this area. The convention, however, is to include only the acreage of pasture, and fodder crops such as pasture, hay, silage, kale and roots. The acreage of cereals used is omitted. The reason is that cereal crops are usually cash crops in their own right and it is a simple matter to calculate a separate gross margin for them. There is indeed nothing to be gained by including the profit from growing cereals with the dairy herd. The cereal crop is therefore credited with the market value of the crop grown and the dairy cows must "buy" the cereals they use at this market price. There is the further point that the farmer has the choice of using home-grown cereals or selling them and buying dairy meal. The implications of the choice are much clearer if the cereals are treated as a separate enterprise.

Assuming that the variable costs (seed, fertilizer etc.) for the pasture, hay, silage and kale are £400, the calculation of Gross Margin is completed as follows—

			£
G.M. (without forage costs)	.	.	.	2800
Variable costs of forage crops .	.	.	400
G.M. (including forage costs) .	.	.	2400
Area utilized—75 acres			

$$\text{G.M. per acre } \frac{2400}{75} = £32.$$

This means that if we regard the cows, young stock and fodder crops as a single unit, the gross margin is £32 per "acre of cows."

The examination of such a cost structure shows how gross margins can be improved. Gross Margin *per acre* depends on the gross margin per cow, the stocking rate and (to a minor extent) on the forage costs. The gross margin per cow in turn depends on the output per cow and the deductions for animal variable costs, especially for concentrates. A rough estimate of the relative importance of these items can be gained by showing the effect on gross margin per acre of improving each factor (reducing costs, increasing output or stocking rate) by 10 per cent—

				INCREASED G.M. PER ACRE £
10% higher stocking rate	.	.	.	3·20
10% higher output per cow	.	.	.	4·50
10% less concentrates	.	.	.	1·90
10% less fodder costs	.	.	.	0·50
10% less other variable costs	.	.	.	0·40

It is thus apparent that stocking rate and output per cow, followed by the cost of purchased concentrates, are by far the most important items; the others are of negligible importance. This fact is illustrated for dairy cows, but similar conclusions can be drawn from a study of beef cattle and sheep. Concentrates in these latter enterprises may be relatively less important and stocking rate more so, but by and large the same factors operate.

It will also be observed that of the original output of dairy cows, nearly half is absorbed by variable costs. An increase of 20 per cent in variable costs would thus reduce gross margins by 18 per cent. This is quite different from cash crops. Cereals, for example, with an output of £40 an acre might have variable costs of only £8. Thus an increase of 20 per cent in variable costs would reduce the gross margin by only 5 per cent. With cash crops, therefore, output or yield per acre is all important. A high-yielding crop usually has a high gross margin and a low-yielding one, a low gross margin.* With livestock, yield per head is only one of several factors affecting gross margins, of which stocking rate and efficiency in the use of feeding-stuffs are the most important. The gross margin from a high-yielding dairy herd, for example, can be quite low owing to extravagant use of feeding-stuffs, and a moderate-yielding one can have a high gross margin because feeding costs are cut to a minimum.

---

* A high-yielding crop (e.g. potatoes) can, of course, have a low Gross Margin if casual labour costs are excessive.

It is thus worth listing the most important factors determining the gross margin per acre from dairy cows, beef cattle and sheep—

Output per head
Stocking rate
Efficiency in use of feeding-stuffs
Availability of by-products.

OUTPUT PER HEAD. Other things being equal, the greater the output per head the better. High yields in the case of cows and rapid growth in the case of fattening animals is important for two reasons. Firstly, food required for maintenance is an overhead that has to be paid for by production. For this reason a bullock that gains 100 lb. in 50 instead of 70 days saves the cost of 20 days' maintenance. Secondly, livestock on hand occupy land and buildings and tie down capital. The more rapid the turnover, therefore, the greater the return per unit of land, buildings and capital.

STOCKING RATE. This point has already been illustrated in the case of dairy cows. The relative importance of stocking rate and output can be illustrated with sheep. The table below shows the gross margin per acre on arable farms in Eastern England with varying lambing rates (output) from 110 to 170 lambs per 100 ewes. The stocking rate varies from two to four ewes per acre.

GROSS MARGIN PER ACRE*

LAMBS PER 100 EWES	EWES PER ACRE		
	2	3	4
	£	£	£
110	8·10	12·30	16·40
130	9·60	14·30	19·40
150	11·10	16·80	22·50
170	12·80	19·10	25·50

* B. G. Jackson: *Economic Position of Sheep*, Cambridge.

As can be seen, an increase in ewes per acre from two to four and in lambing rate from 110 per cent to 170 per cent trebles the G.M. per acre from £8·10 to £25·50 per acre. The relative importance of these two factors in raising G.M. per acre can, however, be assessed by noting that with 3 ewes per acre the G.M. per acre can be raised from £12·30 to £19·10 per acre by increasing the lambing rate from 110 per cent to 170 per cent—a quite formidable task. Almost exactly the same result could be obtained (with 170 per cent lambs) by improving the pasture and increasing the stocking rate from 2 to 3 ewes per acre. This is a much simpler task than that of increasing the lamb crop and serves to emphasize the importance of improving grassland and fodder crops.

If one type of stock is kept, the calculation of gross margin per acre is a comparatively simple matter. A complication arises however when two types of stock, e.g. cattle and sheep, share the same pasture or fodder crops. One way is to attempt to allocate the acreage used and the fodder costs between them by calculating the number of animal units for each enterprise and dividing the fodder costs in proportion. If only a few acres are shared, this may be a reasonable solution. But if most of the fodder crops and pasture are shared, a small error in estimation can tilt the balance quite unfairly between the two enterprises. A better way in such a case is to admit that we are dealing with a joint enterprise and present the results as such. Suppose, for example, that a farmer has a herd of 30 cows and a flock of 150 ewes sharing 150 acres. The procedure is to calculate the gross margin in two stages, first deducting livestock variable costs from the cows and ewes separately and then deducting fodder crop variable costs from both together.

STAGE 1

	Cows			*Sheep*	
30 cows and followers			150 ewes		
		£			£
Output		4500			1425
Less animal variable costs—					
Concentrates . .	£1800			£150	
Vet, miscellaneous .	300			75	
		2100			225
G.M. (without forage costs) .	£2400				£1200
i.e. £80 per cow			i.e. £8 per ewe		

STAGE 2

JOINT ENTERPRISE

							£
Cows .	.	.	.	.	.	.	2400
Sheep .	.	.	.	.	.	.	1200
Total G.M. (without fodder costs) .					.	.	3600
Less fodder costs .	.	.	.		.	.	525
G.M. (with fodder costs)			.	.	.		£3075

i.e. $\pounds\dfrac{3075}{150} = \pounds20\cdot50$ per acre.

At Stage 1 the gross margin (without fodder costs) is £80 per cow and £8 per ewe. This means a loss of £80 for every cow removed from the enterprise and (provided the fodder crops can carry it) a gain of £80 for every cow added. For sheep, the corresponding figure is £8 a head. The joint enterprise has a gross margin of £20·50 an acre for the area devoted to pasture and fodder crops such as silage, hay, kale, mangolds, etc. This figure of £20·50 can then be compared with cash crops or beef cattle or any other alternative enterprise. Having set the information out in this form it is easy to see how the total G.M. per acre can be altered by making adjustments. Suppose we wish to substitute cows for sheep. If 10 cows displace 60 ewes, then the effect would be—

		£
Gain: 10 cows at £80	. . .	800
Loss: 60 ewes at £8 .	. . .	480
Net Gain		£320

As the fodder costs are unchanged, the gain on balance would be £320. It will be seen that cows (£80 each) have a gross margin (without fodder costs) ten times as great as sheep (£8). Thus, if an extra cow displaces ten ewes, the margin would remain unchanged. But if a cow displaces fewer than ten ewes, then the gain from the cows will more than offset the loss from the sheep. In such a situation, it would pay to change over entirely to dairy cows. In practice, however, such a substitution may be limited by lack of dairy buildings or shortage of labour. If so, the best solution is to stock up with cows to the limit and use the remaining fodder acreage for sheep.

The effect of changing the livestock density can also be calculated quite easily. Suppose that by spending £300 more on fertilizer the farmer could carry 5 more cows and 15 more ewes on the same area of fodder crops as before—

		G.M. £
35 cows at £80 .	. . . .	2800
165 ewes at £8 .	. . . .	1320
G.M. (without fodder costs)	. .	£4120
Fodder costs (£525 + 300)	. .	825
Gross Margin		£3295

i.e. $\dfrac{3295}{150} = £22$ per acre.

The new gross margin of £22 per acre is £1·50 more than before.

THE FOOD CONVERSION RATE depends on a variety of factors. It depends on the environment: cattle and sheep in cold and wet conditions use far more food for maintenance, leaving less for production. Food conversion also depends on the age of the animal: the amount of food consumed per 1 lb. liveweight gain falls steadily as the animal grows older. For this reason, it may pay to fatten a young animal on a concentrated and expensive diet and to stop before the conversion rate rises too high. This is the basis of systems such as barley beef.

Individual animals also vary greatly in their ability to convert food into liveweight gain. It is to some extent an inherited characteristic. The ability to select stock likely to fatten quickly and efficiently is thus an important element in success.

AVAILABILITY OF BY-PRODUCTS. In calculating gross margin per acre from cattle and sheep it is customary to count only the acres used primarily by them, i.e. pasture and fodder crops. It is not usual to include the acreage of cash crops from which they derive sugar-beet tops, residues of vegetable crops, or aftermath from grass seed crops. (These acres have already been counted in calculating the gross margins per acre from cash crops and should not be counted again.) A small sheep flock on an arable farm with a large supply of such by-products may thus obtain a substantial "bonus" of fodder at no cost in money or acres. In these conditions, the cattle and sheep are "charged" only with the few acres of pasture and fodder they use exclusively. In consequence the return from these acres may be £30 or £40 an acre or more.

It might seem fairer in such a case to apportion the acres from which the sheep obtain by-products between cash crops and sheep. It should be remembered, however, that if there had been no sheep these by-products would not have been used. The return from the sheep as calculated thus measures their contribution to the total gross margin of the farm.

One word of warning should, however, be added. The high gross margin per acre applies only within the limit of the by-products available. If existing stock are using all the by-products and the farmer introduced more cattle or sheep, they would require a full complement of grazing and fodder crops to sustain them. The extra stock might thus produce a much lower gross margin per acre than the original livestock.

Another point of importance is competition between dairy cows on the one hand and beef cattle and sheep on the other. As already mentioned, beef cattle and sheep commonly show a gross

margin per acre of £10 or £15 compared with £25 to £35 from
dairy cows. On what grounds, therefore, can one justify cattle or
sheep when dairy cows could be kept? The answer is that dairy
cows also require more specialized buildings and specialized
labour than do cattle and sheep. Thus although dairy cows have
a higher gross margin per acre than cattle and sheep, they also
require more common costs for labour and buildings. Therefore,
unless the buildings are already available or the enterprise is large
enough to justify their erection and the employment of full-time
cowmen, the extra fixed costs of introducing dairy cows would
offset the higher gross margin per acre. There is also the consideration that dairy cows require far more care and attention
and much longer hours of work than beef cattle.

The point about size of enterprise can be illustrated by a simple
example. Suppose that a farmer has 50 acres devoted to beef
cattle managed part time by the field staff.

		TOTAL G.M.
		£
(a)	50 acres beef cattle at £12 . .	600

If the farmer changed this to twenty dairy cows, employing a
cowman and altering the buildings to suit, the result might be—

			£
(b)	50 acres dairy cows at £30 . .		1500
	less cowman . . .	850	
	alterations (20 cows at £8) .	160	
			1010
	G.M. less extra common costs .		£490

The dairy cows thus contribute a net addition of £490, which is
substantially less than the £600 from beef cattle. On the other
hand, if 100 acres were available—

| | | £ |
| (a) | 100 acres beef cattle at £12 . . | 1200 |

If the 100 acres were devoted to 40 cows, one cowman could
still deal with them.

			£
(b)	100 acres dairy cows at £30 . .		3000
	less cowman . . .	850	
	alterations (40 cows at £8)	320	
			1170
	G.M. less extra common costs .		£1830

With 100 acres, the dairy herd begins to show a substantial advantage over beef cattle. It is obvious, therefore, that unless it is large enough a dairy herd is not worth while on a mixed farm, and small areas of pasture and leys are more efficiently utilized by beef cattle and sheep.

As already stated, the size of the gross margin from livestock can be changed quite markedly by the system of management. This point can be demonstrated in milk production. There are three main systems of managing cows. There are traditional dairy farmers, who make up the bulk of milk producers, and there are progressive farmers who concentrate on raising output with high milk yields per cow, or reduce costs by using improved pasture and cheap bulky foods. The gross margins that might be expected from these groups are shown in Fig. 36. After charging forage costs the gross margin per cow is £83 for the traditional herd, £100 for the well-managed, bulk-feed herd and £108 for the high-yield herd. Per acre, the figures are £42, £50 and £57 respectively. The young dairy stock give a gross margin of £35 per head for the whole rearing period of £14 per acre. Young stock, as might be expected, have returns per acre close to those for rearing beef cattle.

It now remains to give the return for a dairy herd as a whole and to show how this can be influenced by the system of management.

DAIRY COWS	TRADITIONAL	BULK FED	HIGH YIELD
Gallons per cow	800	830	1020
Use of land—grazing . . .	0·8	0·6	0·7
hay and silage . .	1·0	1·2	1·0
kale etc. . .	0·2	0·2	0·2
Total acres per cow . .	2·0	2·0	1·9
	£	£	£
Output—milk	126	131	157
calf	17	17	17
culls (25%) . . .	14	14	14
	157	162	188
less replacements . . .	22	22	22
Total output . . .	135	140	166
Variable costs—concentrates .	36	22	42
vet, A.I. etc. .	6	6	6
G.M. (excluding forage costs) .	93	112	118
Forage costs . . .	10	12	10
G.M. (including forage costs) .	83	100	108
G.M. per acre	£42	£50	£57

YOUNG DAIRY STOCK		PER 3 YEARS*	PER HEIFER
		£	£
Per heifer calved: value into herd . . .		90	30
less calf		15	5
Output		75	25
less variable costs: concentrates . . £27			
miscellaneous . . 3			
		30	10
G.M. (excluding forage costs)		45	15
Forage costs		10	3
G.M. (including forage costs)		35	12
Acres used		2·5	0·8
G.M. per acre		£14	

FIG. 36. GROSS MARGINS FROM DAIRY COWS

* These costs are for the full rearing period of nearly three years. Alternatively, it can be regarded as the annual costs of a "rearing unit" of three young stock—calf, yearling and down-calving heifer, producing one heifer per year for the dairy herd. *One* young dairy animal thus costs one third of the above per year.

1. Average traditional dairy herd. Followers equal the cows in numbers, i.e. enough heifers are reared to replace 33 per cent of the herd each year.

	G.M.	ACRES
1 cow	£93	2·0
1 young heifer	15	0·8
	108	2·8
less forage, 2·8 acres at £5 . . .	14	

£94 ÷ 2·8 = £33 per acre

2. Farmer retains all the young stock, selling the surplus as stores or dairy heifers.

	G.M.	ACRES
1 cow	£93	2·0
3 young stock	45	2·5
	138	4·5
less forage, 4·5 acres at £5	22	

£116 ÷ 4·5 = £26 per acre

A large proportion of young stock reduces the gross margin per acre from £33 to £26.

3. Poorly-managed herd—uses 1 lb. concentrates per gallon more than No. 1 (say 8 cwt. extra at £1·40 = £11). Cow and follower use 3½ acres.

	G.M.	ACRES
1 cow	£82	2·5
1 heifer	15	1·0
	97	3·5
less forage, 3·5 acres at £4 . . .	14	

£83 ÷ 3·5 = £24 per acre

4. Well-managed, bulk-fed herd on productive pasture; three young stock to every four cows, i.e. enough to replace 25 per cent of the herd each year.

	G.M.	ACRES
1 cow	£112	1·4
¾ heifer	11	0·5
	123	1·9
less forage, 1·9 acres at £8 . . .	15	

£108 ÷ 1·9 = £57 per acre

As can be seen, better management raises the gross margin from £33 to £57 per acre.

5. A small farm. Standards as for No. 4 but the farmer rears no young stock. (G.M. per cow reduced by £5 to allow for extra cost of buying heifers.)

	G.M.	ACRES
1 cow	£107	1·4
less forage, 1·4 acres at £8 . . .	11	

£96 ÷ 1·4 = £68 per acre

6. Badly-managed herd. Yield 700 gallons. Farmer uses on average 4 lb. concentrates per gallon throughout the year.

	COW £		HEIFER £
Milk	102	Value	80
Calf	14	*less* calf . . .	14
Culls	14		—
	—		66
	130	Conc. and misc. . .	33
Replacements . . .	20		—
	—	G.M. (excl. forage) . .	33
Output	110		—
		G.M. per year . . .	11

			Acres
less Concentrates (25 cwt at			
£1·50) . . .	38	1 cow	3
Vet., A.I. etc. . .	6	1 heifer	1
G.M. (excl. forage) .	66		–
1 heifer . . .	11		4
	77		
Forage costs 4 acres at £2 .	8		
	£69 ÷ 4 = £17 per acre.		

The standards of management given above are by no means extreme. The yields from Nos. 1, 2 and 3 are 800 gallons, from Nos. 4 and 5 are 830 gallons and from No. 6 is 700 gallons. Many herds are better managed and give higher yields than Nos. 4 and 5. Many others are far worse than No. 6. Nevertheless, the gross margin per acre on the best (£68) is four times as great as the worst (£17).

This example thus emphasizes the point that within a single enterprise there are many alternatives and there is as much scope for planning on a specialist farm as there is in mixed farming.

EXAMPLE I

The farm is a dairy farm of 205 acres. The buildings are substantial but inconvenient. There are standings for 40 cows and ample space to rear young stock. Most of the farm is in grass but most of it could be ploughed. The farmer ploughs up 15 acres each year and puts it through a rotation of wheat, potatoes and kale, oats, long ley. Two cowmen are employed who also tend the young stock. The farmer does the field work and can replace a cowman on holiday. The cowmen help in the field when necessary. Casual workers lift the potatoes; a contractor bales the hay. Surplus young stock are sold as stores or heifers at varying ages.

The farmer has been making a bare living of £600 or £700 a year, but as the rent has been recently doubled, he has difficulty in breaking even. He asks the help of the local Agricultural Adviser, who begins by preparing a normalized budget of his present position as follows—

COMMON COSTS	£	GROSS MARGINS	Acres	£
Wages	1600	Dairy cows . . .	100	2404
Machinery	850	Young cattle . .	70	596
Rent	1000	Potatoes . . .	5	305
Miscellaneous . .	650	Wheat . . .	15	602
	4100	Oats	15	340
Net Profit .	147			
	4247		205	4247

The next step is to calculate the gross margins per acre and compare them with local averages—

G.M. PER ACRE

				THIS FARM	AVERAGE
				£	£
Dairy cows	.	.	.	24	31
Young cattle	.	.	.	8½	12
Potatoes	.	.	.	61	55
Wheat	.	.	.	40	35
Oats	.	.	.	23	22
Barley	.	.	.	—	30

Crops such as potatoes, wheat and oats compare favourably with the average. Oats, however, give a very poor return in comparison with wheat and barley and could be discarded. The gross margin from dairy cows (£24 per acre) and young cattle (£8½ per acre) are well below average. As the cattle account for over two thirds of the total gross margin, it is on them that attention must be focussed. If the gross margin per acre from cows is low, then either the margin per head is low or the cows use too many acres. The details of the gross margin per cow, taken from the farm records, were as follows—

PER COW

				£						£
Concentrates	.	.	.	39	Milk .	.	.	.	.	114
Replacements*	.	.	.	22	Calf .	.	.	.	.	7
Vet., A.I. etc.	.	.	.	10	Cull cows*	.	.	.	.	15
Gross margin	.	.	.	65						
				£136						£136

* Cow replaced every four years.

According to the Agricultural Adviser, £65 per cow is fairly typical of traditional herds but those with good grass and good quality silage attain £80. The yield of milk per cow is 830 gallons, which again is typical. The utilization of the forage crops is as follows—

ACRES

				Cows	Young Stock	Total
Grazing	.	.	.	60	40	100
Hay	.	.	.	32	28	60
Kale	.	.	.	8	2	10
				100	70	170

The amount of land used is—

	ACRES	ACRES PER HEAD	LOCAL AVERAGE
40 cows . . .	100	2·5	1·9
60 young stock . .	70	1·1	0·8

It is thus evident that the dairy cows are using too much land. A further point is that young stock have a much lower gross margin per acre than either cows or cash crops. It seems sensible, therefore, to reduce the number of young stock reared in favour of milking cows or cash crops. Indeed, the farmer might go further and dispense with young stock altogether and buy replacements. The farmer is, however, most reluctant to do so. With the prospect of losing one of the cowmen, the farmer asks the landlord whether he would be prepared to install more labour-saving buildings. The landlord is willing to convert the cowshed into cubicles and build a parlour for an additional rent of £400. This would raise the capacity to 50 cows, which could be managed by one cowman. About 12 heifers will be required each year for replacement. This could be supplied by 40 young stock.

The next step is to make a plan including the dairy herd of 50 cows. The Agricultural Adviser used the following list of requirements for a good bulk food system—

ACRES	FORAGE PER COW	YOUNG STOCK	TOTAL FOR 50 COWS	40 YOUNG STOCK		TOTAL
Grazing . .	0·60	0·45	30	18		48
Hay }					say	28
Silage } . .	1·10	0·33	55	13	,,	40
Kale etc. . .	0·20	0·03	10	1¼	,,	12
	1·90	0·81				128

Of this total of 128 acres, 116 are pasture or leys, leaving 89 acres for arable. The latter would fit a three-year shift of 30 acres a year. The first can be wheat (G.M. £35 per acre and the best cereal), the second can include 12 acres kale and the quota of 10 acres of potatoes. The remaining 8 acres of the second year and the third year (30 acres) can be barley.

Wheat . .	30 acres		Hay . .	28 acres
Barley . .	38 ,,		Silage . .	40 ,,
Potatoes . .	10 ,,		Grazing . .	47 ,,
Kale . . .	12 ,,			
				205 ,,

Average forage costs (fertilizers, seeds, etc.) are as follows—

Kale	12 acres at £8	. . .	96
Hay	28 ,, at £5	. . .	140
Silage	40 ,, at £5	. . .	200
Grazing	47 ,, at £1·50	. .	70
			£506

On average, bulk-fed cows have a gross margin of £80 a head (without forage costs) and young stock of £13 a head. On this basis, the total gross margin can be estimated as follows—

		£
50 cows at £80 .	. . . .	4000
40 young stock at £13	. . .	520
		4520
less forage costs .	. . . .	506
Total gross margin	. . . .	£4014

The gross margin of £4014 will be attained from the use of 127 acres, i.e. nearly £32 per acre including young stock. This seems satisfactory.

Average labour requirements in the area are—

MAN DAYS PER ACRE			EARLY SPRING	LATE SPRING	SUMMER	EARLY AUTUMN	LATE AUTUMN
Potatoes	.	. .	2	$\frac{1}{4}$	$\frac{1}{4}$	—	$2\frac{1}{2}$
Wheat .	.	.	$\frac{1}{4}$	—	—	$\frac{1}{2}$	$\frac{1}{2}$
Barley .	.	.	$\frac{1}{2}$	—	—	$\frac{1}{2}$	$\frac{1}{4}$
Hay (2 cuts) .	.	.	$\frac{1}{10}$	—	1	1	—
Silage (2 cuts)	.	.	$\frac{1}{10}$	—	$\frac{1}{2}$	$\frac{1}{2}$	—
Kale .	.	.	$\frac{1}{4}$	—	$\frac{3}{4}$	—	—
Pasture	.	.	$\frac{1}{10}$	—	$\frac{1}{10}$	—	—
One man supplies .		.	42	36	31	39	49

In this case, labour requirements (in man days) are—

				EARLY SPRING	LATE SPRING	SUMMER	EARLY AUTUMN	LATE AUTUMN
Potatoes	10 acres	.	.	20	$2\frac{1}{2}$	$2\frac{1}{2}$	—	25
Wheat	30 ,,	.	.	$7\frac{1}{2}$	—	—	15	15
Barley	38 ,,	.	.	19	—	—	19	$9\frac{1}{2}$
Hay	28 ,,	.	.	3	—	28	28	—
Silage	40 ,,	.	.	4	—	20	20	—
Kale	12 ,,	.	.	3	—	9	—	—
Pasture	47 ,,	.	.	5	—	5	—	—
	205 ,,			$61\frac{1}{2}$	$2\frac{1}{2}$	$64\frac{1}{2}$	82	$49\frac{1}{2}$
2 men supply		.	.	84	72	62	78	98

If one of the cowmen becomes a field worker, he and the farmer can deal with all the crop work. The following is a budget for this plan—

COMMON COSTS	£	GROSS MARGINS	£
As before	4100	Potatoes, 10 acres at £61 .	610
Extra rent	400	Wheat, 30 acres at £40 .	1200
Extra machinery (say) . .	200	Barley, 38 acres at £30 . .	1140
	——	Dairy cows	4014
	4700		
Net Profit . . .	2264		
	£6964		£6964

Wheat and potatoes are assumed to give the same gross margins as before; barley is inserted at the local average.

The estimated profit of £2264 compares favourably with £147 before. The success of this plan depends on—

1. An increase in cash crops from 35 acres to 78 acres.
2. Better utilization of fodder crops and grazing. This is a technical point and the Agricultural Adviser must decide whether this is feasible, and whether the farmer can carry it out successfully.
3. A reduction in the number of young stock.

This is not necessarily the optimum plan for this farm. It is, however, one that the farmer will accept, and that seems to be within his capabilities. The plan is given only in outline. Further discussions would be necessary on the details of feeding, improvement of grassland, design of the yard and parlour and the use of machinery. These are, however, technical matters that need not concern us now.

QUESTIONS

1. Produce alternative plans for this farm, including some of the following—

   (a) Assume no alterations to the buildings, one cowman tending 25 cows, the other helping with the cropping.
   (b) One cowman leaves and cannot easily be replaced.
   (c) The landlord will provide a larger yard and parlour.
   (d) The farmer gives up rearing heifer replacements.

2. A farmer with sheep on an arable farm was told that their G.M. per acre was £15 on land where he could have grown cereals with a G.M. of £35 per acre. He justified their retention on the ground that the yield of the two barley crops following the sheep was improved.

   (a) What increase in yield would be necessary to justify this argument? How likely is this result to be obtained?
   (b) Reconsider this proposition on poorer land with a higher rainfall. (G.M. from sheep £20 an acre, from cereals £28.)

CHAPTER 18

SPECIALIZATION

TRADITIONALLY, mixed farming was the mainstay of British agriculture. Diversification brought many advantages because crops and livestock were often complementary to each other, and advantage was taken of this in designing the traditional crop rotations. Cultivation of root crops eliminated weeds in the grain crops that followed. The grain crops in turn produced straw for bedding livestock and the farmyard manure produced enriched the crops to which it was applied. These considerations helped to ensure a mixture of crops and livestock on a farm.

There were other advantages in diversification. Bad weather or disease could wipe out one crop but the farmer who had several crops could hope that the loss on one would be made up by the gain on another. Mixed farming thus helped to spread risks. Exactly the same consideration applied to price fluctuations and the farmer could hope that if the price of one product declined steeply, others would remain steady or even rise.

On the other hand, there are advantages in specialization, and these are becoming steadily more important as time passes. The level of skill required for enterprises such as milk or fat pig production is continuously rising, and it is no longer possible to expect one man to be really expert in more than one or two of them. Specialized machinery and equipment is becoming steadily more expensive and requires a fairly large output to justify its purchase. In consequence, the farmer tends to drop small enterprises so that he can concentrate his time and resources on the remainder.

There is also the fact that scientific discoveries have weakened the technical advantages of mixed farming. Herbicides have made cereals a cleaning crop and the farmer need no longer include a root crop in the rotation merely to eliminate weeds. He can buy nitrogen as a fertilizer and need not grow clover merely to enrich the soil. Pests and diseases are under better control and the farmer can take liberties in growing one grain crop after another that would have been considered impossible twenty years ago.

One consequence of these changes has been to give the farmer far more freedom in choosing his crops and types of livestock. He can therefore choose crops and livestock because they pay, and for no other reason. Economic considerations are thus much more important in determining farming systems than was the case in the past. It is thus much easier to specialize.

If specialization is easier to put into effect, is there still any reason for maintaining a mixture of enterprises on a farm? So far as arable farming is concerned, there is another reason for diversity that has not so far been mentioned in this chapter. Different crops and livestock are often complementary in their labour requirements. Barley needs labour in early spring and early autumn, whereas sugar-beet needs it in late spring and late autumn. The two crops thus hardly ever compete for labour and the same field staff can deal as readily with both crops as with either separately. A carefully chosen mixture of crops can thus utilize labour much more efficiently than can one crop alone. Indeed, a large part of Chapter 16 was occupied in showing how to choose the optimum combination of crops for this very purpose. This is the chief justification for a mixture of crops under modern conditions and, as wages rise, it becomes steadily more important.

The next point to consider is: if some mixture of crops is justified, how many crops should be included? This is a point on which it is impossible to generalize because the answer depends on the circumstances. By and large, however, three to five crops are usually sufficient on a general farm to provide as reasonable a distribution of labour as is likely to be achieved.

So far as livestock is concerned, labour requirements are usually fairly uniform throughout the year. When this is so, one live-stock enterprise can utilize the time of a stockman efficiently without any need for diversification and, as a result, the stockman becomes much more of an expert. It is for this reason that the single enterprise livestock farm, such as the dairy farm or poultry farm, is much more common than the single enterprise crop farm.

The final point to consider is the extent to which a mixture of enterprises really does offset risk and uncertainty. So far as arable farming is concerned, two crops will be less risky than one if their yields or prices fluctuate in different directions so that the loss on one is compensated by a gain on the other. A wet August that spoils the barley crop might augment the yield of potatoes or sugar-beet in October. On the other hand, weather conditions that spoil barley at harvest time would also spoil wheat, and these two crops together might be nearly as risky as either separately. Some diversity is therefore justifiable, and this applies particularly to the fruit and vegetable producer because his prices and yields fluctuate so sharply from one season to the next. In general farming, however, fluctuations are less violent and the main crops have price guarantees. A large selection of crops is thus less neces-sary. Again it is difficult to generalize, but the three or four crops justified by the need to employ labour efficiently will generally provide all the hedging against risk that is profitable to pursue. To increase the number usually means the addition of enterprises further down the priority list in suitability and profitability. If so, the loss in profit can easily outweigh the gain in reduced risk.

On balance there can be little doubt that the tendency is towards specialization. The efficient use of labour and expensive equipment, the need for skill and the advantages of buying and selling larger quantities all pull in this direction. Some risk is inevitable, and the farmer must accept this as the price of efficiency, taking meantime such precautions as he can against loss.

The methods of planning for more specialization without sacrificing the advantages of diversification will be discussed in the examples that follow.

EXAMPLE I

A young farmer with 200 acres has a wide diversity of interests. As can be seen from the budget, he has ten enterprises. In addition to cereals, sugar-beet and potatoes, he grows two acres of vegetables on contract. He has a few cattle and pigs, and his wife has laying hens and turkeys. He employs one stockman and three field workers and works in the field himself. He has three problems to solve, however.

(a) Two of his men are leaving to work in a neighbouring satellite town and it is doubtful if they can be replaced.

(b) The canning factory have told him that they are no longer interested in two acres of vegetables—if the farmer wants a new contract, he must grow at least ten acres.

(c) In spite of satisfactory gross margins per acre, the farm is showing a profit of only £500 a year.

BUDGET OF PRESENT PLAN

COMMON COSTS	£		GROSS MARGINS	£
Wages (stockman, 3 field workers)	3300	55 acres	Wheat at £40 .	2200
		45 ,,	Barley at £35 .	1575
Machinery and fuel . .	1880	10 ,,	Oats at £25 . .	250
Rent	1000	15 ,,	Potatoes at £55 .	825
Other overheads . . .	760	22 ,,	Sugar-beet at £60 .	1320
	———	2 ,,	Vegetables at £70 .	140
	6940	4 ,,	Fallow . . .	—
		47 ,,	Cattle at £5 . .	235
			Pigs . . .	777
			Laying hens . .	80
Net Profit . . .	527		Turkeys . .	65
	———			———
	£7467	200 acres		£7467

An estimate of the labour requirements is given in Fig. 37.

The farmer decides that with only two workers he must simplify and streamline his farming. The enterprises to eliminate are—

(*a*) Those with a low return per acre such as oats, which compare unfavourably with barley.

(*b*) Those with a small return in relation to the time and responsibility required, such as the turkeys, laying hens and vegetables.

LABOUR REQUIRED IN MAN-DAYS

	ACRES	1 EARLY SPRING	2 LATE SPRING	3 SUMMER	4 EARLY AUTUMN	5 LATE AUTUMN
Wheat . . .	55	7	—	—	14	23
Barley . . .	45	22	—	—	11	6
Oats . . .	10	5	—	—	3	1
Potatoes . .	15	30	4	4	—	38
Sugar-beet . .	22	22	88	22	—	44
Vegetables . .	2	—	—	6	37	47
Fallow . . .	4	—	1	1	—	—
Leys . . .	12	3	—	12	—	—
Pasture . . .	35	4	—	3	—	2
Straw . . .	(50)	—	—	—	12	—
		93	93	48	77	161
3 men and farmer supply		140	120	120	120	160

FIG. 37. LABOUR PROFILE FOR ARABLE FARM—PRESENT PLAN WITH TEN ENTERPRISES AND FOUR MEN

It is also necessary to trim enterprises to be within the capacity of the labour that will be available. So far as crops are concerned a comparison of the present labour requirements and the amount supplied by two men is as follows—

PERIOD	1	2	3	4	5
Present requirements (man-days)	93	93	48	77	161
Farmer + 1 man supply . .	70	60	60	60	80
Deficit (−) or excess (+) . .	−23	−33	+12	−17	−81

The greatest problem is late autumn and the labour requirements must somehow be reduced. The largest items in Period 5 are the potatoes, the sugar-beet and the vegetables. If, as seems likely, labour in late autumn is the most limiting factor, then the vegetables and potatoes, which give the lowest return per man day, should go first. The farmer, also, prefers to discard potatoes rather than sugar-beet because potato harvesting gangs are becoming scarce. The discarding of the vegetables is in fact inevitable because the farmer cannot undertake the ten acres that the processor wants with only two men. If he keeps sugar-beet, however, he will mechanize the crop further to save labour. He will buy a precision drill and a mechanical thinner, which he will use once each spring, finishing the thinning by hand. This should halve the labour required in Period 2. He will also buy a tanker harvester in place of the present one. This should enable him to harvest with a gang of two instead of three.

If there are no potatoes, more cereals can be grown. Indeed, cereals should be pushed to the limit so long as they do not impinge on the sugar-beet. With a five course rotation—2 wheats,

LABOUR REQUIREMENTS FOR NEW PLAN (MAN-DAYS)

	ACRES	1 EARLY SPRING	2 LATE SPRING	3 SUMMER	4 EARLY AUTUMN	5 LATE AUTUMN
Wheat . . .	72	9	—	—	18	36
Barley . . .	72	36	—	—	18	9
Sugar-beet . .	22	22	44	22	—	28
Leys . . .	14	3	—	14	—	—
Pasture . . .	20	2	—	2	—	1
Straw . . .	(36)	—	—	9	—	—
	200	72	44	47	36	74
Farmer + worker supply		70	60	60	60	80

FIG. 38. LABOUR PROFILE FOR ARABLE FARM—IMPROVED PLAN WITH FIVE ENTERPRISES AND TWO MEN

2 barleys and a break—the labour requirements are as shown in Fig. 38.

The farmer has no definite cattle policy at the moment and he buys calves and store cattle whenever they seem cheap. The total gross margin from cattle however is only £235 for the use of 20 acres of permanent pasture and 27 acres of leys and fodder crops. This is a return of only £5 an acre, which is poor. A better enterprise, which would require very little labour, would be single suckling beef cows, selling the calves at eight months. This should give a return of at least £12 an acre. The cattle could then use the permanent pasture and such acres of the break shift as were not used for sugar-beet.

As can be seen, the new programme is within the capacity of the field worker and the farmer.

The remaining enterprise is the pig herd. At present, the farmer has 15 sows and he rears the progeny to bacon weight. The present gross margin of £777 is equivalent to £50 per sow. A margin of £777 is, however, insufficient to pay the wage of the stockman. If the farmer intends to keep the stockman he must either build up the pig enterprise to a full-time unit (say 40 sows) or discard it altogether. If the first step is to build the herd up to 30 sows this would require buildings costing £2000. At £50 per sow, the gross margin for 30 sows would be £1500. After paying £900 as wages to the pigman, the farmer would be left with £600 with which to build the herd up to full capacity. The budget for the new plan (including the pig herd) is as follows—

BUDGET FOR NEW PLAN

COMMON COSTS	£		GROSS MARGINS	£
As before	6740	72 acres	Wheat at £40 .	2880
less 2 men . . .	1600	72 „	Barley at £35 . .	2520
	——	22 „	Sugar-beet at £60 .	1320
	5140	34 ,	Cattle at £12 . .	408
Pig housing + extra for harvesting*	480		Pigs . . .	1500
	5620			
Net Profit . . .	3008			
	£8628			£8628

* 20 per cent of £2400—say 5 per cent for upkeep and 15 per cent for repayment of capital in 7 years.

The estimated profit is £3008, an increase of £2481 over the present profit of £527. It should be noted that the gross margins per acre are the same as in the original plan except for the cattle. The increase in profit is thus due mainly to a better organization. The necessary changes are—

1. Elimination of less profitable and small, time-consuming enterprises.
2. Expansion of cereals and pig enterprises.
3. Better deployment of crops to utilize labour, aided by the improvement of sugar-beet equipment.

EXAMPLE II

As has been shown, specialization can bring advantages to the farmer. It is not, however, an automatic key to success. Specialization must be in the right enterprise—in the wrong enterprise it can be disastrous. Properly used, specialization can produce savings, but equally it can bring increased costs for new equipment, and unless this is accompanied by improved technical efficiency the farmer can find himself in a worse position than before.

These points can be brought home by an example. Assume that a farmer has a mixed arable and dairy farm of 160 acres. He has a herd of 25 cows in an old-fashioned cowhouse tended by a stockman. He also has one field worker who deals with 90 acres of cash crops. The farmer helps with the cows or field crops as necessary. A budget of the present position is as follows—

BUDGET—PRESENT POSITION

COMMON COSTS	£		GROSS MARGINS	£
Wages (2)	1700	20 acres	Potatoes at £65 .	1300
Machinery and fuel .	1465	40 „	Wheat at £36 .	1440
Rent	800	32 „	Barley at £28 .	896
Other overheads . .	488	68 „	Cows at £26 . .	1768
	4453			
Net Profit . . .	951			
	£5404	160		£5404

The present profit of £951 is not enough and the farmer is anxious to increase it. The gross margins for cash crops and cows are quite reasonable for the area. The faults in the present system are, however, obvious enough. A full set of arable machinery for 90 acres of cash crops is uneconomic. A herd of 25 cows is too small to justify a cowman. It would thus be best to specialize in either cash crops or dairying.

Let us assume that the farmer decides to specialize in dairying. The landlord is prepared to convert the buildings to a labour-saving yard and parlour for 60 cows that can be operated by one man. The landlord expects an extra rent of 10 per cent on the cost of £4800.

PLAN I. SPECIALIZE IN DAIRY COWS

The farmer dispenses with the cash crops and the field worker. The entire farm will be devoted to pasture and fodder crops for sixty cows and followers. The farmer will grow the fodder crops and relieve the cowman when on holiday. The gross margin from dairy cows remains unchanged. It is assumed that with no cash crops machinery costs will fall by £500.

BUDGET FOR PLAN I

OOMMON COSTS	£	GROSS MARGINS	£
Wage (cowman) . . .	900	160 acres Cows at £26 . .	4160
Machinery	965		
Other overheads . . .	488		
Rent (existing) . . .	800		
Extra for new buildings £4800			
at 10%	480		
	3633		
Net Profit . . .	527		
	£4160		£4160

The result is a disastrous fall in income to £527. The reason is that the gross margin per acre for cows is less than for cash crops. Thus, although the wage of one man is saved in Plan 1, the returns from dairy cows cannot carry the extra rent and loss of cash crop revenue.

PLAN 2. SPECIALIZE IN CASH CROPS

The farmer specializes in cash crops and discards the dairy cows and cowman. The whole farm is arable and the farmer adopts a rotation of wheat—barley—barley—break. The few acres of ley support beef cattle or sheep with a modest gross margin of £12 an acre.

BUDGET FOR PLAN 2

COMMON COSTS	£	GROSS MARGINS	£
Wage (field worker) . .	800	40 acres Wheat at £36 .	1440
Machinery* . . .	1365	80 „ Barley at £28 . .	2240
Rent	800	20 „ Potatoes at £65 .	1300
Overheads	488	20 „ Leys at £12 . .	240
	3453		
Net Profit . . .	1767		
	£5220		£5220

* Assume a fall of £100 for dairy equipment no longer required.

The result is an estimated profit of £1767—£816 better than the present one. The reason is that the extra cash crops have a better gross margin than the cows they displace. There is also a saving on the wages of the cowman, who is no longer required. The weakest part of Plan 2 is the low return of £12 an acre for the 20 acres of leys. In time, however, the farmer and the field worker may be able to develop a more intensive beef cattle or other enterprise to increase this return.

The verdict is that the farmer is more skilled at arable farming than dairying, and if the whole farm is potentially arable, that is the line in which he should specialize.

PLAN 3. SPECIALIZE IN CASH CROPS

Let us assume that the circumstances are different. Forty acres of the farm are in permanent pasture and cannot easily be ploughed. If the farmer specializes in cash crops the pasture is put into cattle or sheep with a gross margin of £12 an acre. The rotation, wheat—barley—barley—break, is the same as in Plan 2.

BUDGET FOR PLAN 3

COMMON COSTS	£	GROSS MARGINS	£
As in Plan 2 . . .	3453	30 acres Wheat at £36 .	1080
		60 „ Barley at £28 .	1680
		20 „ Potatoes at £65 .	1300
		10 „ Leys ⎫ at £12 .	600
Net Profit . . .	1207	40 „ Pasture⎭	
	£4660		. £4660

The estimated profit of £1207, which is only £256 better than the present one of £951. The advantage of this plan is that the wage of one man is saved. The disadvantage is that by dispensing with the dairy cows the gross margin from 50 acres of leys and fodder crops has dropped from £26 to only £12 per acre. Specialization in cash crops in this case can succeed only if the farmer can find some more profitable use for the pasture—say an intensive beef or sheep enterprise.

PLAN 4. SPECIALIZE IN DAIRY COWS

If the farm has 40 acres of permanent pasture and the farmer, with no cash crops to distract his attention, is prepared to concentrate on improving the fodder crops and increasing the yield from 750 to 850 gallons a cow, it should be possible to raise the gross margin per acre to at least £35. Making the same assumptions as in Plan 1, the budget shows an estimated profit of £1967, an improvement of £1016 over the present level of £951.

BUDGET FOR PLAN 4

COMMON COSTS		£	GROSS MARGINS		£
As in Plan 1	. .	3633	160 acres at £35 .	.	5600
Net Profit	. .	1967			
		£5600			£5600

It is therefore evident that successful specialization is not simply a matter of dropping some enterprises from the farm system. It means concentration on an enterprise for which the farm or the farmer has some inherent advantage. A reduction in the number of enterprises does simplify management and the farmer should use this opportunity to concentrate his attention on improving the technical efficiency of the enterprises retained. In the example given, Plan 1 failed because the farmer concentrated on an indifferent dairy enterprise. Plan 2 succeeded because the farm was naturally suited to arable farming and the change was a simple one. Plan 3 was disappointing because the permanent pasture limited the cash crop enterprise. Plan 4 succeeded because the farm was suited to dairying and the farmer was able to concentrate on improving the herd and the fodder crops.

QUESTIONS

1. In Example 1, assume that the farmer will lose only one man and can obtain a contract for 10 more acres of sugar-beet. Prepare a plan.
2. In Example 2, assume that the farmer has carried out Plan 4 successfully. The pasture and fodder crops have been improved and he finds that he can carry a cow and follower on 2 acres instead of 2½ acres. How would you advise him to ultilize this improvement?

CHAPTER 19

FARM PLANNING IN PRACTICE

IN the chapter on programme planning, the aim was to produce the optimum plan with the highest possible income. When an Agricultural Adviser is helping to plan a farm, however, a little more flexibility is permissible. The farmer may not indeed require the optimum plan but merely one that solves the difficulties that confront him at the time. Indeed, he may not welcome a plan very different from his present system because he lacks the knowledge or ability to put it into operation. Even if he has the means to carry it out, he may not have the courage to make a drastic change—or at least not too quickly. A farmer's attitude also depends on his age and circumstances. A young man will embark on an ambitious plan that will produce long-term results, whereas an old man with no son would have little interest in such a plan. Account must also be taken of the farmer's likes and dislikes. A farmer may dislike pigs and, however profitable they may be in theory, it is pointless to include them in a plan if the farmer has no intention of trying them. Allowance must sometimes be made for the farmer's prejudices. The Agricultural Adviser should, of course, try to persuade the farmer to change his mind, but if he will not some concession may be necessary to make the plan acceptable. This is important because, unless the farmer agrees to the plan, he will not act on it.

But even if the plan recommended is not the optimum one, it will be nearer optimum than the present one. Indeed, the plan may be one of a series, allowing the farmer time to acquire the skill or accumulate the capital to move further in the desired direction. Thus, although the Agricultural Adviser may not formally programme a farm plan as described in Chapter 16, he will use the optimizing techniques described there to choose plans likely to be successful.

There is a further point. In the programming exercises, restrictions were strictly applied. Thus, if the labour force on a farm were reduced and insufficient time left in October to harvest the sugar-beet, it might be necessary to reduce the area of sugar-beet. It should not be forgotten, however, that restrictions can sometimes be overcome. If the farmer were reluctant to give up his sugar-beet contract, he and the Agricultural Adviser might succeed in finding some means of breaking the bottleneck. More time might be made available for harvesting by extending overtime working, or the rate of work improved by reorganizing the system of harvesting, or an improved harvester might be purchased if the extra capital costs could be justified.

EXAMPLE I

The giving of advice on farm planning can best be illustrated by taking an example. Mr. Robinson rents Barleycorn Farm of 610 acres for £3000 a year. He makes a profit of £4000 to £5000 a year, or £8 an acre. This is a reasonably satisfactory profit for a farm of this type but Mr. Robinson would like to improve it still further. He asks his District Agricultural Adviser for advice. The D.A.A. tells him to ask his accountant to extract information from the records on yields, receipts and variable costs over the last two or three years. From this, the D.A.A. prepares average gross margins and a budget.

BUDGET—PRESENT ORGANIZATION

COMMON COSTS		£	GROSS MARGINS		£
Wages (7 men)	. .	5700	180 acres Wheat at £45 .		8100
Machinery	. .	3460	180 ,, Barley at £36 .		6480
Rent	. . .	3000	30 ,, Potatoes at £80 .		2400
Other overheads	. .	3225	20 ,, Cocksfoot at £20		400
		———	200 ,, Livestock at £14		2850
		15385	(200 ewes and 50		
Net Profit	. . .	4845	beef cows)		
		———			———
		£20230	610 acres		£20230

The following is a brief account of the discussion that the D.A.A. might have with the farmer and the plans that he might prepare for him.

The 540 acres of arable land are farmed on three 180 acre shifts of wheat—barley—break, the latter including 30 acres of potatoes, 20 acres of cocksfoot for seed and 130 acres of leys, used by beef cattle and sheep. There are also 70 acres of permanent pasture.

It is evident that the gross margins per acre for the main cash crops (£45 for wheat, £36 for barley and £80 for potatoes) are quite reasonable. It might well be possible to improve yields to some extent but meanwhile it would be prudent to budget on what is known to be possible. The use of 200 acres or one-third of the farm for livestock with a gross margin of only £14 per acre is, however, an obvious weakness. This is the section that should receive first attention. The details of the gross margin calculation are as follows—

	£
50 beef cows at £48	2400
200 ewes at £7	1400
G.M. (without forage costs) . .	£3800
less forage costs	950
G.M. (including forage costs) . .	£2850

The calves from the beef cows are reared and sold at eighteen months of age. The ewes are kept to produce late fat lambs sold in autumn.

The livestock utilize—

Permanent pasture	70
Leys (arable)	130
	200

The G.M. per acre is thus $\dfrac{2850}{200} = £14$ per acre.

This is a poor return, but may be the best obtainable from permanent pasture. These livestock are, however, also using 130 acres of arable land, some of which at least might be growing cash crops. But before deciding whether to replace livestock with cash crops, it is worth estimating which of the two—sheep or cattle—gives the better return. A rough division of acres and costs is as follows—

	G.M.			G.M.
50 cows . . .	£2400	200 ewes . . .		£1400
Forage costs . .	500	Forage costs . .		450
G.M. (incl. forage) .	£1900	G.M. (incl. forage) .		£950
Acres	100	Acres		100
G.M. per acre . .	£19	G.M. per acre . .		£9·50

The cattle thus appear to have a return (£19 per acre) twice as great as the sheep (£9·50). This calculation is approximate but the conclusion that the sheep are the weakest enterprise seems quite definite.

The common costs seem fairly reasonable. Labour will be considered later in relation to the work requirements of the various plans. Machinery costs (£5 per acre) are quite modest.

OPPORTUNITIES. Potatoes have the highest gross margin but are limited by quota to 30 acres. Casual labour is available to lift the potatoes. Wheat and barley have the next highest gross margins per acre and could be expanded. Cocksfoot (£20 per acre) gives a poor return but it is not easy to find alternative break crops. The best available appear to be—

Italian ryegrass for seed .	.	G.M. £25 per acre
Clover for hay and seed .	.	G.M. £20 per acre
Beans	.	G.M. £25 per acre

The gross margins quoted are local averages. These crops are not much better than the cocksfoot already grown.

PLAN I

1. Expand cereals.
2. Give up cocksfoot seed.
3. Give up sheep.
4. Keep the present beef cattle to use the 70 acres permanent pasture; they will also need 30 acres of arable land for hay or silage.

A fairly intensive cereal rotation would be wheat—wheat—barley—barley—break. Eighty per cent of the arable land in cereals with two wheat crops in succession is as much as the D.A.A. feels safe to advise. The "break" shift is made up of potatoes, hay and silage for the beef cattle and beans. With 540 acres of arable land, this means five shifts of 108 acres.

Wheat	216 acres
Barley	216 acres
Potatoes . . .	30 acres ⎫
Hay or silage . .	30 acres ⎬ 108 acres
Beans	48 acres ⎭
	———
	540 acres

It is now necessary to see whether this programme can be managed by the existing staff. The following are the estimated labour requirements—

LABOUR REQUIREMENTS—MAN-DAYS PER ACRE

MAN DAYS	EARLY SPRING	LATE SPRING	SUMMER	EARLY AUTUMN	LATE AUTUMN
Wheat	$\frac{1}{8}$	—	—	$\frac{1}{4}$	$\frac{1}{2}$
Barley	$\frac{1}{2}$	—	—	$\frac{1}{4}$	$\frac{1}{8}$
Potatoes . . .	2	$\frac{1}{4}$	$\frac{1}{4}$	—	$2\frac{1}{2}$
Hay	$\frac{1}{4}$	—	1	—	—
Beans (spring) . .	$\frac{1}{2}$	—	—	$\frac{1}{4}$	$\frac{1}{8}$
Hay and seed . .	$\frac{1}{4}$	—	1	$\frac{1}{2}$	—
Straw	—	—	—	$\frac{1}{4}$	—
One man supplies . .	35	30	30	30	40

REQUIREMENTS FOR PLAN I

	EARLY SPRING	LATE SPRING	SUMMER	EARLY AUTUMN	LATE AUTUMN
216 acres Wheat . .	27	—	—	54	108
216 ,, Barley . .	108	—	—	54	27
30 ,, Potatoes . .	60	8	8	—	75
30 ,, Hay . .	8	—	30	—	—
48 ,, Beans . .	24	—	—	24	6
50 ,, Straw . .	—	—	—	12	—
	227	8	38	144	216
6 men supply . .	210	180	180	180	240

Of the seven men employed, six are field workers. The seventh is a stockman. The farmer helps with the stock or in the field as

required. It is evident that six men can deal with this programme
with some help from the farmer in springtime. As the sheep have
been discarded, the stockman is no longer fully occupied. Indeed,
a stockman is hardly necessary, and if the farmer tended the cattle
in spring and autumn, the field men could deal with them in
winter. The farmer, however, prefers to keep a stockman if he
has any cattle at all. As the acreage of cereals has increased, it
will be necessary to replace the present 10 ft. combine by a 12 ft.
one of high capacity. Some additional storage capacity may also
be required. This will increase machinery costs by about £300 a
year. It may be noted that the sale of the sheep flock will help
to provide capital for this extra equipment. A budget for Plan 1
is as follows—

BUDGET—PLAN 1

COMMON COSTS	£	GROSS MARGINS	£
As before . . .	15385	216 acres Wheat at £45 .	9720
Extra machinery costs .	300	216 „ Barley at £36 .	7776
		30 „ Potatoes at £80 .	2400
		48 „ Beans at £25 .	1200
Net Profit . . .	7311	100 „ Cattle (as now) .	1900
	£22996	610	£22996

The estimated profit is thus £7311, an increase of £2466 over
the existing system. One possible difficulty is the fact that one
combine is expected to cut 432 acres of cereals and 48 acres of
beans. A second combine would, however, require a substantial
amount of extra capital and two small combines would require
more labour to operate them. If the farmer had any doubts about
the ability of the combine to deal with this area of cereals, it
would be cheaper to make arrangements with a contractor well
ahead of harvest time to cut say 50 acres.

PLAN 2

The farmer is not enthusiastic about having as much as 80
per cent of the arable land in cereals. It is therefore worth
exploring a four-course rotation with 75 per cent of cereals and
no sheep; wheat—wheat—barley—break. This means 135 acres
per shift—

Wheat	270 acres
Barley	135 acres
Potatoes . . .	30 acres
Hay or silage . .	30 acres
Beans	50 acres
Ryegrass for seed .	25 acres

135 acres

The D.A.A. is unwilling to suggest more than 50 acres of beans, as this would cause congestion at harvest time. He therefore recommends 25 acres of ryegrass for seed to make up the "break" shift to 135 acres. The labour profile is also given.

LABOUR PROFILE—PLAN 2

			EARLY SPRING	LATE SPRING	SUMMER	EARLY AUTUMN	LATE AUTUMN
270	acres	Wheat . .	34	—	—	68	135
135	,,	Barley . .	68	—	—	39	17
30	,,	Potatoes . .	60	8	8	—	75
50	,,	Beans . .	25	—	—	25	6
25	,,	Ryegrass . .	6	—	25	13	—
30	,,	Hay or silage .	7	—	30	—	—
50	,,	Straw . .	—	—	—	12	—
540			200	8	63	157	233
	6 men supply . .		210	180	180	180	240

Again, six men should be able to deal with it. With more wheat and less barley there is more work in the autumn and less in spring.

BUDGET—PLAN 2

COMMON COSTS	£	GROSS MARGINS	£
As before . . .	15385	270 acres Wheat at £45 .	12150
Extra machinery costs .	300	135 ,, Barley at £36 .	4860
		30 ,, Potatoes at £80 .	2400
		50 ,, Beans at £25 .	1250
		25 ,, Ryegrass at £25 .	625
Net Profit . . .	7500	100 ,, Cattle (as before)	1900
	£23185	610	£23185

The estimated profit is thus £7500, which is £2655 more than the existing system. Although the proportion of low-value break crops is greater (25 per cent of the arable total compared with 20 per cent in Plan 1) this is more than compensated by more wheat (50 per cent of arable land compared with 40 per cent in Plan 1), which has a higher gross margin than barley.

PLAN 3

The farmer is somewhat reluctant to give up the sheep unless this is really necessary. The weakness of this enterprise at the moment is that the 200 ewes occupy 100 acres—only 2 ewes per acre. With a full-time shepherd and intensive stocking the sheep might appear in a more favourable light. To occupy the shepherd fully, however, a flock of 600 ewes would be required. With intensive forward creep grazing it should be possible to keep 4 ewes on an acre. This enterprise can be grafted conveniently into Plan 2, with sheep replacing the cattle—

BUDGET—PLAN 3

COMMON COSTS	£	GROSS MARGINS	£
As in Plan 2 . . .	15685	270 acres Wheat at £45 .	12150
		135 „ Barley at £36 .	4860
		30 „ Potatoes at £80 .	2400
		25 „ Beans at £25 .	625
		150 „ Ewes	
		600 × 7 £4200	
		less Fodder costs 900	
Net Profit . . .	7650		3300
	£23335	610	£23335

It will be noted that with heavier stocking the G.M. from sheep is £3300 from 150 acres, or £22 per acre. This brings sheep up to the level of cattle and nearly up to beans or ryegrass. They are still well below cereals. There is therefore no special advantage to be gained from extending sheep further on to the arable land.

It is also worth considering whether some reduction in sheep numbers would be an advantage. Even if a shepherd is employed, it is not essential to give him 600 ewes. If a smaller number of sheep allowed the release of land for a more profitable use, that would be an advantage. In the present case, 500 in place of 600 ewes would release 25 acres to put into beans, which are fractionally more profitable than sheep.

The estimated profit is £7650, which is nearly the same as for Plan 2. The farmer, however, objects to this plan for two reasons. Firstly, no farmyard manure is produced for the potatoes. The D.A.A. replies that this is not essential if a proper dressing of fertilizer is applied. In any case, the 80 acres of leys used by the sheep could take the form of a two- or three-year ley withdrawn temporarily from the rotation. This land could then be cropped with potatoes. The second objection is that the cattle yards would be left unused. The farmer then suggests that both objections could be met by starting an intensive cattle-rearing and fattening unit. He would, however, then need an extra stockman costing £900. The gross margin from such stock might be £10 to £15 a head, depending on the price paid for calves and the skill of the stockman. If 100 calves were fattened (and this is as many as could be fitted into existing buildings) at £12 per head this would bring in £1200, or £300 after deducting the stockman's wage. This enterprise would also require about £4000 of capital. This in turn would require an overdraft and £200 or more for interest charges. It is not, therefore, an attractive proposition on this scale. The farmer should therefore think of a smaller enterprise that he or the shepherd could tend or a larger one that would justify the employment of a stockman. A part-time unit with say 30 calves would bring in £360, which is not worthwhile. The larger unit is ruled out for the meantime through lack of capital, but the 100-calf unit is worth consideration (as Plan 3a) as a stepping-stone to a larger unit.

PLAN 4

The farmer then puts the suggestion: "Why not have a simple plan? Discard the cattle and sheep, let the permanent pasture to a neighbour for £200 and give up potatoes." This plan will obviously depend on growing the maximum possible acreage of cereals. Assume that the rotation is 2 Wheat—4 Barley—Clover ley.

BUDGET FOR PLAN 4

COMMON COSTS	£	GROSS MARGINS	£
As in Plan 2 . . .	15685	154 acres Wheat at £45 .	6930
less stockman and one other	1700	309 „ Barley at £36 .	11124
		77 „ Clover at £20 .	1540
	13985	70 „ Let . . .	200
Net Profit . . .	5809		
	£19794	610	£19794

The estimated profit—£5809—is nearly £1000 more than the present one, but about £1600 less than Plans 1, 2 or 3. It is a very simple plan and could be operated with five field workers if the farmer is prepared to help. Spring sowing and harvesting are

LABOUR REQUIREMENTS—PLAN 4 (MAN DAYS)

	EARLY SPRING	LATE SPRING	SUMMER	EARLY AUTUMN	LATE AUTUMN
	1	2	3	4	5
154 acres Wheat . .	19	—	—	38	77
309 acres Barley . .	155	—	—	77	39
77 acres Clover . .	19	—	77	38	—
	193	—	77	157	116
5 men supply . .	175	150	150	150	200

bottlenecks and a large combine and seed drill would be a great convenience. There is, however, an element of risk. With a long succession of grain crops, a decline in cereal yields is a possibility, and if this occurred the profit could easily fall below the present level.

COMPARISON OF PLANS

Many more variants are possible on these plans. The four illustrated are, however, enough to show the farmer the way in which he should reorganize the farm. The position can be summarized as follows—

1. The cash crops and livestock are quite well managed. The main fault with the livestock is that while the return *per head* is quite reasonable, the return *per acre*, especially from sheep, is well below that of the cereals or potatoes.

2. The most profitable crop is potatoes. Unfortunately, the acreage cannot be increased. The next most profitable crops are wheat and barley, which should certainly be increased. The practical limits are those of a reasonable rotation—say 75 per cent with a 4-course or 80 per cent with a 5-course one. This is as far as the farmer is prepared to go.

3. The farm includes some permanent pasture and (apart from letting) sheep and cattle are the only way to use it. Cattle give a much better return than sheep and should be preferred. With an effort, the return from sheep could be raised to the level of the cattle or seed crops. With the same effort, however, the return from cattle could also be improved and would probably still be ahead of the sheep.

4. It seems probable that the best plan is one with a high proportion of cereals, particularly wheat, and cattle to use the pasture. Plan 2 answers this description.

5. So far as profit is concerned, there is little to choose between Plans 1, 2, 3 and 3a—all give a net return of £12 to £13 an acre, an increase of more than 50 per cent compared with the present plan. Plans 3 and 3a include intensive sheep. It is by no means certain that the farmer could successfully double the stocking rate and even if he does, the extra return compared with Plan 2 is quite small. The intensive cattle enterprise in Plan 3a requires another skill and more capital, also for a meagre return.

6. Plan 4 (no livestock, no potatoes, cereals maximized) is a simple one. It gives a better profit than the present one but not nearly as much as Plans 1, 2 or 3. If the farmer lost two or three of his staff and could not replace them, some such plan might be worth consideration. Otherwise, it has no special merit.

On balance, the Agricultural Adviser would probably recommend Plan 2. It is a safe and profitable plan that does not depend on some new skill that the farmer or his men may not possess.

The D.A.A. would, however, present the farmer with the alternatives and leave it to him to decide.

If the farmer accepts Plan 2 there is one final service that the D.A.A. can perform for him. The plan includes more cereals and more wheat. It is therefore advisable to make sure that the labour force can deal with the fairly continuous busy period from the beginning of August to the latter part of November. The labour profile already given deals only with the total number of man-days in each period. It is advisable to ascertain that each job can be done within the proper period and that the machinery and gang size is available to carry it out. This is done by going over the main tasks. The acres per day, and the number of men required are given in Fig. 39.

	ACRES	ACRES PER DAY*	DAYS	GANG
Combine beans . . .	50	10	5	3
Combine corn . . .	405	16	25	4
Bale straw	50	17	3	2
Cart straw	50	17	3	4
Plough (wheat) . . .	270	5	54	1
,, (barley) . . .	135	5	27	1
,, (beans) . . .	50	5	10	1
,, (potatoes) . . .	30	5	6	1
Harvest potatoes . . .	30	2	15	3
Drill wheat	270	20(+15)	14	3

* Conservative estimates based on equipment already on the farm.

FIG. 39. CHIEF CROPPING TASKS—AUGUST TO NOVEMBER

The results are then filled in on a sheet as shown in Fig. 40. On the horizontal scale are marked the estimated number of days with suitable weather for crop cultivations. Allowance has been made for short days and bad weather towards the end of the year. A fair estimate of working days by soil type would be—

	L	M	H*			L	M	H*
April . .	22	20	18	October .		22	20	17
May . .	24	22	18	November .		22	18	14
June . .	26	22	18	December .		18	14	10
July . .	26	25	24	January .		14	12	8
August .	26	25	24	February .		10	8	6
September .	24	23	22	March .		18	14	12

* On light, medium and heavy soil.

The vertical scale is for the number of men employed on each task. The area of each block thus represents the man days required for the task concerned. It will be seen that the six men should be able to deal with all the urgent tasks in the autumn with some time to spare as a margin of safety. Indeed, it is possible that with fairly large equipment the labour force could be reduced below six.

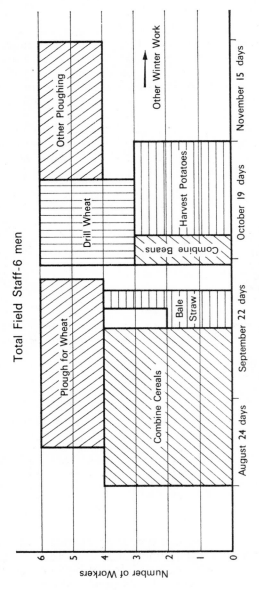

FIG. 40. LABOUR PROFILE FOR PLAN 2

	PRESENT SYSTEM	PLAN 1 80% CEREALS NO SHEEP	PLAN 2 75% CEREALS NO SHEEP	PLAN 3 75% CEREALS INTENSIVE SHEEP	PLAN 3A PLAN 3 PLUS INTENSIVE BEEF	PLAN 4 NO LIVESTOCK
GROSS MARGINS	£	£	£	£	£	£
Wheat	8100	9720	12150	12150	12150	6930
Barley	6480	7776	4860	4860	4860	11124
Potatoes	2400	2400	2400	2400	2400	—
Beans	—	1200	1250	625	625	—
Grass seed	400	—	625	—	—	1740
Total crops	17380	21096	21285	20035	20035	19794
Cattle	1900	1900	1900	—	1200	—
Sheep	950	—	—	3300	3300	—
TOTAL G.M.	20230	22996	23185	23335	24535	19794
Common costs	15385	15685	15685	15685	16785	13985
NET PROFIT	4845	7311	7500	7650	7750	5809
Profit per acre	£7·90	£12·00	£12·30	£12·50	£12·70	£9·50

Fig. 41. Comparison of Plans

QUESTION

You have just taken (as a tenant) a 500-acre farm (420 acres arable, 80 acres permanent pasture) on fertile but light soil. The following standards are suggested to you by your local advisory officer—

	GROSS MARGIN PER ACRE	REGULAR LABOUR REQUIRED (MAN DAYS)				
	£	EARLY SPRING	LATE SPRING	SUMMER	EARLY AUTUMN	LATE AUTUMN
Wheat . .	35	$\frac{1}{4}$	—	—	$\frac{1}{2}$	$\frac{1}{2}$
Barley . .	30	$\frac{1}{2}$	—	—	$\frac{1}{2}$	$\frac{1}{4}$
Potatoes .	60[1]	2	$\frac{1}{4}$	$\frac{1}{4}$	—	$2\frac{1}{2}$
Sugar-beet .	70[2]	1	5	2	—	3
Hay . .	−5[3]	$\frac{1}{4}$	—	1	—	—
Kale . .	−8[3]	$\frac{1}{4}$	1	$\frac{3}{4}$	—	$\frac{3}{4}$
Pasture . .	−3[3]	—	—	—	—	—
One man supplies (man days) . . .	40	35	30	40	50	

[1] £74 per acre less £14 for casuals for lifting.
[2] Machine harvested.
[3] Variable costs per acre. If hay off leys is sold, allow £10 G.M./acre.

Restrictions—

Potatoes—quota 20 acres.
Sugar-beet—you can get a contract for up to 30 acres.
Wheat—not more than once in succession and only after roots or leys.
Cereals—not more than five cereals in succession.

You can assume for ease of working that the variable costs per acre of pasture are all alike (whether long or short ley or permanent pasture). The same is true of hay. The permanent pasture cannot easily be ploughed.

	PER 100 EWES		PER BULLOCK
	EARLY LAMBS	LATE LAMBS	(SUMMER FATTENED)
Output	£750	£900	£12
Variable costs—			
Concentrates . . .	£120	£100	—
Medicines etc. . .	£50	£50	£2
Forage required (acres)—			
Grazing . . .	20	30	1
Hay and aftermath .	4	8	—
Kale	4	—	—

Sheep—farmer can tend up to 100 ewes himself or hire a shepherd (wage £800), who can tend up to 400 ewes, with help from the farmer at lambing time.
Bullocks—time spent on them is negligible.
Arable workers—wage £700 a year.
Machinery and fuel—£4000 (this figure can be reduced at your discretion if you prescribe a very extensive system).
Rent—£2500; *Other overheads*—£1000.

The farmer can do physical work at peak periods but otherwise prefers to concentrate on management and dealing with emergencies.

Make any other assumptions that seem reasonable.

(a) Prepare a profitable and, in your opinion, satisfactory plan within the limits described above, and state your reasons for choosing it.

(b) The previous tenant (rent £1000 a year) tells you that he produced cereals, potatoes, lambs and summer-fattened cattle. He usually included a two- or three-year ley in the rotation and was thinking of giving up potatoes to save labour. Would this be a good system for you to adopt? If not, why not?

(Practical Examination, Postgraduate Diploma, Cambridge 1965.)

CHAPTER 20

STARTING A FARM

THE question is often asked: "I would like to tender for a farm of (say) 300 acres. I believe that I can raise £15000; is this enough capital to take it as a tenant?" Capital requirements have been increasing for many years. Before 1939, a tenant could have established himself for £10 an acre. Now he would need £60 or more, and, if he bought the farm, he would need to add another £200 or £300 for land and buildings.

Average figures of capital requirements are not, however, of much value in individual cases. The amount required varies greatly from farm to farm. Capital depends on the type of farm, and good arable land naturally requires far more per acre than upland pasture. Capital also depends on the intensity of the system adopted and the speed with which the enterprises are built up. A farmer who starts with high-grade stock and a full range of new machinery can easily spend twice or three times as much per acre as another who starts with poorer stock and second-hand equipment. It is certainly possible to start a little understocked and hope to build up numbers out of profits. Indeed a farmer short of capital would be well advised not to spend too lavishly at the beginning because he may modify his ideas after a few months and may need a margin to make a change.

There is, however, a lower limit to the amount of capital needed for any particular farm and below this level the farm business is likely to founder. Too much cheese-paring in the early stages can hamper growth and cause more loss in output than is saved in costs. There is a further point. When a farmer tenders for a tenancy he may have stiff competition, and if he must offer a very high rent to obtain the tenancy and also make enough profit to live on, he may need to farm intensively from the beginning. This in turn implies enough capital to build up the business fairly rapidly.

The aim of this chapter is to show a method of assessing capital requirements. When thinking of taking a farm, the intending farmer should make two separate plans—

1. He should prepare a budget to show how he would like to farm the holding when he is fully established. He should plan the crops and livestock to explore the possibilities. He should estimate the profits and check this against economists' reports for the area and the opinion of the local Agricultural Adviser.

2. Having decided on his goal, he should then make a plan to show how he is to reach it and how much capital this will require.

This entails the preparation of a *Capital Profile* from the *cash flow* of receipts and payments over the first two or three years.

The question may be asked: is it not possible to estimate capital requirements by examining the balance sheets of existing farmers? The Net Capital in a Balance Sheet is certainly an estimate of the amount of capital a farmer could realize by selling up on the day concerned. This is not, however, necessarily the amount that would be required by a new occupier. The implements on an existing farm stand at a well written-down value but a newcomer might have to buy much of his equipment new to obtain exactly what he requires. The inventory, moreover, might contain stocks of grain or other produce ready for sale that the new farmer need not take over because the existing occupier would probably sell them on the market before he left. Above all, however, the new farmer needs enough capital not only to buy the live and dead stock necessary but also enough to run the farm until the flow of receipts can pay for current expenses.

In practice, therefore, an incoming farmer needs enough capital for the following items.

On entry or soon after he will need money to pay for—

1. Tenant right valuation, including cultivations and growing crops left by the previous occupier. In autumn an incoming tenant may also be glad enough to take over fodder crops and litter that he can use for his stock during the first winter.

2. Livestock, especially adult breeding stock. He need not necessarily *buy* a full quota of young stock at the beginning as he may breed his own replacements after entry.

3. Implements to get cultivations under way.
During the year he will also require—

4. Working capital to pay for seeds, fertilizers, wages and other current expenditure until the flow of receipts exceeds payments.

5. Cash to pay living expenses for the same period as (4) above.

EXAMPLE I

The construction of a capital profile can be illustrated by taking an example. Assume that Mr. Brown is about to take over a 320-acre arable farm at Michaelmas. He intends to run it on a five-course shift—wheat, three barleys and a break crop consisting of leys, potatoes and a few fodder roots. He intends to buy 20 beef cows and keep them on 20 acres of permanent pasture and part of the leys. Surplus hay will be sold. The tenant right (including cultivations for winter wheat and some fodder crops) is valued at £1000. Mr. Brown estimates that he must spend £4000 on tractors and implements on entry and a further £2000 on a combine harvester before harvest. He intends to employ

3 men (wage £800). Other costs are estimated as follows: fuel £640, repairs £960, miscellaneous £640. Crop sales and variable costs per acre are as follows—

	ACRES	OUTPUT	SEED	FERTILIZER	SPRAYS	CASUAL LABOUR	GROSS MARGIN
		£	£	£	£	£	£
Wheat . .	60	45	3	4	1	—	37
Barley . .	180	40	3	3	1	—	33
Potatoes . .	20	120	28	12	2	14	64
Hay . .	16	14	2½	1½	—	—	10
Leys . .	20	—	2½	1½	—	—	4*
Mangolds etc. .	4	—	1	7	—	—	8*
Pasture . .	20	—	—	1	—	—	1*

* Fodder costs per acre.

It is assumed that the beef cows will calve in early spring and that 18 calves will be sold at eight months old around October. The cattle use £80 worth of purchased feeding-stuffs and cost £20 for veterinary and other expenses. During the second year, £300 is allowed for replacement of breeding cows, and £960 is also allowed in the second year for machinery replacement.

The next task is to list the payments and receipts and to date them. A monthly profile could be prepared but this is more detailed than is usually necessary because, quite apart from any deliberate granting of credit, there is usually a delay of a few weeks before accounts are sent and paid. It is thus sufficiently exact to divide the year into quarters and to assume that the farmer can use cash received during each quarter to pay expenses in that quarter. It is also assumed at this point that the farmer receives no credit and pays expenses in the quarter in which they are incurred.

Fig. 42 shows a cash-flow profile over the first two years. During the first quarter (October to December) the farmer pays for tenant right, machinery and breeding cows. Seed and fertilizer for winter wheat appear in the first quarter, and for spring-sown crops in the second quarter; crop sprays appear in the third. Purchased feeding-stuffs are placed in the two winter quarters. Most of the other expenses have been spread evenly over the year.

Expenditure in the first quarter (£8075) is unusually high because it includes a number of non-recurrent items on entry. The second quarter is also heavy and includes rent and the bulk of the seeds and fertilizers. The third quarter is less, and the fourth shows an increase due to the purchase of the combine harvester and the second instalment of the rent.

By the end of the year £18516 has been spent but, apart from hay sold, no receipts have been obtained. Crop receipts appear from October onwards, in the fifth quarter. It has been assumed

	FIRST YEAR					SECOND YEAR				
	1 OCT.–DEC.	2 JAN.–MAR.	3 APR.–JUN.	4 JUL.–SEP.	TOTAL FOR YEAR	5 OCT.–DEC.	6 JAN.–MAR.	7 APR.–JUN.	8 JUL.–SEP.	TOTAL FOR YEAR
	£	£	£	£	£	£	£	£	£	£
ON ENTRY—										
Tenant right	1000	—	—	—	1000	—	—	—	—	—
Machinery	4000	—	—	2000	6000	—	—	—	—	—
Beef cows	1200	—	—	—	1200	—	—	—	—	—
	6200				8200					
CURRENT COSTS—										
Cow replacements	—	—	—	—	—	300	—	—	—	300
Seed	180	1194	—	—	1374	180	1194	—	—	1374
Fertilizer	240	882	—	—	1122	240	882	—	—	1122
Sprays	—	—	280	—	280	—	—	280	—	280
Casual labour	—	—	—	—	—	280	—	—	—	280
Regular labour	600	600	600	600	2400	600	600	600	600	2400
Rent	—	900	—	900	1800	—	900	—	900	1800
Fuel	160	160	160	160	640	160	160	160	160	640
Repairs	240	240	240	240	960	240	240	240	240	960
Replacements	—	—	—	—	—	240	240	240	240	960
Feeding-stuffs etc.	45	45	5	5	100	45	45	5	5	100
Other costs	160	160	160	160	640	160	160	160	160	640
Living expenses	250	250	250	250	1000	250	250	250	250	1000
	8075	4431	1695	4315	18516	2695	4671	1935	2555	11856
RECEIPTS—										
Wheat	—	—	—	—	—	1800	900	—	—	2700
Barley	—	—	—	—	—	4800	2400	—	—	7200
Potatoes	—	—	—	—	—	1600	800	—	—	2400
Hay	—	—	—	—	—	—	—	—	224	224
Calves	—	—	—	224	224	900	—	—	—	900
	—	—	—	224	224	9100	4100	—	224	13424
Surplus or Deficit	−8075	−4431	−1695	−4091	−18292	+6405	−571	−1935	−2331	+1568
Cumulative Deficit = Capital	−8075	−12506	−14201	−18292	−18292	−11887	−12458	−14393	−16724	−16724

FIG. 42. CAPITAL PROFILE AND CASH FLOW FOR FIRST TWO YEARS FOR 320-ACRE ARABLE FARM

that two-thirds of the crops are sold before New Year and the remainder after. In practice, of course, the timing of sales depends on circumstances. If the farmer is short of cash, he will sell early, but if he expects prices to rise he will sell later in the season.

In the second-last line the surplus or deficit of receipts over expenses is shown in each quarter. In the last line is the cumulative deficit from the date of entry. At the end of the first year this reaches its maximum total of £18292. In the fifth and sixth quarters this deficit falls to around £12000 and then climbs again to £16724 at the end of the second year. The "deficit" at any point is in fact the amount of money that the farmer has invested in the farm at that date—in other words, the capital. It will be seen that on an arable farm the capital invested rises to a peak at about Michaelmas and then declines as the crops are sold. This is because expenses are a more or less steady flow throughout the year, whereas receipts from cash crops appear from October onwards. An arable farmer thus tends to be short of cash in late summer, just before the crops are ready for sale. In other words, this is the point at which his capital requirements reach a peak. In the second year, the system has become established and the normal ebb and flow of capital investment can be clearly seen. Capital requirements again reach a peak in September of the second year, and this pattern is likely to repeat itself in future years. It will be noted that the peak at the end of the second year is somewhat less than at the end of the first. The reason is that a profit of £2568 has been made during the second year. As only £1000 has been drawn for private purposes, the remaining £1568 has been reinvested in the farm and this has reduced the deficit by that amount.*

It is evident that on a farm of this kind the critical date when capital requirements are at a maximum is around 30th September. Thus if the farmer has enough capital to pass this point, he has enough to continue indefinitely—provided that he continues to make a profit and can finance further expansion out of profits.

On an arable farm of the kind described it is indeed possible to estimate capital requirements without constructing a complete profile. The capital is the sum of the values of—

(a) Tenant right.
(b) Livestock.
(c) Implements.
(d) Working capital, which is estimated as current costs *less* receipts generated in the course of the year and marketed before 30th September.

---

* This assumes that the valuation remains constant.

In this case—

	£
Tenant right	1000
Livestock	1200
Machinery	6000
One year's expenses	9316
Personal expenses	1000
	£18516
Less receipts before 30th September—	
Hay	224
Capital required	£18292

The total of £18292 for 320 acres is £57 an acre. It should be emphasized, however, that this is an estimate for one plan carried out in the way described. With a different programme and different tactics in carrying it out, quite a different answer would be obtained. Indeed, if the farmer is short of capital, one of the main reasons for preparing a capital profile is to enable him to plan and replan in order to keep capital requirements within the total available. If capital requirements exceed the amount of money available he must decide how he is to deal with the situation. He has three alternatives—

1. He can rely on credit. We have assumed so far that all expenses are paid in the quarter in which they are incurred. Suppliers may, however, not press for payment for a few months.
2. He may ask the bank for an overdraft.
3. He may change the farm plan.

Suppose, for example, that Mr. Brown has only £16000. According to the profile, he will exceed this limit about July and will have a deficit until about November. He could therefore take this plan to his bank manager and ask for an overdraft not exceeding £2500 for about four months. It will be noted, by the way, that he will need an overdraft at the same time in the next year. Provided he makes a substantial profit in the second year and does not spend it all, the overdraft will be smaller. But if he invests in some new enterprise it may well be greater.

Merchant credit for a few months is not hard to obtain at the cost of some loss of discounts. If reliance is placed on this source of credit, it is as well to note which bills can be postponed and for how long. The seed merchant might be willing to wait, but unless he can wait from March to November this would not solve the problem. The best one to postpone, if it could be arranged, would be the payment for the combine harvester.

In the long run the farmer should shape his farm plan to maximize his profit. But if he is short of capital, he may be compelled to modify his plans to some extent to keep within the limit of his resources. How much can be accomplished by changing the farm plan? As will be shown, the tactics adopted can affect capital requirements quite substantially. This can happen for two reasons. In the first place, some crops and livestock give a much *quicker* return on money invested than others and will naturally be preferred by the farmer short of capital. In the second place, some crops and livestock are *complementary* to others in capital requirements. On an arable farm, for example, store cattle fattened in winter can be complementary to cash crops. Stores can be bought in autumn when crops are being sold and cash is plentiful and sold again in spring when cash is short. In this case the cattle do not need additional capital because they are using capital that would otherwise be idle.

It is thus worth considering farm enterprises in terms of the size and timing of the cash flow to which they give rise.

CASH CROPS. Most farm crops absorb capital over the year and give a cash return from September onwards. As already mentioned, such crops produce a shortage of capital in spring and summer and an ample supply in autumn and winter. Peas and some fruit and vegetables marketed in summer are thus complementary to crops marketed in autumn because they provide cash that helps to finance the late summer period.

DAIRY COWS. These require a large fixed investment but give a quick return on money invested in feeding-stuffs. They also provide a flow of receipts throughout the year that may be very useful in providing working capital.

CATTLE. Beef cows require a fixed investment and give a slow return, with a time lag of twelve to twenty-four months or more. Store cattle, on the other hand, need capital for only a few months and can be timed to be complementary to crops and other enterprises.

SHEEP. Breeding ewes require a fixed investment and give a return after nearly twelve months. Late lambs marketed in autumn coincide with cash crops but early lambs can provide a useful flow of cash in late spring and summer.

PIGS. Sows resemble dairy cows in requiring a large fixed investment for buildings and working capital. They also provide a flow of cash throughout the year. If the farmer starts with gilts, he can expect a cash return from fat pigs in about seven to ten months. A fattening unit using weaners could give returns in three to five months. A new pig enterprise can therefore be timed to be complementary in its capital requirements to other enterprises.

LAYING HENS. Point-of-lay pullets give a return within a few weeks of purchase. Day-old chicks do so in about five months, and also need capital for rearing equipment. A new poultry enterprise can therefore be timed to be complementary to other enterprises.

Returning now to our example, it can be seen that all the enterprises chosen have a time lag of about twelve months and all produce a flow of receipts in the following autumn. None of them is therefore complementary to another. In other words, the total amount of capital required is more or less the sum of all the enterprises included. With care, it would have been possible to make one enterprise finance another. For example, if Mr. Brown had purchased store cattle for winter fattening in place of beef cows, the sale of fat cattle in spring would have released capital for expenses and the grazing could have been let for the summer. It might also have been possible to start a poultry enterprise from point-of-lay pullets that would have provided a useful flow of cash throughout most of the year.

EXAMPLE II

Mr. Green is about to take over a 150-acre dairy farm. He intends to have a 50-cow herd and to start by buying good down-calving heifers (average £95 each) that should calve within a month or two of purchase. He will rear some heifer calves as replacements and sell the remainder. The cropping is—

Hay	.	. 43 acres	Mangolds	.	. 3 acres
Silage	.	. 7 acres	Leys grazed	.	75 acres
Kale	.	. 8 acres	Barley	.	. 16 acres

He hopes to grow good quality fodder crops and supplement this with 3 lb. concentrates per gallon in winter and $1\frac{1}{2}$ lb. in summer. Tenant right costs £800, machinery and equipment £3000, and a parlour and alterations to the yard £2500. The farmer hopes to run the farm himself with the aid of a cowman (wage £900). The rent is £1050.

The capital profile is shown in Fig. 43. It is quite different in form from the previous example. Capital requirements reach a peak very quickly and remain at this level with very little seasonal variation. This is to be expected because milk produces a flow of receipts throughout the year. As the heifers will calve for the first time in late autumn, more milk is produced in the second than in the third or fourth quarter. In future years, however, the tendency will be for the milk supply curve to flatten out. The

	FIRST YEAR					SECOND YEAR				
	1 OCT.–DEC.	2 JAN.–MAR.	3 APR.–JUN.	4 JUL.–SEP.	TOTAL FOR YEAR	5 OCT.–DEC.	6 JAN.–MAR.	7 APR.–JUN.	8 JUL.–SEP.	TOTAL FOR YEAR
	£	£	£	£	£	£	£	£	£	£
ON ENTRY—										
Tenant right	800				800					
Heifers	4750				4750					
Machinery	3000				3000					
Yard and parlour	2500				2500					
	11050				11050					
CURRENT COSTS—										
Heifer replacements		380			380	475	475			950
Seeds		175			175		175			175
Fertilizer		620			620		620			620
Feeding-stuffs	315	540	240	190	1285	565	590	250	220	1625
Misc. costs 50 cows at £10	125	125	125	125	500	125	125	125	125	500
Wages	225	225	225	225	900	225	225	225	225	900
Rent		525		525	1050		525		525	1050
Machinery	112	113	112	113	450	187	188	187	188	750
Other costs	150	150	150	150	600	150	150	150	150	600
Living expenses	200	200	200	200	800	200	200	200	200	800
	12177	3053	1052	1528	17810	1927	3273	1137	1633	7970
RECEIPTS—										
Milk	875	2188	1417	1062	5542	1750	2188	1417	1204	6559
Calves	50	335	50		435	50	335	50		435
Cull cows		240			240	350	350			700
Barley						252	250			502
	925	2763	1467	1062	6217	2402	3123	1467	1204	8196
Surplus or Deficit	−11252	−290	+415	−466	−11593	+475	−150	+330	−429	+226
Cumulative Deficit = Capital	−11252	−11542	−11127	−11593	−11593	−11118	−11268	−10938	−11367	−11367

FIG. 42. CAPITAL PROFILE AND CASH FLOW FOR FIRST TWO YEARS FOR 150-ACRE DAIRY FARM

purchase of concentrates is greater in winter than summer but this is largely balanced by higher receipts per gallon. Peak requirements are, in fact, £11893 at the end of the year, but this figure is very little more than that of £11692 at the end of six months.

Capital requirements for such a farm could be estimated briefly as follows—

					£
Tenant right	.	.	.	.	800
Livestock .	.	.	.	.	4750
Yard and parlour	.	.	.	.	2500
Machinery and equipment .		.	.	.	3000
Working capital—					
3 months expenses (including private drawings) .		.	.	.	1127
Total capital		.	.	.	£12177

This calculation differs in one respect from the estimate for the arable farm. In that example, working capital was calculated as one year's current costs less receipts during the year. A similar calculation here would be £6760 less £6217 = £543. This is obviously too little to finance current costs in the early stages until the heifers calve and milk receipts pay for current costs. The delay until a flow of receipts is obtained depends on the type of stock purchased. It could be quite short if cows in milk are purchased. As a matter of prudence, however, it is wise to have in hand at least enough cash for three months' current costs (£1202). A reasonable estimate for working capital is thus: *either*, one year's current costs less receipts during the year; *or*, first three months' current costs, and to use whichever is the greater. This calculation is, however, no more than an approximation; a capital profile is a more reliable guide.

Another point should be noticed in the capital profile. During the second year, the net surplus was only £226 after allowing £800 for personal expenditure. Unlike the previous example, however, the valuation has increased during the second year. At the end of the first year there is a batch of heifer calves being reared as replacements. After two years there is a second batch of replacements up to two years of age. Assuming that on balance the valuation has increased by about £800, the profit is approximately £1800 (£226 + £800 + £800), which is very reasonable for a farm of this size. It will be noted, however, that during this period of building up stock, the cumulative deficit has hardly changed and is nearly as large at the end of the second year as at the end of the first. It would thus be impossible to pay off any large debt. Indeed, if this farmer had started with only £10000 and had been allowed by his bank to have an overdraft, this would have been £1252 at the end of three months and £1593 at the end of the first year. At the end of the second year it would still have been £1367. Even if he made a profit of £1800 in the third year and continued to live frugally on £800, it is doubtful whether the overdraft would be paid off.

The maximum capital requirement (at the end of the first year) is £11593, or £77 per acre. This is the cost of carrying out this plan in the way described. There are other possibilities. Instead of buying down-calving heifers, the farmer could buy older cows at a lower price. If a number of these were in milk, there would be a flow of receipts almost from the beginning. This, coupled with two or three months' credit from a sympathetic feeding-stuffs merchant, might substantially reduce working capital requirements.

EXAMPLE III

So far we have been dealing with starting a farm. There is also the problem of estimating the amount of capital required to start a new enterprise on an existing farm. The process is essentially the same as that already described. The first step is to prepare a budget to show the profit expected from the enterprise. If the return seems sufficiently attractive, plans can then be made to show how the enterprise can be built up, how much it will cost and how these capital requirements fit in with those of the farm as a whole. The process can best be demonstrated by taking an example.*

Assume that a farmer wishes to start a pig enterprise producing fat baconers on an existing farm. He intends to erect efficient new buildings to ensure a good food conversion rate. He intends to build up the herd over six months, buying on average six in-pig gilts each month. He will employ one full-time pigman.

Fig. 44 shows the enterprise fully established. It will be noted that the budget is self-sustaining. Allowance is made for the replacement of sows by breeding gilts and of boars by purchase. Allowance is also made (in depreciation) for replacement of buildings. The valuation can thus be assumed to remain constant. The profit is estimated at £1604 and, as this seems a reasonable return, the farmer then calculates the amount of capital required (Fig. 45). The fixed capital consists of the buildings (estimated at £5790), the equipment (mill and mix, food trolleys, etc., £900) and the gilts and boars (£1540), totalling £8230. The next problem is to calculate the working capital required. This is

---

* The author is indebted to Mr. R. F. Ridgeon for preparing these budgets.

shown in Fig. 46. It will be seen that as each batch of gilts farrow, their food requirements double until the young pigs are weaned. Provision is then made for food for the fattening pigs. This cost builds up until the first batch of pigs is ready to go, in the seventh month after purchasing the first gilts. In the eighth and succeeding months enough cash is being received from the sale of baconers

558 pigs weaned	528 sold for bacon
540 pigs reared	12 kept as gilts

COSTS	£	RECEIPTS	£
Food—		Sales—	
Sows, 36 × 26 cwt. at £1·50	1404	528 baconers at £17 . .	8976
Boars, 2 × 20 cwt. at £1·50	60	10 cull sows at £18 . .	180
Creep, 558 × ¼ cwt. at £2·10	293	1 cull boar at £8 . .	8
Feeders, 540 × 5¼ cwt. at			
£1·40	3969		
Gilts, 12 × 3 cwt. at £1·50	54		
	——		
	5780		
Labour	800		
Housing depreciation . .	460		
Other costs . . .	470		
1 replacement boar . .	50		
	——		
Total costs . . .	7560		
Profit	1604		
	——		——
	£9164		£9164

FIG. 44. BUDGET FOR PIG ENTERPRISE
(WHEN FULLY ESTABLISHED)

to finance working capital for food and other costs. The peak requirement of working capital is £1595.

The total fixed and working capital is thus £9825, or £273 per sow. Of this total, nearly two-thirds is fixed equipment. The estimated profit of £1604 represents a return of $\dfrac{1604 \times 100}{9825} =$ 16½ per cent, which appears reasonably promising.

The final point to consider is the rate at which the farmer could repay a loan from such an enterprise. The key factor is the net cash flow—its size, timing and duration. In this context, the cash flow is even more important than the net profit, because the farmer must actually possess the cash to make repayments when necessary. It will be seen from Fig. 46 that from the seventh month current receipts are £765 and expenses £587, leaving a cash balance of £178 a month, or £2136 per year. These are, of course, estimates and will be subject to fluctuation. Nevertheless, if plans mature as expected, the enterprise will be producing a cash surplus of some £2000* a year after seven months. If the farmer borrowed £10000 it would take nearly six years to repay it with interest at six or seven per cent. A bank might be unwilling to give a loan for so long a period. An alternative would be to raise a mortgage for the buildings—say £5000 repaid over ten

FIXED CAPITAL	£	£
Stock—		
36 in-pig gilts at £40 . . .	1440	
2 boars at £50	100	
		1540
Housing—		
12 farrowing huts at £70 . .	840	
Dry sow accommodation . .	750	
2 boar pens at £100 . . .	200	
200 feeder house at £20 . . .	4000	
		5790
Equipment—		
Sow feeders, weighers trolley etc. .	400	
Mill and mixer	500	
		900
		8230
WORKING CAPITAL		
Food costs	990	
Labour costs	469	
Other costs	136	
		1595
Total Capital . . .		£9825

FIG. 45. CAPITAL REQUIRED TO START 36-SOW HERD PRODUCING BACONERS

years and costing £700 a year. The farmer might borrow £2000 from the bank and produce the remaining £2800 from his own resources. After paying the mortgage instalment, the farmer would have £1300 in cash, which would repay the bank loan about two years after the enterprise was started. After this point the farmer would have an additional income of £1300 until the mortgage was repaid.

As in the previous examples, there is no single "correct" answer for the amount of capital required. The amount spent on fixed equipment could be reduced if the farmer already had buildings that could be cheaply converted. With care, the figure of £20 per fat pig for new buildings could be reduced. On the other hand,

* Building repairs are included in "other costs." Depreciation of equipment can be largely ignored in the early stages with new equipment.

	Month	1	2	3	4	5	6	7	8	9	10	11	12
		£	£	£	£	£	£	£	£	£	£	£	£
Sows Food Batch 1 (A)		15	F30	30	15	15	15	15	F30	30	15	15	15
,, ,, 2			15	F30	30	15	15	15	15	F30	30	15	15
,, ,, 3				15	F30	30	15	15	15	15	F30	30	15
,, ,, 4					15	F30	30	15	15	15	15	F30	30
,, ,, 5						15	F30	30	15	15	15	15	F30
,, ,, 6							15	F30	30	15	15	15	15
Boars Food													
Creep Feed				5	5	5	5	5	5	5	5	5	5
Feeders Batch 1				25	60	75	90	105		25	60	75	90
,, ,, 2					25	60	75	90	105		25	60	75
,, ,, 3						25	60	75	90	105		25	60
,, ,, 4							25	60	75	90	105		25
,, ,, 5								25	60	75	90	105	
,, ,, 6									25	60	75	90	105
Total Food Costs (B)		15	45	105	180	270	375	480	480	480	480	480	480
Labour Costs		67	67	67	67	67	67	67	67	67	67	67	67
Other Costs		6	12	19	26	33	40	40	40	40	40	40	40
Payments Made (B)		67	88	124	191	273	370	482	587	587	587	587	587
Value Pigs Sold									765	765	765	765	765
Working Capital (C)		67	155	279	470	743	1113	1595	1417	1239	1061	883	705

Notes: (A) It is assumed that 6 in-pig gilts are purchased monthly for the first 6 months and that they farrow (F) the following month.

(B) Food and Other Costs are paid one month in arrears but Labour must be paid as incurred.

(C) Working Capital increases until the 7th month, after which the value of pigs sold will exceed costs each month.

Fig. 46. Working Capital Required by 36-sow Herd Producing Bacon Pigs

(Cash flow estimate for first 12 months.)

if inferior buildings raised the food conversion rate, such an economy could be dearly bought.

Another point to be taken into account is the size of the enterprise. If a pigman is employed, then the herd must be large enough to justify his wages. This means a one-man unit of 30 to 40 sows. On the other hand a farmer short of capital might build a herd up gradually to say 12 sows tended part-time by himself or a member of the family. If he is successful and can accumulate capital he could then consider further expansion to a one-man unit employing a full-time pigman.

QUESTIONS

1. Assume that in Example I the farmer has £14000 and can borrow not more than £3000 at six per cent. Prepare a new plan and estimate the time required to repay his loan.

One of the following may be tested—

(a) Fattening of store cattle.
(b) Intensive fattening of purchased calves.
(c) A sheep flock.
(d) A small dairy herd (assume that the landlord will convert buildings to take dairy cows for an extra rent of £7 a cow).

2. Prepare an alternative plan for Example II. Assume that you can buy older cows in milk giving 850 gallons a year and costing £70 each. A third of these cows must be replaced each year.

Try the effect of—

(a) Buying all cows at entry.
(b) Spreading the purchase of cows over the first twelve months.

3. Assume that in Examples I and II you enter the farm in spring. Assume that the tenant right is £2500 (Example I) and £1500 (Example II).

4. Try the effect of introducing a pig herd on to the arable farm. How should the starting of this unit be timed to minimize capital requirements? Try the effect of feeding home-grown barley.

5. Compare the capital requirements for Example III with the following—

(a) 36-sow herd built up over a longer period.
(b) 48-sow herd.
(c) 12-sow herd (tended by the farmer).

6. Prepare a capital profile for a flock of laying hens starting with (a) point-of-lay pullets, and (b) day-old chicks and rearing equipment. How would you time the introduction of such an enterprise on either an arable or a livestock farm?

7. Prepare a capital profile for a type of farm with which you are familiar.

CHAPTER 21

CAPITAL INVESTMENT

THERE is a constant need for more capital in farming—to take advantage of new techniques, to intensify production and (all too often) to finance the replacement of stocks whose value has been increased by inflation. Indeed, unless the farmer is careful, capital investment can become a bottomless pit which continues to absorb a large part of his income. It follows, therefore, that capital expenditure should be incurred only when the cost can be genuinely justified. A large part of this book has been concerned with planning changes on the farm and preparing budgets to show whether the farmer is likely to gain as a result. The criterion used so far has been a fairly simple one—when the change has been carried out, will it increase the farmer's profit? We have still to consider the question of how the change is to be financed. Some changes involve no more than a switch from one crop or type of livestock to another and are fairly easily financed. Others are more fundamental and involve the investment of substantial amounts of capital. This raises the point of whether the results are likely to justify the capital required.

There are three reasons why project evaluation is important. In the first place, few farmers have the reserves to finance large projects and must borrow at least part of the capital required. If so, the farmer should be able to prepare a convincing case for his bank manager or whoever is lending the money. Secondly, the project should be profitable enough to repay interest on any loan and allow the farmer to recover the capital invested during the lifetime of the project. Thirdly, the project should provide a large enough surplus to reward the farmer for the risk and responsibility of managing the new enterprise.

SIMPLE CRITERIA FOR INVESTMENT

To show how an investment can be assessed, let us take a simple case. Suppose a farmer invests £1000 in a new enterprise and obtains a profit of £250 a year. This is a return of 25 per cent on the capital originally invested. If the farmer could borrow the £1000 at 10 per cent interest, it would pay him to do so because after paying interest, he would have 15 per cent or £150 a year left. If the income continued indefinitely and the loan were not repaid, the 25 per cent return quoted would be an adequate assessment of the project.

Unfortunately, cases are seldom as simple as this. The amount is often by no means clear-cut. Even if a farmer invests £1000, this is the peak investment and as the equipment and buildings deteriorate the amount invested declines. If the value declines eventually to £500, the average amount invested might be only £750. In this case, a return of £250 on an average investment is 33 per cent compared to 25 per cent on the peak investment.

One fairly simple criterion is the *pay back period*. In our example, a net return of £250 would pay back the £1000 invested in four years. This is a simple test and the shorter the period, the better the investment. As a test, it is likely to appeal to a lender whose main interest is the return of his loan. The disadvantage is that it gives no credit for the later stages beyond the pay-back stage. This test might therefore rate a project giving a quick return above another that took longer to become established but gave higher returns in the long run.

Discounted Cash Flow

With small projects, such criteria may be quite adequate. But if they are large, more precise standards are required. These take into account a number of considerations which have so far been ignored. For example—

(*a*) Receipts and payments are often not spread evenly over the years. Investment may not be confined to one point but be spread over a period and overlap the first returns. The return may also vary, rising to a peak after a number of years and then declining.

(*b*) Investments tend to have a definite life. After a certain period, equipment wears out and additional capital may be necessary to replace it. Even if a project could be continued indefinitely, it may eventually become uneconomic for some reason not at present foreseen. The investment should therefore be profitable enough to allow for recovery of capital invested within the life of the project.

These points can be illustrated by means of an example. Suppose that a farmer starts a new enterprise such as a laying flock or a beef herd. He invests £6000 during the first year in housing and stock and a further £1500 in the second year. Revenue begins in the second year (£500) and grows steadily to give a net cash flow of £2000 in the second and third years. In the fourth year, the unit is enlarged and an additional £3500 is invested. Revenue reaches a peak of £3000 in the fifth, sixth, seventh and eighth years and then declines in the ninth year. The enterprise is finally wound-up in the tenth year and the stock and equipment sold for £4000.

The payments and receipts for each year are set out and the difference tabulated as the *cash flow*. No distinction is made between capital and current items. As will be seen later, this is not necessary when we are dealing with the whole life of a project at one time.

	CAPITAL EXPENDITURE £	NET* RECEIPTS £	NET CASH FLOW £
Year 0 .	6000	—	−6000
1 .	1500	500	−1000
2 .	—	2000	+2000
3 .	—	2000	2000
4 .	3500	2500	−1000
5 .	—	3000	+3000
6 .	—	3000	3000
7 .	—	3000	3000
8 .	—	3000	3000
9 .	—	2000	2000
10 .	—	4000†	4000
	£11000	£25000	£14000

* Receipts, *less* annual costs (feeding-stuffs, repairs, etc.).
† Salvage value of building and equipment, *plus* sale value of livestock.

How is one to judge the success of this enterprise? The net cash flow has fluctuated from year to year. In three years there was a deficit; in seven years there was a surplus. In all, the farmer has paid out £11000 and received £25000, leaving a surplus of £14000. This alone, however, is not a sufficient criterion of success. In particular, one consideration has so far been ignored—the cost of using capital. The farmer has borrowed money to start this enterprise and this has cost him 8 per cent a year. Even if he had owned the capital invested, the farmer could have invested the money quite safely at 8 per cent in government stocks. It would thus be reasonable to charge interest at that rate on the amount invested in the business. It would also be reasonable to credit the enterprise with interest on any surpluses that emerge. One way of putting the investments and surpluses from different dates on the same footing would be to carry them forward with interest to the date when the project ended and judge its performance accordingly. But in most cases, the farmer is not holding a post mortem on the past but is framing a plan for the future. He is therefore looking at the project from the starting point when he must decide whether or not to invest. It would, therefore, be more useful to carry the value of investments and returns back to the starting date. But if items are carried back, interest could not be added but deducted. This is known as *discounting*.

The process may be explained as follows. Suppose you own £100 and the interest rate is 10 per cent. If this £100 were invested, it would earn £10 in interest in the next year, making £110 in all. If this £110 were then invested for a second year, it would earn £11 interest making £121 at the end of two years or, to carry the process further, £161 at the end of five years. In other words, if money can be invested at 10 per cent, then £100 now is worth £121 in two years and £161 in five years. But if £121 in two years time is worth £100 now, what is the value of £100 in two years time? The answer is $\frac{100}{121}$ or £82·60. Thus £82·6 is the *discounted value*, at present, of £100 promised or expected in two years time. Similarly, £100 in five years time is worth $\frac{100}{161}$ or £62·10 now. This is because £62·10 invested now would become with interest £100 in five years time. To save trouble in calculating this sum, discount tables are published (*see* Appendix, page 256) which give the Net Present Value (N.P.V.) of £1 at one, two or more years at various rates of interest. For example, £1 in five years time at 8 per cent is worth £0·681 now.

This process of discounting provides a means of assessing the present value of a cash flow at various future dates. The net cash flow in our example has thus been discounted at 8 per cent in the following way.

EXAMPLE I

	CASH FLOW £	DISCOUNT FACTOR £	DISCOUNTED CASH FLOW £
Year 0* .	−6000	× 1·000	−6000
1 .	−1000	× 0·926	−926
2 .	2000	× 0·857	1714
3 .	2000	× 0·794	1588
4 .	−1000	× 0·735	−735
5 .	3000	× 0·681	2043
6 .	3000	× 0·630	1890
7 .	3000	× 0·583	1749
8 .	3000	× 0·540	1620
9 .	2000	× 0·500	1000
10 .	4000	× 0·463	1852
	£14000		+£5795

* This assumes that the project starts from the date when the £6000 capital is spent. Year one states the result one year later.

It will be seen that the value of future receipts and expenses dwindle as they recede into the future—in this case down to only 50 per cent in year nine. Discounted in this way, the value of the total cash flow of £14000 falls to £5795. This means that £5795 in hand now has the same value as £14000 over the next ten years. This is so because the £1852 given for year ten, if invested now would with interest, be worth £4000 in ten years. This statement could be repeated for all the other sums quoted in column 3 which, if invested now, would by the year quoted amount to the sum in column 1.

The £5795 is in fact the net present value of this enterprise. It represents the surplus the farmer can expect (if the budget is reliable) after allowing for the recovery of capital invested and for the current rate of interest. If there is no surplus, the investment is not worth undertaking. If there is a surplus, it is for the farmer to decide whether it is large enough to compensate for the risk and responsibility entailed.

INTERNAL RATE OF RETURN

The question now arises of what rate of interest should be used in preparing such budgets? If the capital is borrowed, then the rate charged is an obvious choice. Even if the farmer is using his own capital, he should allow the interest rate he would have obtained if he had not used it for the project concerned. If the money would otherwise have been invested in stocks or shares, he should allow the current rate, say 5 per cent. If the money would otherwise have been invested in another project on the farm, he should allow the return he gets on tenant's capital on his farm (say 15 per cent).

However, instead of stating the answer as a lump sum after allowing some arbitrary rate of interest (e.g. £1000 after allowing 8 per cent), there is some advantage in stating the outcome simply as a percentage rate of return on the capital invested (e.g. 16 per cent). This has the merit of allowing the farmer to compare this rate directly with other projects or investments. The method used is to calculate the *Internal Rate of Return* (I.R.R.). The procedure is as follows. When the N.P.V. is calculated the size of the surplus depends on the interest rate used. Thus, if a higher rate of interest is used the surplus diminishes. It follows, therefore, that a point will be reached when the surplus disappears. The interest rate at this point is the return or I.R.R. from the enterprise. Finding the proper rate is a matter of trial and error. It is done by trying one rate and, if it is too low, trying another which is just too high (or vice versa). When the answer is bracketed between two rates the actual figure can be estimated.

In this case, the answer is obviously far above 8 per cent because there is a large surplus of £5795. For this reason, 20 per cent is tried as a first estimate. As this produces a deficit of £180, this is too high. The calculation is therefore repeated for 15 per cent. This produces a surplus of £1554. It is evident that the rate of return is between 15 per cent and 20 per cent and nearer 20 per cent. The exact rate is estimated by interpolation. If a rise

	NET CASH FLOW £	DISCOUNT FACTOR	20% D.C.F. £	DISCOUNT FACTOR	15% D.C.F. £
Year 0 . .	—6000	× 1·000	—6000	× 1·000	—6000
1 . .	—1000	× 0·833	—833	× 0·870	—870
2 . .	2000	× 0·694	1388	× 0·756	1512
3 . .	2000	× 0·579	1158	× 0·658	1316
4 . .	—1000	× 0·482	—482	× 0·572	—572
5 . .	3000	× 0·402	1206	× 0·497	1491
6 . .	3000	× 0·335	1005	× 0·432	1296
7 . .	3000	× 0·279	837	× 0·376	1128
8 . .	3000	× 0·233	699	× 0·327	981
9 . .	1000	× 0·194	194	× 0·284	284
10 . .	4000	× 0·162	648	× 0·247	988
			—£180		+£1554

of £1734 (from —£180 to £1554) is produced by a change of 5 per cent (from 20 per cent to 15 per cent) then a rise of £180 would be produced by $\frac{5 \times 180}{1734} = 0.5\%$. The I.R.R. is thus $20\% - 0.5\% = 19.5\%$. This return of $19\frac{1}{2}$ per cent is reasonably satisfactory and somewhat above the average return on tenant's capital. If money has to be borrowed at 8 per cent, there is a margin of $11\frac{1}{2}$ per cent as a reward for risk and enterprise. On the whole, the farmer should probably not embark on an enterprise giving less than 15 per cent and if he is really short of capital, not less than 18 to 20 per cent. If the return falls below these levels, he should try to devise another plan that is more profitable.

PREPARING A D.C.F. BUDGET

In drawing-up estimates of Discounted Cash Flow, the question arises of the number of years that should be included in the budget. Some enterprises have predictable lives. An apple orchard, for example, might start bearing in seven years, rise to a peak in eighteen years and be ready for grubbing in forty years. In the case of livestock, however, it is more difficult to set a limit. The farmer should be able to budget the costs and returns for establishing a new herd for the first two or three years with a fair degree of accuracy. By that time, the net cash flow will have levelled out and will presumably remain at that level, at least so far as can be foreseen. Even if the farmer hopes that his new enterprise will continue indefinitely, he would be wise to set a time limit. With new buildings, this could be ten or at the most fifteen years. The buildings will no doubt last longer, but as new techniques are introduced, the farmer will almost certainly wish to make alterations that will require more capital.

Quite apart from this, economic conditions can change and dairy cows or pigs that seem so successful now may no longer be profitable on that farm. It follows, therefore, that the farmer should budget to recover capital sunk in fixed assets within a reasonable period. For this reason, specialized equipment should be valued at the final date at no more than its scrap value. In the case of buildings this might be a nominal value for storage. Livestock are less of a problem because they are saleable and the capital sunk in them can usually be recovered. They can, therefore, be treated as if sold at valuation in the final year.

When dealing with an enterprise in which the cash flow remains constant for some years, time can be saved by using an annuity table (see Appendix, page 257) to calculate the discounted return for a group of years. Suppose, for example, a farmer intends to build up a pig herd with money borrowed at 8 per cent—

	CASH FLOW	DISCOUNT FACTOR @ 8%	D.C.F.
Year 0	−£5000	× 1·000	−£5000
1	+500	× 0·926	463
2 to 9*	+1000	× 5·320	5320
10	+3000	× 0·463	1389
			N.P.V. +£2172

* Annuity of £1 per year @ 8 per cent for nine years (£6·246), less year one (£0·926).

When dealing with machinery and equipment, a shorter period than ten years may be prudent. A farmer offered a contract for some new crop (e.g. vegetables for freezing) would have to buy special harvesting or processing machinery. If this equipment has a life of eight years the budget should write off the value in this time. It might also be wise to repeat the calculation using five years in case the farmer might want to withdraw after that time.

Choosing Between Projects

So far, discussion has centred round whether or not an investment is justified. Sometimes a farmer may be faced with a choice between two enterprises that are mutually exclusive—either because they would occupy the same land or buildings or because there is not enough capital to finance them both.

The two criteria already described, Net Present Value (N.P.V.) or Internal Rate of Return (I.R.R.), can be used to rank enterprises in order of priority. If the enterprise requires nearly the same amount of capital, these two criteria will usually rank them in the same order. But if one enterprise is much larger than another, this may not be so.

To take an example, assume that a farmer has to choose between two projects giving the following returns—

	PROJECT A CASH FLOW	PROJECT B CASH FLOW
Year 0	−£1000	−£3000
1	+200	+300
2–9 . . .	300	600
10	400	1600
I.R.R.	25%	15%
N.P.V. (discounted @ 8%)	£966	£1211

In this case Project A gives a higher return on capital: 25 per cent, compared to 15 per cent for Project B. On the other hand, Project B gives a larger N.P.V. (£1211 compared to £966). Which test should be used? In fact, these two tests measure different qualities. The productivity per unit of capital is measured by I.R.R. Thus, if one project gives a return of 15 per cent and another gives 20 per cent, then the latter makes better use of each unit of capital. The I.R.R. does not, however, measure the size of the contribution that each scheme is expected to make to the profit of the farm as a whole. By contrast, N.P.V. measures the size of the contribution but ignores the amount of capital. This means that if the N.P.V. is used the farmer will choose a large project giving a large N.P.V. in preference to a small one with a smaller N.P.V. even if the latter has a higher percentage return on capital. One justification for ignoring the amount of capital involved is that if the money has been borrowed it does not belong to the farmer. His responsibility is to pay the interest and, having done so, he need not be concerned with the amount involved. On the other hand, if things go wrong, the farmer would soon find the repayment of a large sum more of a burden than a small one. On the whole, the author is inclined to favour I.R.R.

In the present case, it is easy to see that Project B has no great advantage over A because it needs £2000 extra capital to produce an extra £245 N.P.V. (£1211 *less* £966), which means a poor return. This conclusion can be proved formally by deducting the returns of A from B and discounting the difference.

	CASH FLOW B−A	DISCOUNT FACTOR @ 10%	D.C.F.
Year 0 .	−£2000	× 1·000	−£2000
1 .	+100	× 0·909	+91
2–9 .	300	× 4·849	1455
10 .	1200	× 0·386	463
			+£9

It is obvious that the return from the extra £2000 is only 10 per cent. This is hardly enough. It would thus be advisable to choose Project A and (if the farmer wished to invest an additional £2000) increase the size of Project A or look for some other project with a better return than 10 per cent. There are other occasions when the conclusion is not so obvious, especially if the projects are of different lengths. For this reason, we need a method of comparison such as that given above.

In choosing between projects, some consideration should also be given to the risk involved. The farmer should look for a higher I.R.R. from a risky enterprise than from a safe one.

CAPITAL GEARING

Another point worth mention is the case where the farmer has the choice of starting a new venture on a small scale with his own capital or on a larger scale with borrowed capital. Suppose the farmer has prepared a budget for a new livestock enterprise. The estimated results are as follows, using his own capital of £5000—

	CASH FLOW	DISCOUNT FACTOR @ 20%	D.C.F.
Year 0 .	−£5000	× 1·000	−£5000
1–9 .	+1100	× 4·031	+4434
10 .	3000	× 0·162	486
			−£80

The I.R.R. is 20 per cent and the enterprise seems quite a desirable one. The farmer considers that, with an extra £5000, he could double the size of the enterprise and the returns from it. Half the capital required is for new buildings. He could, therefore, borrow an extra £5000 for the buildings on a 10-year mortgage at, say, 8 per cent or £745 a year. What is the return on this larger enterprise? The I.R.R. on the whole £10000 is also, of course, 20 per cent. But half the capital is costing the farmer only 8 per cent. The extra profit (£355, i.e. £1100 *less* £745 mortgage) could thus be said to accrue to the farmer and to the £5000 of capital he has invested. The larger enterprise can thus be presented as follows (including only the farmer's capital and treating the mortgage as an expense):

	CASH FLOW
Year 0 .	−£5000
1–9 .	+ 1455
10 .	5255*

* (£3000 × 2) − £745

This yields a return of 29 per cent, which is even more attractive than 20 per cent. It will be appreciated that such a calculation is for the farmer's own information. The lender would be interested only in the 20 per cent return for the whole venture which appears to provide ample cover for the 8 per cent he expects. The fact that the farmer is providing half the capital would also reassure him. He might even think, "Even if the return on the whole enterprise falls by two thirds, there will be almost enough to repay my loan." (In this eventuality the unfortunate farmer would be left with no return.)

The device of using borrowed capital at a fixed interest rate to augment the return on capital owned by the business is known as *gearing*. If the return from the whole business is well above the cost of the borrowed capital, the return on the capital provided by the business is greatly increased. Indeed, the higher the ratio of borrowed capital the higher the gearing and the greater the return on the capital owned by the business. Working on borrowed capital is, of course, risky and the higher the gearing, the greater the risk. If profits fall *below* the cost of borrowed capital, losses are also geared-up and exaggerated. Used with discretion, however, by a farmer confident of his ability to make profits, it is a legitimate way to accelerate the growth of a business.

EXAMPLE II
A CASE IN DETAIL

Having dealt with farm planning, cash flow and project appraisal, it now remains to put these techniques together in a single example. Let us assume that a farmer already has a mixed farm and would like to start a new livestock enterprise (say a pig or beef herd). He has prepared a budget of the enterprise as it should appear when fully in operation—

PRELIMINARY BUDGETS
YEAR 2 AND LATER

	£		£
Opening Valuation . .	4000	Sales . . .	5000
Purchases (food etc.) .	3000	Closing Valuation .	4000
Depreciation of buildings .	500		
Estimated Profit	1500		
	£9000		£9000

The capital expenditure at the beginning will be—

	£
Buildings (net of grant) .	5000
Livestock . . .	3000
	£8000

The purchase of livestock is shown as—

YEAR 0

Purchase (stock) . .	£3000	Closing Valuation . £3000

During the first year, the herd will become established. It should increase in value to £4000, and some stock will have been sold before the end of the year.

YEAR 1

	£		£
Opening Valuation . .	3000	Sales	1500
Purchases (food etc.) .	2000	Closing Valuation .	4000
Depreciation of buildings .	500		
	£5500		£5500

At first sight, an enterprise that requires £8000 of capital and provides an annual profit of £1500 seems reasonably attractive. If the farmer had savings of £8000 to invest he could be earning

	0	1	2	3	4	5	6	7	8	9	10	11	12
CASH FLOW	£	£	£	£	£	£	£	£	£	£	£	£	£
In													
Receipts	—	1500	5000	5000	5000	5000	5000	5000	5000	5000	5000	5000	5000
Income Tax (rebates)	—	—	240	—	—	—	—	—	—	—	—	—	—
Overdraft (at end)	8000	9300	7990	6960	5866	4694	3437	2090	646	—	—	—	—
	8000	10800	13230	11960	10866	9694	8437	7090	5646	5000	5000	5000	5000
Out													
Overdraft (at beginning)	—	8000	9300	7990	6960	5866	4694	3437	2090	646	—	—	—
Expenditure	8000	2000	3000	3000	3000	3000	3000	3000	3000	3000	3000	3000	3000
Interest (to bank)	—	800	930	799	696	587	469	344	209	65	—	—	—
Income Tax paid	—	—	—	171	210	241	274	309	347	387	430	450	600
Cash Withdrawn	—	—	—	—	—	—	—	—	—	902	1570	1550	1400
	8000	10800	13230	11960	10866	9694	8437	7090	5646	5000	5000	5000	5000
TRADING ACCOUNT	£	£	£	£	£	£	£	£	£	£	£	£	£
Sales and Receipts	—	1500	5000	5000	5000	5000	5000	5000	5000	5000	5000	5000	5000
Closing Valuation	3000	4000	4000	4000	4000	4000	4000	4000	4000	4000	4000	4000	4000
Net Loss	—	800	—	—	—	—	—	—	—	—	—	—	—
	3000	6300	9000	9000	9000	9000	9000	9000	9000	9000	9000	9000	9000
Purchases and Expenses	3000	2000	3000	3000	3000	3000	3000	3000	3000	3000	3000	3000	3000
Interest (bank)	—	800	930	799	696	587	469	344	209	65	—	—	—
Depreciation	—	500	500	500	500	500	500	500	500	500	500	500	500
Opening Valuation	—	3000	4000	4000	4000	4000	4000	4000	4000	4000	4000	4000	4000
Net Profit	—	—	570	701	804	913	1031	1156	1291	1435	1500	2000	2000
	3000	6300	9000	9000	9000	9000	9000	9000	9000	9000	9000	9000	9000

FIG. 47. FEASIBILITY STUDY No. 1 FOR NEW LIVESTOCK ENTERPRISE FINANCED BY BANK OVERDRAFT

an extra £1500 a year in cash within two years. Unfortunately, his capital is already committed in the farm and he must borrow. He visits his bank manager, who is sympathetic but asks for a feasibility study to show how large an overdraft will be required and how long repayment will take. The first attempt (Fig. 47) shows the cash flow and trading accounts for the first twelve years. The appraisal is made, however, on the cautious assumption that the project lasts only ten years. The marginal rate of tax is 30 per cent. (This is the rate paid on the last of the present profits and will also apply to any additional profits from this enterprise.) The interest on the overdraft is 10 per cent.

CALCULATION OF N.P.V. AND I.R.R.

The procedure is as follows (see Fig. 47).

1. Fill in receipts, payments and valuations in the Cash Flow statements and the Trading Account from the preliminary budgets already given.

2. Under Income Tax rules, the building can be written off in ten equal instalments. Enter £500 depreciation in the Trading Account years one to ten.

3. In each year, complete first the Cash Flow and then the Trading Account.

4. The balance in the Cash Flow is the closing overdraft. This is also the opening overdraft next year and from it is calculated the interest.

5. Each Trading Account gives a profit or loss. Income Tax (30 per cent of the profit) is paid the next year and is entered in the Cash Flow. The loss in year one reduces tax from other sources and is entered as a credit in the Cash Flow year two.

The following points should be noted—

(a) The bank overdraft which starts at £8000 rises to £9300 at the end of year one. This is due to interest (£800) and the fact that expenditure (£2000) exceeded income (£1500) by £500.

(b) At the end of year two, the overdraft (£7990) is still nearly as high as at the beginning. Thereafter, it falls slowly until it disappears during year nine.

(c) The profit in year two is only £570 compared to £1500 in the preliminary budget. It has been reduced by the cost of interest. As the overdraft falls, the profit rises slowly to £1500 in year ten and then to £2000 in year eleven after the buildings have finally been written-off.

(d) As the overdraft is extinguished, a cash surplus emerges in year nine. This can be used to enlarge the enterprise. It is assumed, however, that it is withdrawn for private consumption or investment elsewhere.

(*e*) Year twelve shows the long-term result which will continue indefinitely so long as the buildings are satisfactory. The farmer might, of course, wish at some point to reorganize the enterprise and inject more capital.

The next task is to calculate the I.R.R. and N.P.V.—

	EXPENDITURE £	RECEIPTS £	NET CASH FLOW £	DISCOUNT FACTOR @ 10%	N.P.V. £
Year 0 .	−8000	—	−8000	× 1·000	−8000
1 .	−2000	+1500	−500	× 0·909	−455
2–9 .	−3000	+5000	+2000	× 4·849	+9698
10 .	−3000	+9000	+6000	× 0·386	+2316
				NET PRESENT VALUE:	£3559

The N.P.V. is £3559 and the I.R.R. is 17·2 per cent. These are satisfactory results and are easily calculated.

Some business consultants, however, prefer to use N.P.V. net of **tax**. The justification is that different methods of financing an operation might incur different amounts of tax and the return net of tax might reveal the effect. If income tax is deducted from the net cash flow given above, the result is as follows—

	NET CASH FLOW (*less* TAX) £	N.P.V. @ 10% £	N.P.V. @ 15% £
Year 0 .	−8000	−8000	−8000
1 .	−500	−454	−435
2 .	+2240	+1850	+1693
3 .	1829	1373	1203
4 .	1790	1223	1024
5 .	1759	1092	874
6 .	1726	973	746
7 .	1691	867	636
8 .	1653	772	541
9 .	1613	684	458
10 .	5120*	1976	1265
		£2356	+£5

* £2000, *less* £880 (tax on years nine and ten), *plus* stock sold for £4000. Buildings are written-off.

The N.P.V. at 10 per cent is now £2356 and the I.R.R. is almost exactly 15 per cent. It may seem surprising that the deduction of tax at 30 per cent makes so little difference and reduces the return only from 17·2 per cent to 15 per cent. The reason is that in this case, there is a large amount of interest to pay. For this reason, profits (and the income tax paid on them) are quite low.

THE APPRAISAL

The next point is to decide whether a return of 17·2 per cent can be regarded as satisfactory. It can be compared with the cost of capital (10 per cent), the return on equities (say 5 per cent), government bonds (say 9 per cent) or the return on tenant's capital on the rest of the farm (say 15 per cent). If the I.R.R. of 15 per cent (net of tax) is used instead, it must of course be compared with other returns net of tax at the same rate as the farmer pays. Deducting tax at 30 per cent, the cost of borrowing capital is 7 per cent, the return on equities 3½ per cent, on bonds 6⅓ per cent, and on tenant's capital in the rest of the farm 10½ per cent.

It is understandable that large companies should wish to deduct levies such as Corporation Tax before calculating the I.R.R., but the benefit of deducting income tax from farming projects is rather less obvious. The return without deducting tax is simple to calculate and easier to compare with other rates which are usually quoted without deduction of tax.* Whatever the merits of deducting tax, it is not customary to deduct interest or depreciation when calculating N.P.V. or I.R.R. Depreciation is not included, because it is allowed for in the salvage value of buildings and equipment included at the end of the project. Interest is not deducted, because this would confuse the picture. It is best to calculate the rate of return, e.g. 20 per cent, and compare this with the cost of borrowing (say 8 per cent) or alternative uses (say 15 per cent). If interest were deducted first, such clear-cut comparisons would be difficult to make.

When the budget was completed, the farmer took it to his bank manager. The latter agreed that a return of 17 per cent seemed reasonable and would cover the cost of borrowing (10 per cent) by a slim but (if all went well) an adequate margin. He objected, however, to the size of the loan and the eight years required to repay it. Bankers prefer short-term loans and like to see the sum borrowed covered by new assets that can easily be realized. In this case, the peak overdraft of £9300 is far above the £4000 that could be realized by selling the livestock. If the farmer has other assets such as title deeds, there should be ample security. Nonetheless, the banker would like to see this debt paid off reasonably

---

* One anomaly caused by deducting tax is the following. A farmer who borrows heavily will pay more interest and less tax than another who is debt-free. As tax is deducted for any given project, but interest is not, a farmer heavily in debt would show a higher I.R.R. than one who was not.

soon because the farmer is quite likely in a year or two to ask for a loan for some other improvement not at present foreseen. The bank manager would also prefer to see the farmer investing some savings of his own in the venture.

The bank manager, therefore, suggested that the farmer should obtain a mortgage for the buildings (£5000) using the title deeds of the farm as security. This would reduce the maximum overdraft to just over £4600. The overdraft, however, would still last for seven years. The farmer then offered to save £500 a year from his income from the rest of the farm and use this to reduce the overdraft more quickly. The new budget is shown in Fig. 48.

A Revised Budget

Two new items have been introduced. The annual mortgage repayment of £815 includes both interest and repayment of capital. In the early years, the repayment is mainly interest and in later years, it is mainly capital (*see* Appendix, page 258). The interest (which is chargeable against profits) is entered in the Trading Account. The whole of the repayment (£815) is entered in the cash flow. The £500 a year which the farmer intends to save is also entered there. These savings reduce the maximum overdraft to £4115 and it disappears entirely in the fourth year. This proposition satisfies the bank manager.

One point should be noted. The paying in of £500 a year does not change the amount of capital invested, because the money put in by the farmer is balanced by a withdrawal of a similar amount by the bank. The N.P.V. and I.R.R. is the same as that already calculated.

It now remains to appraise the project from the point of view of the farmer. In theory, the new herd produces an extra profit of £1500 a year from year two. In fact, the farmer will have his income reduced by £500 a year for four years and after that will see it increased in cash by only about £800 a year until year eleven. There can be little doubt that the accumulation of capital out of profits can be a slow and painful process. On the other hand, the farmer has acquired substantial assets—stock worth £4000 and buildings that should have enhanced the value of the farm. As a precautionary measure, the buildings have been written off after ten years, but if the farmer keeps the herd, they will undoubtedly have some value after that date.

The real difficulty is that the farmer is borrowing at 10 per cent and making only 17 per cent. This does not leave much margin from which to pay off a large loan. With lower rates of interest, the picture would be quite different. If money could be borrowed at 7 per cent, the overdraft would be cleared in about five years

YEAR

CASH FLOW	0	1	2	3	4	5	6	7	8	9	10	11	12
	£	£	£	£	£	£	£	£	£	£	£	£	£
In													
Receipts	—	1500	5000	5000	5000	5000	5000	5000	5000	5000	5000	5000	5000
Income Tax (rebate)	—	—	240	—	—	—	—	—	—	—	—	—	—
Overdraft (at end)	3000	4115	2602	1362	54	—	—	—	—	—	—	—	—
Cash paid in	—	500	500	500	500	—	—	—	—	—	—	—	—
	3000	6115	8342	6862	5554	5000	5000	5000	5000	5000	5000	5000	5000
Out													
Overdraft (at beginning)	—	3000	4115	2602	1362	54	—	—	—	—	—	—	—
Expenditure	3000	2000	3000	3000	3000	3000	3000	3000	3000	3000	3000	3000	3000
Interest (bank)	—	300	412	260	136	5	815	815	815	815	815	—	—
Mortgage	—	815	815	815	815	815	342	357	372	390	408	428	600
Income Tax	—	—	—	185	241	291	843	828	813	795	777	1572	1400
Cash Withdrawn	—	—	—	—	—	835							
	3000	6115	8342	6862	5554	5000	5000	5000	5000	5000	5000	5000	5000
TRADING ACCOUNT													
Sales and Receipts	—	1500	5000	5000	5000	5000	5000	5000	5000	5000	5000	5000	5000
Closing Valuation	3000	4000	4000	4000	4000	4000	4000	4000	4000	4000	4000	4000	4000
Net Loss	—	800	—	—	—	—	—	—	—	—	—	—	—
	3000	6300	9000	9000	9000	9000	9000	9000	9000	9000	9000	9000	9000
Purchases and Expenses	3000	2000	3000	3000	3000	3000	3000	3000	3000	3000	3000	3000	3000
Interest (bank)	—	300	412	260	136	5	—	—	200	140	75	—	—
Interest (mortgage)	—	500	470	435	395	355	310	260	500	500	500	—	—
Depreciation	—	500	500	500	500	500	500	500	500	500	500	4000	4000
Opening Valuation	—	3000	4000	4000	4000	4000	4000	4000	4000	4000	4000	4000	4000
Net Profit	—	—	618	805	969	1140	1190	1240	1300	1360	1425	2000	2000
	3000	6300	9000	9000	9000	9000	9000	9000	9000	9000	9000	9000	9000

FIG. 48. FEASIBILITY STUDY No. 2 OF NEW LIVESTOCK ENTERPRISE FINANCED BY BANK OVERDRAFT, MORTGAGE AND CURRENT SAVINGS

without any extra savings. With loans at 10 per cent, the proposition is marginal and if conditions are less favourable than was assumed, the new enterprise could be a liability. Before embarking on it the farmer should consider whether there is any way in which capital costs could be reduced. Buildings, for example, are often unnecessarily massive and expensive and may in fact impede alterations at a later date. The returns can also be improved by having better stock or a better system, because the rate of return depends on the efficiency of production. Quite a modest improvement in the food conversion rate could increase the I.R.R. from 17 per cent to 20 per cent or more. A fall in the interest rate (which at the time of writing is at peak levels) could reduce the burden of repayments. If there is a sharp fall in interest rates in two or three years time, it might be worth repaying the balance of the mortgage and taking out a newer one at the lower rate. Such a change will cost a fee but might well be worthwhile.

When a project is somewhat marginal, the decision is apt to depend on temperament. If pride of possession is the motive, the plan is quite feasible and the farmer can have his new herd at not too great a personal cost. If, however, a higher standard of living is his motive, then he must be prepared for a long wait, or he must find a more profitable alternative.

THE SCOPE FOR CAPITAL APPRAISALS

One final comment should be made on the reliability of the results. All budgets dealing with the future are liable to error and this applies particularly to estimates of returns in eight or ten years time. Discounting does nevertheless reduce the importance of estimates of results some years ahead. In consequence, they bear much less weight in the final result than estimates of the immediate future which should be fairly firm.

It will be appreciated, moreover, that capital budgets are not in fact a forecast of the future. This is not possible. Their purpose is simply to estimate the outcome of a particular plan. The results are therefore only as reliable as the assumptions on which they are based. These assumptions, particularly about the level of efficiency to be expected, depend on the judgment of the farmer (or his adviser) and on whether he has the skill to carry out the project as planned. There are other uncertainties, particularly about prices, which are beyond the power of the farmer to influence. But as one of the professed aims of agricultural policy is to help to stabilize prices, the risk of sharp fluctuations should not be too great, at least for the main farm products.

There is, however, another hazard that can be the most crippling of all—the lack of finance to complete a project already begun. Borrowing on the basis of optimistic plans without adequate preparation can easily lead a farmer into undertaking more than he can accomplish and promising repayment when this is plainly impossible. Even if the enterprise is successful, the farmer short of funds may be driven to short-term expedients to raise cash such as selling-off stock or equipment at a loss. Worse still, he may find repayment almost impossible and be left with a burden that takes a lifetime to repay. This is a hazard than can be largely avoided by the means described in this chapter. If a plan appears to be feasible and profitable with a reasonable margin for contingencies, the odds are in favour of success unless conditions are much less favourable than could reasonably be expected. On the other hand, if it fails on either count (of profitability or feasibility) then the odds are against success unless conditions are unusually favourable. In an uncertain world, this is as much as the farmer can expect and it should enable him to plan ahead with a reasonable degree of confidence.

These in outline are the chief methods used in assessing a capital investment. Similar methods are employed in business for large industrial projects. They are also used by developing countries to justify international loans (e.g. from the World Bank) for irrigation and reclamation schemes. In such cases, other considerations such as the social cost of labour and the effect on the balance of payments have to be introduced, but in principle, the methods are the same.

Assets and Liabilities

To conduct a business successfully, it is not enough to make a profit—the capital position must be sound so that the business remains solvent and able to meet its liabilities as they arise. A number of tests employed in business and industry are sometimes used in farming—particularly in large companies and partnerships. The tests are mostly based on the balance sheets and the net profit. These are a few—

Liquidity Ratio: ratio of liquid assets (cash and debtors expected to pay soon) to current liabilities (creditors, short-term loans, bank overdraft). This shows whether there is enough ready cash to pay short-term debts.

Current Ratio: similar, but includes easily realizable assets such as crops and livestock for sale.

Capital Gearing: ratio of long-term loans to net capital. This shows the extent to which the business is operating on borrowed capital. (*See* Chapter 14.)

RETURN ON CAPITAL: net profit as percentage of net capital. With high gearing this return is much greater than if calculated on total assets.

RATIO OF NET CAPITAL TO TOTAL ASSETS: this shows the proportion of the capital that belongs to the farmer. (The remainder is debts and loans.) If net capital falls to zero, the business is insolvent.

RATIO OF FIXED ASSETS TO TOTAL ASSETS: This shows the proportion of the capital tied up in equipment, buildings, land etc. that cannot quickly be turned into cash.

Such tests can be useful to someone examining a business from the outside, e.g. a sleeping partner or a possible purchaser of a business. He should note if any ratios are deteriorating from year to year. This might indicate that the business is getting into difficulties. They are of less interest to the farmer who operates on his own without many debts or loans.

QUESTIONS

1. Assuming that you have only a limited amount of capital, which project (A or B) would you prefer—

	CASH FLOW	
	A	B
	£	£
Year 0 .	−3000	−3000
1 .	+300	+2000
2 .	700	1500
3 .	1000	1000
4 .	1500	700
5 .	2000	500

You intend to borrow the capital at 7 per cent.

Both projects cease after year five.

2. If the projects in Question 1 continue until year ten with the same cash flow as in year five, which project would you prefer?

3. In Example I in this chapter, extra capital was invested in year four. Assume that this is a separate investment. Compare the returns from this and the original project.

4. Recalculate Example II on the assumption that money can be borrowed for 8 per cent. With use of farm labour, you can reduce the cost of buildings by £1000. Prepare an assessment.

5. Prepare an assessment of the capital invested in the pig herd described in Example III, Chapter 20.

6. Assume that you already have a 700-acre farm and are considering whether to rent in addition the 320-acre arable farm described in Example I, Chapter 20. Prepare an assessment for one of the following situations—

(a) The farm is next door. You will need only one extra man and £2000 of additional machinery.

(b) The farm is 50 miles away and you will need to employ a manager.

(c) You can buy the farm at £250 an acre. If you expect land values to increase by 3 per cent a year, would this change your assessment?

7. You wish to tender a rent for the 320-acre farm as described in Question 6 (a). Giving yourself a reasonable return on capital, how much rent could you afford to offer?

8. Prepare a budget to justify the expenditure of capital to introduce one of the following on a mixed farm—

(a) A laying flock of 10000 poultry (using either purchased or home-grown food).

(b) A barley beef unit.

(c) A contract for 50 acres of vining peas.

If you had to choose one of these projects which would you prefer?

CHAPTER 22

TAXATION

INCOME Tax is the most important of the taxes levied by the Government and the farmer is called upon to pay his share in common with other members of the community. The assessment and collection of income tax is a complicated matter, and it would be impossible to deal with all aspects of the subject in the account given here. Emphasis has been laid on the general principles on which income tax is assessed, and the application of these principles to the farmer. The examples given are calculated on the rates in force in 1970–71, but the details are constantly changing and the reader should concentrate on the method of calculation rather than on the actual figures used.

DEVELOPMENTS IN FARM TAXATION

A tax on income has been imposed in this country for more than a hundred years. In most trades the tax is levied on the actual profits made. The farmer, perhaps because he seldom kept satisfactory records, was for long given special treatment, being taxed, not on his profits, but on the rental value (the so-called "annual value" of his farm).

Although the farmer had special treatment, his profits were then small and it is doubtful whether any other system of taxation would have collected much revenue from the farming industry. After the outbreak of war in 1939, the need for increased revenue led to a change and from 1941 the larger farms with a rental value of more than £300 were for the first time assessed on profits. In 1942 the limit was lowered to £100, thus bringing in the middle-sized farmers, and finally, in 1948, all farmers were made taxable, like any other business, on their profits as shown by a set of accounts.

SCHEDULES OF ASSESSMENT

According to its source, income is taxed by different sets of rules or schedules. Schedule A was formerly the landlord's tax but receipts from rents are now included in Schedule D. Schedule B was formerly the farmers' schedule, under which farmers were allowed to pay on the rental value of the farm. Now it applies only to some commercial woodlands. Schedule C deals with interest and dividends taxed at source.

Schedule D is the ordinary business tax and includes profits from farming. Schedule E deals with wages and salaries and applies to farm workers. Schedules D and E are thus the two that mainly concern the farmer.

Schedule D

Schedule D deals with the taxation of business profits and income from professions. So far as the farmer is concerned, he is taxed on the net profit shown in a properly prepared Trading Account.

The farmer can prepare his own accounts and submit them for taxation purposes if he is sufficiently expert to do so. Unfortunately, income tax law becomes steadily more complex as time passes, and most farmers prefer to leave the matter to a professional accountant. This costs a fee, but in return the accountant can use his skill to ensure that his client pays no more tax than is necessary. It is, perhaps, worth noting that although the accountant certifies the accounts this is on the basis of the information submitted to him. The accountant will try to ensure that the accounts are complete, but he cannot be held responsible for items omitted altogether. The onus is thus on the farmer to provide the accountant with all the information necessary to make the accounts correct. The deliberate omission of income is of course heavily penalized.

Tax is levied on profits made during the previous year. The Income Tax year ends on 5th April, but accounts ending on other dates during the previous year will normally be accepted. For the 1970–71 year of assessment (commencing 6th April, 1970), accounts closing on, for example, 28th May or 29th September, 1969, would serve.

For income tax purposes the following items must not be charged in the Trading Account—

1. Interest on the farmer's own capital.
2. Interest on loans (except for interest on a bank overdraft or on a mortgage to the Agricultural Mortgage Corporation).
3. Household and private expenses.
4. Income Tax, which is regarded as a private and not a business charge.
5. Salary to the farmer himself.

It is permissible to include in farm expenses the cost of boarding farm workers (at rates prescribed by the Agricultural Wages Board), meals given to casual workers, and the keep of working dogs. Wages paid to the farmer's family, including his wife, for work done, may be included, provided the payments are reasonable in amount, and are recorded in the books of the business as and when paid.

On the receipts side of the Trading Account, credit must be made for benefits that the farmer as a private person receives from the farm. The value of the following items is therefore added to the farm receipts in the Trading Account—

1. Farm stores used in the house, e.g. fuel.
2. Farm produce used, e.g. milk, eggs, poultry.
3. Two-thirds of the value of the farmhouse if included in the rent of the farm (the remaining one-third is an allowance for the use of part of the house as a farm office or other business use).
4. Farm labour used in the house, private garden, etc.
5. A share of motor-car and telephone expenses for private or other use not connected with the farm.

CAPITAL EXPENDITURE

For taxation purposes the Inland Revenue Department draws a careful distinction between capital expenditure and other expenses. Capital expenditure, so far as the farmer is concerned, includes the purchase of implements, machinery, buildings, and land. Capital expenditure (apart from the concessions mentioned below) is not allowable as an expense when arriving at the profit of a farm. Thus, if a farmer spends £1000 on erecting a cowhouse, he is not allowed to charge this sum against profits. Once it is erected, however, he is allowed to charge the cost of repairs necessary to keep the cowhouse in good condition. But if he enlarges or improves it, the cost would again be capital expenditure and not chargeable against profits.

It will be seen, therefore, that the farmer who wishes to buy new machinery or to modernize and extend his buildings has to find the money out of his profits or reserves. Once the equipment is purchased or the buildings erected, he is able to charge repairs in later years, but this does not help him to find the ready cash when the capital expenditure is incurred. This difficulty has been recognized by the Government, and in order to encourage the re-equipment and modernization of industry and agriculture, some assistance is provided: there are various allowances, called *Capital Allowances*, that can be set against profits before Income Tax is assessed.

CAPITAL ALLOWANCES

AGRICULTURAL BUILDINGS AND WORKS. A tenant or owner who erects agricultural buildings or works can claim, in addition to any Investment Grant received, an allowance of ten per cent of the cost a year for ten years. (The definition includes the construction and improvement of farm buildings, cottages, fences and sewerage works, water and electricity installations, walls, shelter belts of trees, reclamation of former agricultural land, and

up to one third of the expenditure on farm houses.) This allowance can be charged against profits as if it were an expense.
Suppose, for example, that a farmer erects a piggery costing
£4000—

	£
Cost of construction	4000
Investment Grant (say 30%) . .	1200
	£2800

In addition the farmer can charge £280 (10 per cent of £2800)
each year for ten years as a deduction from profits.

In the first year, the farmer thus gets a grant of £1200 and a
deduction of £280 from his profits. If he is paying 40 per cent
income tax, the latter is worth £112. If the rate of tax continued
unaltered he would have received at the end of ten years £1120
in rebate of income tax and £1200 grant—£2320 in all. The net
cost of the building to the farmer after ten years would then be
£1680 (£4000 less £2320). This capital allowance "goes with
the land." If the farm were sold during these ten years, the new
owner can claim the balance of the rebate.

MACHINERY AND PLANT. If a farmer buys implements or machinery, new or secondhand, after 26 October 1970 he can claim—

(a) A first-year allowance of 60 per cent.

(b) An allowance of 25 per cent of the remaining value, each
year until the equipment is sold or scrapped.

(c) One exception is motor cars. They qualify for a 25 per cent
allowance each year (the 60 per cent allowance does not apply).

EXAMPLE I. A farmer buys a tractor for £1000.

	£
Cost	1000
1st Year, allowance—	
60% of £1000	600
Value after one year	400
2nd Year, writing-down allowance—	
25% of £400	100
Value after two years	300
3rd year, writing-down allowance—	
25% of £300	75
Value after three years	225
etc.	

Balancing Allowance and Balancing Charge. When an implement
is finally sold or scrapped, a reckoning must be made to find
whether the annual allowances have been too great or too small.

If the allowances have been insufficient to cover depreciation, the farmer can claim the balance as a "balancing allowance." But if the allowances have been greater than the actual depreciation a "balancing charge" will be made against him. For example—

(1) A farmer bought a tractor for £800 and some years later sold it for £50. The depreciation over this period was therefore £750. If the farmer had received only £600 in allowances, he could charge up £150 as a "balancing allowance."

(2) If the same farmer had sold the tractor for £300, the depreciation would have been £500 (£800 less £300). But he had already received £600 in allowances. The Income Tax authorities would then make a "balancing charge" against him of £100 (£600 less £500).

(3) The "balancing charge," however, will never exceed the allowances already received, e.g. a farmer bought an implement for £100, and, after receiving allowances of £30, he sold it for £120 The "balancing charge" in this case would be limited to the £30 already granted as allowances.

In Part I of this book, implements were included in the Trading Account, and for the beginner this is the simplest method to adopt. The Inland Revenue Authorities, however, regard implements as fixed capital. They exclude purchases, sales and valuations of implements from the Trading Account and prefer to make the allowance for wear and tear as a separate deduction. There is no objection to presenting the accounts as already described, leaving the Inspector to make such adjustments afterwards.

ALLOWANCES FOR LIVESTOCK. It will be recalled (page 77) that methods were shown by which fixed or productive stock, such as a dairy herd, could be raised or lowered in value as the cost of rearing livestock rose or fell. Because the value of livestock appears in the opening and closing valuations, however, an increase or decrease in the valuation raises or lowers the net profit. This system, whereby the value of livestock is included in the Trading Account, is called the "stock-in-trade" method.

It would, however, be possible to argue that a dairy herd (or other breeding stock) was fixed capital and that any change in valuation should not be taken into account in calculating the profit.

If a farmer wishes to have his permanent breeding flocks and herds treated as fixed capital, he can choose what is called the "herd basis." Suppose, for example, that a farmer has a dairy herd and chooses the herd basis. The value of the young stock appears in his Trading Account but not the adult dairy cows. Thus if the value of his dairy cows rises or falls, his profit is unaffected.

It is apparent that the herd basis will attract less taxation if the general price level is rising or if the farmer gradually improves his herd over a long period. The stock-in-trade method on the other hand will attract less taxation during a period of falling prices.

If the herd basis is adopted the following points should be noted—

1. The method applies to adult cows, sheep, pigs, and poultry kept for breeding purposes. It does not apply to flying flocks of cows or ewes (even if they calve or lamb while on the farm), or young stock (except hill sheep where replacements are reared on the farm). In practice, the herd basis is most often used for dairy cows.

2. The cost of replacing animals in the herd can be charged as an expense, e.g. if a farmer buys a cow for £90 to replace an old one sold for £60, he can charge £30 as "cost of replacing one cow."

3. If heifers are reared on the farm, they must be entered as a "sale" in the Trading Account when they enter the dairy herd. This is quite logical because they then disappear from the Trading Account and the cost of rearing them (e.g. food, labour, etc.) has appeared as part of the farm expenditure.

4. If the herd is increased in size, the cost is regarded as capital expenditure and cannot be entered as an expense in the Trading Account.

5. If the herd is sold, the proceeds do not appear in the Trading Account as a receipt. This concession applies only if at least a fifth of the herd is sold during the year.

6. A farmer starting in business can choose either method. Having made his choice, however, he must normally adhere to it.

PERSONAL ALLOWANCES

We have shown how business profits are assessed for taxation. These, together with other forms of income such as dividends, fees, salaries, wages, and in the case of a married man, his wife's income, give the taxpayer's total income on which tax is levied. Before calculating the tax, however, certain allowances are made, of which the following are the most important, the rates being those current in 1970–71.

1. *Earned Income.* Income derived from wages, salaries, directors' fees and farm or business profits is considered to be "earned" income, and a deduction of two-ninths is allowed (up to £4005) and one-ninth (up to £9945). Receipts from rents and dividends on shares are "unearned" income.

2. *Personal and family allowances.* If the taxpayer is single the first £325 of income is tax free. If he is married, the allowance is £465 with an addition of £155 for a child up to 11 years, £180 up to 16, and £205 over 16 if still a student. Under certain circumstances relief may also be claimed for dependent relatives.

3. *Life Insurance.* An allowance is also made on premiums paid on a life insurance policy.

After deducting all allowances, the remainder is "taxable income" which is taxed at the rate of 38·75 per cent.

Using the details given, the following examples illustrate the method by which Income Tax is worked out in practice.

1. *Mr. Whitley is a tenant at Fairview farm. He is a bachelor, and his accounts show a net profit of £720.*

Assessment under Schedule D		£720
Less allowances for—		
Earned income (⅔ of £720)	£160	
Personal allowance	325	
		485
Taxable income		£235
Tax on £235 at 38·75%		£91·06

2. *Mr. Warren is the tenant of Wideacre farm at a rent of £1500. His accounts show a net profit of £2700. He is married and has two children aged between 11 and 16 years.*

Assessment under Schedule D		£2700
Less Earned income (⅔ of £2700) . . .	£600	
Personal Allowance (married) . . .	465	
Allowance for children	360	
		1425
Taxable income		£1275
Tax on £1275 at 38·75%		£494·06

SURTAX

In addition to income tax, persons with large incomes also pay Surtax, with each additional "slice" of income paying at a steadily rising rate of duty. For the year 1969–70, Surtax will be charged only when surtaxable income exceeds £2500, but when it does it is imposed at the rates for the excess over £2000. However, where the income exceeds £2500 but not £2681, the Surtax payable will be limited to 40 per cent of the income over £2500.

INCOME						£
First £2000	.	.	.	.	.	Nil
2001–2500 on last £500		.	.	.	.	10·0
2501–3000 ,,	,, 500	.	.	.	.	12·5
3001–4000 ,,	,, 1000	.	.	.	.	17·5
4001–5000 ,,	,, 1000	.	.	.	.	22·5
5001–6000 ,,	,, 1000	.	.	.	.	27·5
6001–8000 ,,	,, 2000	.	.	.	.	32·5
8001–10000 ,,	,, 2000	.	.	.	.	37·5
10001–12000 ,,	,, 2000	.	.	.	.	42·5
12001–15000 ,,	,, 3000	.	.	.	.	47·5
Over 15000		.	.	.	.	50·0

If we include income tax at 38·75 per cent, the total rate thus varies from 48·75 per cent for income exceeding £2500 a year (but chargeable at the rates for £2000) up to 88·75 per cent for income exceeding £15000 a year.

STARTING A FARM

As already mentioned, income tax during any one tax year is normally levied on the profit made during the previous year. In the first year of farming, however, there is no "previous" year. For this reason, there are special rules for the first and second years. The normal rule is—

1st year—taxed on profits between date of entry and 5th April following.

2nd year—taxed on first complete year.

3rd and later years—taxed on profits of previous year (or to be more exact, on the profit shown in a set of accounts finishing during the previous year).

To take an example, suppose that a farmer takes over a holding at September, 1967. His accounts for the first three years show the following profits—

Year ending 30 September, 1968 £400
        ,,   ,,   ,,   ,,   1969 £1200
        ,,   ,,   ,,   ,,   1970 £2000

The tax year ends in April each year. The assessments for taxation would thus be as follows—

1st Assessment—Tax year 1967–8 (ending April, 1968). Taxed on profit made up to April, 1968. At that date he has been farming for six months. As he made £400 in the first twelve months, he is presumed to have made £200 by April.   Assessment £200

2nd Assessment—Tax year 1968–9 (ending April, 1969). Taxed on profit in first complete year, i.e. year ending September, 1968.
Assessment £400

3rd Assessment—Tax year 1969–70 (ending April, 1970). Taxed on profits shown in accounts finishing during the previous year, i.e. year ending September, 1968.   Assessment £400

4th Assessment—Tax year 1970–1 (ending April, 1971). Taxed on profits in accounts finishing during the previous year, i.e. year ending September, 1969.   Assessment £1200

It will be seen that, in this case, the accounts for the year ending September, 1968, appeared in three different assessments. It follows, therefore, that if (as is likely) the profit in the first year is a modest one, the farmer will pay very little tax for the first three years. He can, however, choose in the second and third year to be assessed on the actual profits made during the tax year (April to April). In this case—

2nd Assessment—Tax year 1968–69, ending April, 1969.

April, 1968, to September, 1968, half of £400	£200	
September, 1968, to April, 1969, half of £1200	£600	
		£800

3rd Assessment—Tax year 1969–70, ending April, 1970.

April, 1969, to September, 1969, half of £1200	£600	
September, 1969, to April, 1970, half of £2000	£1000	
		£1600

In this case the second alternative is less favourable to the farmer than the first. If, however, the farmer had made a larger profit in the first year and a poorer one in the second or third year, the second alternative might have been preferable.

GIVING UP FARMING

It will be noticed that when one is starting a farm, parts of the first financial year are assessed two or three times. When a farmer is giving up, the process is reversed and a period is never effectively taxed. The choice, however, of which section is omitted lies with the Inland Revenue.

TAXATION ON CAPITAL GAINS

Formerly, taxation was mainly confined to income and any increase in capital values was exempt from tax, except for Estate Duty on the estates of persons who have died. Taxation on capital gains was, however, begun by the Finance Act, 1962, and the scheme was further modified in 1965 and 1971. From 1971–72, capital gains tax will be abolished for short-term gains (i.e. property, including land, resold at a higher price within twelve months, and at present liable to Income Tax and Surtax), and all capital gains will then be subject to long-term gains tax. This tax is thirty per cent of the gain. If the property was bought before 5 April, 1965, only the gain after that date is taken into account. If property is resold at a loss, the loss can be set against other capital gains in the same year or later years. For the year 1970–71 exemption is given where total gains in the year do not exceed £500. The charge to capital gains tax on death was abolished in April, 1971.

PAY AS YOU EARN

In addition to paying his own income tax an employer is responsible for collecting the income tax payable by his employees. Unlike the farmer, who is taxed on profits earned in the previous year, the farm labourer pays as he earns. This method of collecting tax, which applies to all persons receiving wages or salaries, was introduced in April, 1944, and from the point of view of the wage earner has some advantages, particularly if earnings are variable. Under the previous system the deduction of tax lagged behind the wages on which the tax was levied, and as a result, an employee might still be paying the tax on high earnings at a time when his wages had declined. Under P.A.Y.E. the deductions vary each week according to the amount earned.

To understand the method employed, two points should be clearly understood. The first is the "gross pay," which is the amount on which tax is assessed. Normally this is the cash wage before deducting the worker's share of insurance stamps, and includes bonuses, piecework, overtime, holiday pay and other cash payments. On the other hand, payment in kind, such as free milk, cottage, or board, is not included.

The second point is that (except in the first week) the tax charged each week depends not only on the amount earned in that particular week, but also on the total earnings since the beginning of the tax year in April. Each employee is given a code number according to his personal allowances. From 6th April the wages are noted by the employer each week on a card, which is ruled as shown in Fig. 49. An example will show how this is done.

John Smith is a farm worker, and the Income Tax Inspector sent notification to his employer that Smith's code number was 500. He earned £18 in the first week, £18·50 in the second, and so on, as shown in Column 2. In Column 3, his total pay since the beginning of the year was entered.

Before paying the wage, the farmer looked up the tables supplied by the Inland Revenue Department. Table A gives the tax free allowance (according to the code number), and table B gives the tax payable on the remainder of the income.

In the first week, Smith earned £18, and on looking up Table A (week 1), the farmer found that a man with Code 500 was entitled to £11·50 free of tax (entered in Column 4). This left £6·50 of taxable pay (Column 5), and on looking up Table B, he found that the tax on £6·50 was £2·05. He then deducted £2·05 from Smith's wage before paying him.

CODE NO. 500

WEEK NO.	GROSS PAY IN THE WEEK	TOTAL GROSS PAY TO DATE	TOTAL FREE PAY TO DATE AS SHOWN BY TABLES	TOTAL TAXABLE PAY TO DATE	TOTAL TAX DUE TO DATE AS SHOWN BY TABLES	TAX DEDUCTED IN THE WEEK	TAX REFUNDED IN THE WEEK
	(2)	(3)	(4)	(5)	(6)	(7)	(8)
	£	£	£	£	£	£	£
1 .	18·00	18·00	11·50	6·50	2·05	2·05	—
2 .	18·50	36·50	23·00	13·50	4·30	2·25	—
3 .	18·00	54·50	34·50	20·00	6·40	2·10	—
4 .	Nil (sick)	54·50	46·00	8·50	2·70	—	3·70
5 .	25·00	79·50	57·50	22·00	7·05	4·35	—

FIG. 49. JOHN SMITH'S P.A.Y.E. CARD, 1970–71

At the end of the second week, the farmer looked up the tables for week 2. The man had earned £18·50, making £36·50 to date. The tax free pay for two weeks was £23, leaving £13·50 taxable pay, on which the tax was £4·30. As Smith had already paid £2·05, the remaining £2·25 was deducted from his second week's pay.

In the third week, the same routine was followed, and his earnings to date then totalled £54·50. The tax free allowance was £34·50, leaving £20 on which a total of £6·40 had been deducted as tax.

There is only one other difficulty likely to be found in practice. When a man's wages fall to a low level, he may be entitled to a *refund* of tax. During the fourth week, Smith was ill and earned no wage. His earnings to date were still £54·50, but his tax free allowance had risen to £46, leaving £8·50 on which only £2·70 tax was due. As Smith had already paid £6·40 in tax, he was given a refund of £3·70.

In the fifth week, he resumed work, and tax deductions were continued as before.

At first sight it might appear that a flat deduction each week would be simpler. Unfortunately, unless previous earnings are taken into account, the deductions will not add up at the end of the year to the correct amount due.

At regular intervals the farmer forwards the tax collected to the Income Tax authorities. If an employee leaves during the course of the year, he takes to his new employer a form showing the amount of tax paid thus far. Full details of the scheme are explained in booklets issued by the Inland Revenue Department.

ESTATE DUTY

This is a tax levied at the rates shown below on the estate of an individual who has died. As duty on agricultural land and buildings is reduced by forty-five per cent, land has become a popular investment for wealthy men who wish to reduce the Estate Duty payable by their heirs. This fact has doubtless helped to increase the market price of land.

The duty payable for deaths occurring before April, 1969, was calculated on the *total value* of the estate. Since then, duty has been calculated on the amount exceeding £12500 with each additional "slice" bearing a steadily higher rate of tax—

SLICE OF NET CAPITAL VALUE		TAX RATE
EXCEEDING £	NOT EXCEEDING £	(%)
—	12500	Nil
12500	17500	25
17500	30000	30
30000	40000	45
40000	80000	60
80000	150000	65
150000	300000	70
300000	500000	75
500000	750000	80
750000	. .	85*

* With a ceiling of 80 per cent overall.

CORPORATION TAX

This tax was introduced in 1965. It is paid by limited companies but not by partnerships. The present rate is 40 per cent and is levied on profits. Reasonable fees to directors can be charged as an expense before tax is assessed. Directors and shareholders are, of course, personally liable for income tax and surtax on fees and dividends distributed to them. As partners pay only income tax, the introduction of this tax has made the limited company less attractive to the farmer if profits are large enough to incur Corporation Tax, This is, however, a complex matter and the farmer thinking of forming a limited company would be well advised to obtain professional advice to find whether it would be advantageous in his case.

NATIONAL INSURANCE

Employers are expected to buy stamps from the Post Office and put them on National Insurance Cards for each of their employees. Part of the cost is paid by the employer and part by the employee. The proceeds help to pay for the health service unemployment and sickness allowance, industrial injuries insurance, redundancy payments and pensions. Selective Employment Tax (S.E.T.) is also collected as part of the same stamp. Farmers, however, can recover their contributions.

The Conservative Government have announced their intention to abolish S.E.T. from April, 1973.

Plant and Machinery (see p. 243)

As we go to press, the Government has announced that the first year allowance will be increased between 19 July, 1971 and 1 August, 1973 from 60 to 80 per cent as an encouragement to investment.

APPENDIX 1

GROSS MARGINS

WHENEVER possible, local standards should be used. The following gross margins are, however, given as an indication of the levels to be expected (1969)—

CROPS	YIELD	OUTPUT £	SEEDS, FERTILIZER SPRAYS, ETC. £	GROSS MARGIN		
				AV.	LOW	HIGH
Winter Wheat . .	33 cwt.	45	8	37	31	43
Spring Wheat . .	29 cwt.	39	9	30	25	35
Spring Barley . .	29 cwt.	35	7	28	24	32
Spring Oats . .	30 cwt.	37	8	29	25	34
Field Beans . .	23 cwt.	35	7	28	24	33
Field Peas . .	22 cwt.	55	14	41	27	58
Potatoes . . .	9 tons	141	58	83	52	107
Sugar Beet . .	14 tons	94	17	77	65	88

LIVESTOCK: Dairy cows (average) . . . £50–£80 per acre
Young dairy stock and Store cattle . £15–£30 per acre
Cattle (more intensive) . . . £30 or more per acre
Sheep (lowland) . . . . £15–£25 per acre

High and low approximate to upper and lower quartiles in the Eastern Counties of England, i.e. one farm in four will be above "high" and one in four will be below "low." Casual labour (e.g. for harvesting potatoes) has not been charged. As some farmers use it and others do not, this is best when comparing farms. When using gross margins for planning an individual farm, casual labour and contract charges should be deducted.

The returns per acre from grazing livestock depend on the quality of grazing and management and are much more variable than for crops (see Chapter 17). Some intensive forms of cattle rearing apparently show very high returns "per acre" because (apart from a little hay) very little of their food is coming from the land.

STOCKING DENSITY

Grazing livestock units—

Dairy cow	1·0	unit
Beef cows, other cattle over 2 years	0·8	,,
Cattle 1–2 years	0·6	,,
Cattle under 1 year . . .	0·4	,,
Lowland ewe (plus lambs) . .	0·2	,,
Hill ewe (plus lambs) . . .	0·1	,,
Other sheep over 6 months . .	0·1	,,

Forage acres: pasture, silage, hay, kale and other fodder (but not grain crops)—

$$\text{Stocking density} = \frac{\text{Forage acres}}{\text{Grazing livestock units}}$$

A reasonable average is about $1\frac{1}{2}$ acres per livestock unit. If the figure is high, it indicates under-stocking or poor quality grazing or fodder. A low figure may indicate very productive grazing and fodder. It may, however, mean that the farmer is depending heavily on the use of concentrates. For this reason, some authorities prefer "Feed acres per grazing livestock unit." Feed acres are forage acres plus an acreage allowance for purchased and home-grown concentrates and cereals.

Work Units

A Work Unit is the average amount accomplished in one man day of eight hours.

Work units attempt to measure the *physical* labour required to operate a farm. Crops and livestock are therefore weighted according to the average amount of labour required for each. Unlike output per £100 labour, this measure is not affected by differences in yields or prices which have no very direct link with labour requirements. The aim of this factor is to measure the amount of productive work accomplished by each man employed.

Work units—	PER ACRE		PER HEAD
Wheat, barley . . .	2	Dairy cows . . .	10
Oats, beans . . .	3	Beef cows, heifers in calf .	3
Potatoes	15	Bulls	6
Sugar beet . . .	10	Other cattle and calves .	2·5
Mangolds . . .	11	Lowland sheep . . .	0·7
Turnips, swedes . .	9	Hill sheep	0·4
Kale	1·5	Sows, gilts, boars . .	4·0
Grass and clover . .	0·75	Fattening pigs . . .	1·0
Peas, can or freeze . .	3	Laying hens . . .	0·1
Brassicas	20	Pullets	0·05

Divide work units by number of men employed (including an allowance for casuals and farmer's manual work). The average is about 275, but on a well-organized farm should be well over 300. The standards are suited to a mixed farm. Some specialized units (e.g. poultry) use much less labour than these standards imply.

An alternative method that requires rather more arithmetic is—

(*a*) Add 15 per cent (for general maintenance, time lost in bad weather, etc.) to the productive work units calculated above to give "work units required."

(*b*) Multiply the number of workers by 275 (300 for stockmen) to give "work units used."

$$\text{Man work index} = \frac{\text{work units required} \times 100}{\text{work units used}}$$

An index of 100 or more indicates good utilization of labour. Work units are similar to Standard Man Days (s.m.d.) used by the Ministry of Agriculture, Fisheries and Food to classify farms—

NUMBER AND TYPES OF FARMS† IN ENGLAND AND WALES
(FULL-TIME FARMS,* BY MINISTRY REGION, 1968)

TYPE OF FARM	DAIRY	LIVE-STOCK	CROPPING	MIXED	HORT.	PIGS AND POULTRY	TOTAL
East	1323	293	9723	1242	4948	1890	19419
South East	4576	1356	2311	1289	3290	1560	14382
East Midlands	4159	1456	4791	1299	745	823	13273
Yorks. and Lancs.	6288	1176	3576	1187	1525	1637	15389
Sub-total (East)	16346	4281	20401	5017	10508	5910	62463
West Midlands	8468	2552	2047	1790	1680	945	17482
South West	14441	3934	1260	3171	1504	1289	25599
Northern	5527	3705	1932	1668	334	480	13646
Wales	8632	7536	261	1194	277	279	18179
Sub-total (West)	37068	17727	5500	7823	3795	2993	74906
TOTAL	53414	22008	25901	12840	14303	8903	137369

* Over 275 s.m.d's (work units) per farm.
† Dairy farms include 29690 "specialist dairy"; pig and poultry farms include 3289 "predominantly poultry"; cropping farms include 9977 "mainly cereals." Adapted from M.A.F.F. *Farm Classification*.

APPENDIX 2

NET PRESENT VALUES

Discount factors for computing the present value of £1 in *n* years from now.

YEAR	PERCENTAGE (*r*)													
n	5%	6%	7%	8%	9%	10%	12%	15%	20%	25%	30%	40%	50%	60%
1	0·952	0·943	0·935	0·926	0·917	0·909	0·893	0·870	0·833	0·800	0·769	0·714	0·667	0·625
2	0·907	0·890	0·873	0·857	0·842	0·826	0·797	0·756	0·694	0·640	0·592	0·510	0·444	0·391
3	0·864	0·840	0·816	0·794	0·772	0·751	0·712	0·658	0·579	0·512	0·455	0·364	0·296	0·244
4	0·823	0·792	0·763	0·735	0·708	0·683	0·636	0·572	0·482	0·410	0·350	0·260	0·198	0·153
5	0·784	0·747	0·713	0·681	0·650	0·621	0·567	0·497	0·402	0·328	0·269	0·186	0·132	0·095
6	0·746	0·705	0·666	0·630	0·596	0·564	0·507	0·432	0·335	0·262	0·207	0·133	0·088	0·060
7	0·711	0·665	0·623	0·583	0·547	0·513	0·452	0·376	0·279	0·210	0·159	0·095	0·059	0·037
8	0·677	0·627	0·582	0·540	0·502	0·467	0·404	0·327	0·233	0·168	0·123	0·068	0·039	0·023
9	0·645	0·592	0·544	0·500	0·460	0·424	0·361	0·284	0·194	0·134	0·094	0·048	0·026	0·015
10	0·614	0·558	0·508	0·463	0·422	0·386	0·322	0·247	0·162	0·107	0·073	0·035	0·017	0·009
11	0·585	0·527	0·475	0·429	0·388	0·350	0·287	0·215	0·135	0·086	0·056	0·025	0·012	0·006
12	0·557	0·497	0·444	0·397	0·356	0·319	0·257	0·187	0·112	0·069	0·043	0·018	0·008	0·004
13	0·530	0·469	0·415	0·368	0·326	0·290	0·229	0·163	0·093	0·055	0·033	0·013	0·005	0·002
14	0·505	0·442	0·388	0·340	0·299	0·263	0·205	0·141	0·078	0·044	0·025	0·009	0·003	0·001
15	0·481	0·417	0·362	0·315	0·275	0·239	0·183	0·123	0·065	0·035	0·020	0·006	0·002	0·001

For the general case, the discount factor is given by $\dfrac{1}{(1 + r)^n}$

Example: if interest is 8 per cent, a promise to pay £100, 10 years from now, is worth at present £1 × 0·463 = £46·30.

ANNUITY TABLES

Discount factors for computing the present value of a future annuity.

| YEAR | PERCENTAGE (r) | | | | | | | | | | | | | |
n	5%	6%	7%	8%	9%	10%	12%	15%	20%	25%	30%	40%	50%	60%
1	0·952	0·943	0·935	0·926	0·917	0·909	0·893	0·870	0·833	0·800	0·769	0·714	0·667	0·625
2	1·859	1·833	1·808	1·783	1·759	1·735	1·690	1·626	1·527	1·440	1·361	1·224	1·111	1·016
3	2·723	2·673	2·624	2·577	2·531	2·486	2·402	2·284	2·106	1·952	1·816	1·588	1·407	1·260
4	3·546	3·465	3·387	3·312	3·239	3·169	3·038	2·856	2·588	2·362	2·166	1·848	1·605	1·413
5	4·330	4·212	4·100	3·993	3·889	3·790	3·605	3·353	2·990	2·690	2·435	2·034	1·737	1·508
6	5·076	4·917	4·766	4·623	4·485	4·354	4·112	3·785	3·325	2·952	2·642	2·167	1·825	1·568
7	5·787	5·582	5·389	5·206	5·032	4·867	4·564	4·161	3·604	3·162	2·801	2·262	1·884	1·605
8	6·464	6·209	5·971	5·746	5·534	5·334	4·968	4·488	3·837	3·330	2·924	2·330	1·923	1·628
9	7·109	6·801	6·515	6·246	5·994	5·758	5·329	4·772	4·031	3·464	3·018	2·378	1·949	1·643
10	7·723	7·359	7·023	6·709	6·416	6·144	5·651	5·019	4·193	3·571	3·091	2·413	1·966	1·652
11	8·308	7·886	7·498	7·138	6·804	6·494	5·938	5·234	4·328	3·657	3·147	2·438	1·978	1·658
12	8·865	8·383	7·942	7·535	7·160	6·813	6·195	5·421	4·440	3·726	3·190	2·456	1·986	1·662
13	9·395	8·852	8·357	7·903	7·486	7·103	6·424	5·584	4·533	3·781	3·223	2·469	1·991	1·664
14	9·900	9·294	8·745	8·243	7·785	7·366	6·629	5·725	4·611	3·825	3·248	2·478	1·994	1·665
15	10·381	9·711	9·107	8·558	8·060	7·605	6·812	5·848	4·676	3·860	3·268	2·484	1·996	1·666

For the general case, the discount factor is given by $\dfrac{1-(1+r)^{-n}}{r}$ where r = rate of discounting

n = year of cash flow

Example: if interest is 8 per cent, a promise to pay £1 a year for 10 years is now worth £6·709.

ANNUAL MORTAGE REPAYMENT

Annual repayment per £1000 borrowed (including interest and repayment of loan).

YEAR	RATE OF INTEREST (r)										
n	7%	8%	8½%	9%	9½%	10%	10½%	11%	11½%	12%	15%
1	1070	1080	1085	1090	1095	1100	1105	1110	1115	1120	1150
2	553	562	565	569	572	576	580	584	588	592	617
3	381	388	392	395	398	403	406	409	413	417	439
4	296	302	305	309	311	316	319	322	326	330	351
5	244	251	253	257	260	264	268	271	274	278	299
6	210	216	219	223	226	230	233	237	240	243	265
7	186	192	195	199	202	206	209	212	216	219	240
8	168	174	177	181	184	188	191	194	198	202	223
9	154	160	163	167	170	174	177	181	184	188	210
10	142	149	152	156	159	163	166	170	174	177	200
11	134	140	143	147	150	154	158	161	165	169	191
12	126	133	136	140	143	147	150	154	158	162	185
13	120	127	130	134	137	141	145	148	152	156	179
14	114	121	125	129	132	136	140	143	147	151	175
15	110	117	120	124	128	132	135	139	143	147	171
20	94	102	106	110	113	117	122	126	130	134	160
30	81	89	93	97	101	106	109	113	118	124	152
40	75	84	88	93	97	102	107	111	116	121	150

For the general case, the annual charge is given by $\dfrac{Cr(1+r)^n}{(1+r)^n-1}$

where C = capital investment

r = rate of interest

n = years of repayment

Example: if you borrow £1000 at 8 per cent for 20 years, you repay £102 each year for 20 years.

MORTGAGE REPAYMENT DATA

Breakdown of repayment per £1000 borrowed: I = Interest
R = Repayment of loan
L = Loan outstanding

LOAN THROUGH 10 YEARS	6%			7%			8%			9%			10%			12%		
	I	R	L	I	R	L	I	R	L	I	R	L	I	R	L	I	R	L
1	60	76	924	70	72	928	80	69	931	90	66	934	100	63	937	120	57	943
2	55	80	844	65	77	850	74	75	856	84	72	862	94	69	868	113	64	879
3	51	85	758	60	83	767	69	81	776	75	78	784	87	76	792	106	71	808
4	46	90	668	54	89	679	62	87	689	71	85	699	79	84	709	97	80	728
5	40	96	572	48	95	584	55	94	595	63	93	606	71	92	617	87	90	638
6	34	102	471	41	102	482	48	101	494	55	101	505	62	101	516	77	100	538
7	28	108	363	34	109	374	39	110	384	45	110	394	52	111	405	65	112	425
8	22	114	249	26	116	257	31	118	266	35	120	274	40	122	282	51	126	299
9	15	121	128	18	124	133	21	128	138	25	131	143	28	134	148	36	141	158
10	8	128	0	9	133	0	11	138	0	13	143	0	15	148	0	19	158	0

LOAN THROUGH 20 YEARS	6%			7%			8%			9%			10%			12%		
	I	R	L	I	R	L	I	R	L	I	R	L	I	R	L	I	R	L
1	60	27	973	70	24	976	80	22	978	90	20	980	100	17	983	120	14	986
2	58	29	944	68	26	950	78	24	955	88	21	959	98	19	963	118	16	971
3	57	31	913	66	28	922	76	25	929	86	23	936	96	21	942	116	17	953
4	55	32	881	65	30	892	74	28	902	84	25	911	94	23	919	114	19	934
5	53	34	847	62	32	860	72	30	872	82	28	883	92	26	893	112	22	912
6	51	36	810	60	34	826	70	32	840	79	30	853	89	28	865	109	24	887
7	49	39	772	58	37	789	67	35	805	77	33	820	87	31	834	106	27	860
8	46	41	731	55	39	750	64	37	768	74	36	784	83	34	800	103	31	829
9	44	43	688	52	42	708	61	40	727	71	39	745	80	37	763	100	34	795
10	41	46	642	50	45	663	58	44	683	67	42	703	76	41	722	95	38	756
11	38	49	593	46	48	615	55	47	636	63	46	657	72	45	676	91	43	713
12	36	52	541	43	51	564	51	51	585	59	50	606	68	50	627	86	48	665
13	32	55	487	39	55	509	47	55	530	55	55	557	63	55	572	80	54	611
14	29	58	429	36	59	450	42	59	471	50	60	491	57	60	512	73	61	550
15	26	61	367	31	63	387	38	64	407	44	65	426	51	66	445	66	68	483
16	22	65	302	27	67	320	33	69	337	38	71	355	45	73	372	58	76	407
17	18	69	233	22	72	248	27	75	262	32	78	277	37	80	292	49	85	322
18	14	73	157	17	77	171	21	81	182	25	85	193	29	88	204	39	95	226
19	10	78	82	12	82	88	15	87	94	17	92	100	20	97	101	27	107	120
20	5	82	0	6	88	0	8	94	0	9	100	0	11	107	0	14	120	0

Example: if you borrow £1000 for 20 years at 8 per cent, you will repay £102 a year, including (in 1st year) £80 interest and £22 repayment of capital and (in 20th year) £8 interest and £94 capital. Interest is usually chargeable for Income Tax, capital repayment is not.

INDEX

HERD BASIS, 244
HIRE PURCHASE, 50

IMPLEMENTS—
income tax allowances for, 243
valuation of, 82
IMPREST SYSTEM FOR PETTY CASH, 54
INCOME TAX, 240
income tax year, 241
investment grants, 242
Schedule D, 241
Schedule E (pay as you earn), 240, 249
INSOLVENCY, 24, 26
INTERNAL RATE OF RETURN (I.R.R.), 223 et seq.
INVESTMENT GRANTS, 242
INVESTMENT APPRAISAL, 233
INVOICE BOOK, 59

JOINT PRODUCTS AND COST ACCOUNTING, 101

LEASE BACK, 52
LIABILITIES, 12, 23
LIMITED COMPANIES, 71
taxation on, 73
LINEAR PROGRAMMING, 162
LIQUIDITY RATIO, 237
LIVESTOCK—
movement book, 58
output, 106
planning a livestock farm, 164 et seq.
valuation of, 76, 244

MANAGEMENT AND INVESTMENT INCOME, 107
MAN WORK UNITS, 112, 254
MANURIAL RESIDUES—
valuation of, 80, 101
MEMORANDUM OF ASSOCIATION, 72
MORTGAGES, 51, 66

NET CAPITAL, 12, 25
NET FARM INCOME, 107
NET OUTPUT, 106
NET PRESENT VALUE (N.P.V.), 223

OUTPUT—
crop, 105
gross, 104
livestock, 106
net, 106
per £100 labour and machinery, 107
OVERDRAFTS—
security for, 49
OWNER-OCCUPIERS—
accounts for, 67
return on capital, 69

PARTNERSHIPS, 69
PAY AS YOU EARN, 249
PAY BACK PERIOD, 220
PAYEE (of cheques), 43
PAYING-IN SLIP, 45, 53
PAYMENTS—
classification of, 16
PERSONAL ALLOWANCES—
income tax, 245
PETTY CASH BOOK, 53
PLANNING—
for specialization, 180 et seq.
in practice, 190 et seq.
on livestock farms, 164 et seq.
programme, 149 et seq.
PRIORITY LIST OF ENTERPRISES—
for planning, 153
PRIVATE DRAWINGS, 17, 20
PRIVATE USE OF FARM STORES, PRODUCE, FARM CAR, 34, 242
PROGRAMME PLANNING, 149 et seq.
PROVING ACCOUNTS, 24, 36

RECEIPTS—
classification of, 16
REFERENCE FROM BANKER, 43
REPAIRS, 66, 215
RESIDUAL VALUES, 80–2, 86, 101
RETAIL ROUND—
records for, 59

SCHEDULES—
income tax, 240
SECURITY—
mortgage, 51, 66
overdraft, 49
SELECTIVE EMPLOYMENT TAX, 252
SHORT-CUT CASH ANALYSIS, 94
SOLVENCY, 24, 26
SPECIALIZATION, 180 et seq.
STANDARD MAN DAYS (SMD), 255
STANDARD VALUES, 77
STANDING ORDER TO BANK, 46
STARTING A FARM—
budgeting, 204
taxation, 247
STOCK IN TRADE, 244
STOCKING DENSITY, 112, 253
SURTAX, 246

TIME SHEETS, 56–7, 100
TITHE, 66
TRADING ACCOUNT—
preparation of, 11, 22, 34

UNPAID ACCOUNTS, 20, 32